P9-CRZ-009

Gary F Chapman

THE SELF-MANAGEMENT SERIES
Carl E. Thoresen, Ph.D., *General Editor*
Stanford University

This series of self-help books presents techniques that really work based on scientifically sound research.

Designed with the layman in mind, each book presents a step-by-step method you can readily apply to solve real problems you confront in everyday life. Each is written by a respected behavioral scientist who has achieved success in applying these same techniques.

BOOKS IN THE SERIES

All four authors are clinical psychologists. PETER M. LEWIN-
SOHN is professor of psychology at the University of Oregon.
His colleagues are also faculty members in psychology:
RICARDO F. MUÑOZ is at the University of California, San
Francisco Medical School, MARY ANN YOUNGREN is at Port-
land State University, and ANTONETTE M. ZEISS is at Arizona
State University.

Control Your Depression

Peter M. Lewinsohn
Ricardo F. Muñoz
Mary Ann Youngren
Antonette M. Zeiss

A SPECTRUM BOOK

Prentice-Hall, Inc., *Englewood Cliffs, New Jersey 07632*

Library of Congress Cataloging in Publication Data
Main entry under title:

Control your depression.

(The Self-management psychology series) (A
Spectrum Book)
  Bibliography: p.
  Includes index.
  1. Depression, Mental.   I. Lewinsohn, Peter M.
RC537.C68   616.8′52   78–23217
ISBN 0–13–171702–2
ISBN 0–13–171694–8 pbk.

Editorial/production supervision and interior
design by Norma Karlin
Cover design by Al Pisano
Manufacturing buyer: Cathie Lenard

© 1978 by Peter M. Lewinsohn.

All rights reserved. No part of this book may be reproduced
in any form or by any means without permission in writing
from the publisher and the author.

A SPECTRUM BOOK

10 9 8 7 6 5 4 3 2 1

Printed in the United States of America

PRENTICE-HALL INTERNATIONAL, INC., *London*
PRENTICE-HALL OF AUSTRALIA PTY. LIMITED, *Sydney*
PRENTICE-HALL OF CANADA, LTD., *Toronto*
PRENTICE-HALL OF INDIA PRIVATE LIMITED, *New Delhi*
PRENTICE-HALL OF JAPAN, INC., *Tokyo*
PRENTICE-HALL OF SOUTHEAST ASIA PTE. LTD., *Singapore*
WHITEHALL BOOKS LIMITED, *Wellington, New Zealand*

Contents

9

Using Your Social Skills, 197

10

Controlling Thoughts, 217

11

Constructive Thinking, 240

12

Being Your Own Coach:
Self-Instructional Techniques, 256

Part Three
LOOKING TOWARD THE FUTURE

13

Maintaining Your Gains, 269

14

Changing Your Personality, 282

15

Planning Your Future, 296

Appendix A

Appendix B

Preface

During the past decade many psychologists have found that the social learning approach offers a useful framework for understanding depression. Among the first psychologists to use this theoretical approach to design a comprehensive treatment program for depressed people was Peter Lewinsohn. In the early 1960s he began developing the procedures described in Chapter 7 as a way of helping depressed clients learn to overcome their depression. Over the next several years Dr. Lewinsohn, his colleagues, and many graduate students at the University of Oregon Psychology Clinic used this treatment approach with hundreds of clients. On the basis of this clinical experience and a number of research studies, the treatment program was modified several times. The parts of the program that had been shown to be most effective were kept, and those that seemed least helpful were dropped or substantially revised based on therapists' and clients' suggestions. In recent years we have broadened this treatment program to include components that we have found effective for many—but ,not all—depressed clients: learning how to relax (Chapter 6), improving social skills (Chapter 8) and improving the quantity and quality of social interaction (Chapter 9), and changing thoughts that produce or maintain depression (Chapters, 10–12).

We are confident that the treatment approaches presented in this book can be of real benefit to many depressed people. But a note of caution is in order: Studies on self-help treatment programs show that as many as 50 percent of the participants fail to complete their programs—often because they have not been able to maintain sufficient motivation to work alone on their problems. Studies also show that having minimal contact with a therapist (as little as a 5- or 10-minute phone call per week) can make a tremendous difference in people's ability to follow through and successfully complete self-help treatment programs. This contact often consists only of checking on the person's progress and offering encouragement, but it seems crucial for many people. Therefore, we urge you to make similar arrangements for yourself. In Chapter 1 we suggest guidelines for deciding when it is important to seek assistance from a professional therapist. But even if these guidelines don't apply to you, we would suggest that you select someone to offer an external source of encouragement and motivation. That person could be a professional therapist or counselor, but also could be a clergyman, your family doctor, or someone else whom you like and respect. The resource person's role would be to read this book and to check from time to time on your progress; that way someone other than you will be aware of your efforts and will be able to congratulate you on your success.

Special thanks are expressed to Sandra Smith, Judy Nessen, and Joann Brady, who each spent long hours typing and proofreading at a critical stage during the preparation of this book;

to Carl Thoresen, editor of the Self-Management Psychology Series, for his thoughtful, thorough review of our manuscript; to Lynne Lumsden and Norma Karlin of Spectrum Books for their enthusiasm and patience; to our families and friends for their support and encouragement; and finally, to the many clients and colleagues who—over the years—have helped us develop our treatment approach to depression.

Introduction

Alice has been feeling low for about eight months now. Like everyone else, she has had "down" periods before, but they have usually not lasted this long. She doesn't feel like doing much, has had trouble sleeping and eating, has lost her sense of humor, and is starting to wonder whether she is ever going to feel better.

Her relationship with her family has her worried. She feels that she is a burden on them and that her gloominess is affecting her husband and teenage children. Her job responsibilities are also a source of concern. As a real estate agent, her pace is generally quite fast. But in the last few months, she has slowed down considerably. She is just not functioning as efficiently as she used to. And though she has tried, she can't get herself motivated.

Alice is tired of feeling sad and blue. But even worse, she is afraid that there may be something seriously wrong with her. At times she's even wondered whether she might be losing control, having a "mental breakdown," or even going crazy. She just doesn't understand what is happening to her and doesn't know how to overcome her distress. Yet her doctor tells her that there is nothing physically wrong with her.

Alice is experiencing depression, one of the most common of psychological problems. Mild feelings of depression are experienced by almost all people at some time during their lives. In some cases, feelings of depression become so intense and last so long that professional help becomes necessary.

Psychologists and psychiatrists have not yet discovered all they would like to know about depression. There are many ideas about what produces it and what keeps it going, and there are a number of treatments designed to deal with it.

This book is intended to explain one approach and to give specific steps that are useful in controlling depression. The ideas and techniques presented here are the ones we use in working with people who seek help because they feel seriously depressed.

HOW THE BOOK IS ORGANIZED

The book is divided into three parts:

Part I tells you how we think about depression. Chapter 1 explains what psychologists mean by depression and how to recognize it. Chapter 2 describes the psychological framework we use in making sense out of human behavior—that is, how we explain why people behave the way they do. It is known as the social learning approach. Chapter 3 brings together depression and social learning and explains how to use this approach to deal with depression. Because self-change programs can be hard to implement the first time you try them, Chapter 4 includes a number of basic techniques that are helpful when working on a "self-control" project—that is, when you are trying to change in ways that require sustained effort over time.

Part II is designed to give you step-by-step procedures to control depression. They are presented so that you can use them on your own. Chapter 5 helps you decide which techniques to try first, and Chapters 6 through 12 give detailed instructions on the techniques we have found useful. Here is where you will learn specific ways to control depression.

Part III is about ensuring success. It concerns using the ideas you have learned to deal with future circumstances. Chapter 13 explains ways to maintain your gains and to help prevent the return of serious depression. Chapter 14 describes ways to extend the skills you have learned to other areas of your life. Chapter 15 explores the idea of planning your future and the psychological advantages of having clarified your goals and purposes in life.

SOME CHARACTERISTICS OF THE BOOK

We have attempted to be as concrete as possible in our explanation and instructions, avoiding useless generalities. We have included ways to check whether you are using the techniques properly and how much progress you are making. It is important that you *individualize* what we suggest. Not every technique will be useful to all readers; we have included a variety so that you can find those techniques that will work for you.

Because the book is really intended to teach a way of *thinking* about depression as well as controlling it, you may find it useful even if depression is not a problem. For example, it can give you ideas to prevent depression. Teachers may find the techniques easy to share with their students. Finally, the social learning approach can be helpful as a way of thinking about how you behave in many other situations and how to change behavior that is problematic.

A WORD OF CAUTION

This book is primarily intended to help people control their own depression. However, as noted in the Preface, people often fail to complete self-help programs because it's difficult to maintain sufficient motivation when working alone on problems. Therefore, we encourage you to select a therapist, counselor, or some other resource person to read this book, check on your progress from time to time, offer encouragement, and lend a helping hand if you get bogged down.

Furthermore, there is at least one situation in which we .feel that you should seek help from a professional *immediately*: when you are afraid you might commit suicide. During serious cases of depression, some people give up hope and may do things which they find hard to believe once they no longer feel depressed.

Not every difficult life situation is due to depression or is likely to lead to it. There are other psychological problems that cause distress. These might include relationship problems, difficult decisions, fears of certain objects or situations, economic hardship, physical illness, and so on. You should seriously consider whether you are using this book as a way of avoiding dealing with a serious life situation that requires professional help. Any book, no matter how well written, has its limitations. If you have serious doubts that depression is your major problem, you might profit from a consultation with a mental health professional. To contact a professional helper, consult your local community mental health center, the Mental

Health Association, your physician, or a member of the clergy. In some areas, licensed or certified psychologists, psychiatrists, and social workers are listed in the classified section of the telephone directory.

A FINAL NOTE

If you are sure your problem is depression and have tried conscientiously to use the techniques we suggest but have found no relief, please do not conclude that your case is hopeless. What you have learned is that *this* method did not work for you. There are other methods. You should consider seeing a professional.

part I

The
Concepts

chapter1

Depression

Everyone has times of feeling sad or blue. People often refer to these feelings by saying they are "depressed." We are restricting our discussion to depression that differs from the "down" or "blue" periods that nearly everyone experiences in three ways:

1. The depression is more intense.
2. The depression lasts longer.
3. The depression significantly interferes with effective day-to-day functioning.

By depression we do *not* mean something one *has* like a disease or a broken leg. Rather, we see depression as something one experiences or feels for a period of time. Sometimes the beginning of a period of depression is clear and dramatic and is related to a specific event, such as the death of a loved one. Grief and sorrow in these instances are natural reactions to personal loss. However, if the period of depression seems unduly prolonged, then it is time to do something about it. More often, though, there is no easily identified event that precedes depression. Rather, depression is experienced from time to time without any obvious explanation.

WHAT DEPRESSION IS NOT

First, being depressed is *not* abnormal or crazy. In fact, it is one of the most common problems people experience. It is estimated that at any given time, 3 to 4 percent of the adult population in the United States is clinically depressed. (That's over 6 million people!)

Second, depression is not just *any* bad or upsetting feeling. For example, depression is *not* feeling anxious or nervous, although it is true that depressed individuals frequently feel anxious as well as depressed. The point is that depression is not the only way of being distressed. This book is intended for persons who are depressed.

This chapter is devoted to a discussion of the specific set of behaviors and feelings that make up what we call "the depressive syndrome." We have also included a questionnaire to help you decide if you are experiencing the kind of depression that can be helped by reading and using this book.

THE DEPRESSIVE SYNDROME

A syndrome is a collection of events, behaviors, or feelings that often—*but not always*—go together. The depressive syndrome is a collection of rather specific feelings and behaviors that have been found to be characteristic of depressed persons *as a group*. It is important to recognize that there are large individual differences as to which of these feelings or behaviors are experienced, and to what extent they are experienced. The following are characteristics of the depressive syndrome:

Dysphoria

By dysphoria, we mean an unpleasant feeling state. Dysphoria is the opposite of euphoria (feeling very happy). People who are depressed frequently say they feel very sad, blue, hopeless, or "down" much of the time. Depressed individuals often feel they are worthless or useless, or they see life as meaningless. They may feel gloomy and pessimistic about the future.

Depressed persons frequently describe themselves as deficient or as failures, particularly in regard to areas that are of special personal importance (for example, intellectual pursuits or job performance). Sometimes these feelings of inadequacy appear unjustified to other people. For example, a man may be considered very competent by his co-workers, but because his work falls short of his own standards of perfection, he puts himself down and feels like a total failure.

Low Level of Activity

Depressed persons *do* considerably less overall when they are depressed than when they are not depressed. Sometimes a depressed person's typical day consists largely of "sitting around and doing nothing" or engaging in mostly passive, solitary activities like watching television, eating, or napping. Going to work or taking care of daily household chores may seem to require an almost overwhelming amount of effort.

Often the depressed person feels unmotivated to engage in hobbies or other activities that used to be enjoyable or satisfying. Such activities no longer appeal to the person and seem like "just another chore" that would require too much effort.

Problems Interacting with Other People

Many depressed persons express concern about their interpersonal relationships. This concern may be expressed in a variety of ways. Some individuals are very unhappy or dissatisfied with their marital relationships or with other close, ongoing relationships. Some feel uncomfortable and anxious when they are with other people, especially in groups. Others have difficulty coping with certain kinds of social interactions, especially those requiring them to be assertive (for example, saying "no" to unreasonable demands or being open about their feelings—positive or negative). Finally, some depressed persons feel lonely or unloved, but at the same time they withdraw from people.

Guilt

Some depressed persons express feelings of guilt and believe they deserve to be punished for their "badness" or "sinfulness." Others feel guilt because of their failure—real or imagined—to assume responsibilities in their family lives or jobs. Such persons often feel they are a burden to others and blame themselves for being depressed and thereby failing to meet the needs of their families or others.

Feeling Burdened

Some individuals do not feel at all responsible for their own depression; instead they blame their distress on external causes. Such persons typically complain that others are always putting excessive demands upon them. For example, a housewife may feel constantly burdened by the demands her husband and children place upon her; she may believe that if these demands were suddenly to vanish that she would not be depressed.

Physical Problems

A common problem among depressed individuals is having low energy or feelings of fatigue for long periods of time with no obvious explanation.

Sleep disturbance of some kind also is common. Depressed persons often have trouble falling asleep at night, or they sleep very restlessly with periods of wakefulness throughout the night. Others awaken earlier than they need to arise and are not able to return to sleep.

Depressed persons sometimes experience a loss of appetite and report not enjoying their food anymore or eating irregularly. Depressed persons often show a weight loss.

Other physical problems associated with depression include increased frequency and severity of headaches, stomachaches, and intestinal difficulties. Also, some depressed persons report reduced interest in sexual activity.

Again, it is important to remember that these features of the depressive syndrome are characteristic of depressed persons *as a group*; the depressed individual typically experiences only *some* of them. For example, a person's feelings may be dominated by sadness and hopelessness without experiencing any guilt. Or someone may feel "slowed-down" and fatigued without having headaches.

Another important point is that many characteristics of the depressive syndrome are commonly associated with various physical diseases. A person who has flu, for example, is likely to have a low energy level, not want to be around other people, and generally feel "down." If you are experiencing some of the problems described above and have not had a physical examination for a long time or have reason to question your physical health, we urge you to see your physician.

MEASURING THE LEVEL OF YOUR DEPRESSION

In this section, we provide the Beck Depression Inventory, a questionnaire for you to use in determining whether you are depressed and if so, the level of your depression.[1] *We would like you to complete this questionnaire right now.* The results may not be valid if you read further before checking your responses.

[1] Beck, A. T. *Depression.* New York: Harper & Row (Hoeber Medical Division), 1967, pp. 186–207 and 333–335.

Beck Depression Inventory [a]

Instructions: This is a questionnaire. On the questionnaire are groups of statements. Please read the entire groups of statements in each category. Then pick out the one statement in the group which best describes the way you feel *today,* that is, *right now.* Circle the number beside the statement you have chosen. If several statements in the group seem to apply equally well, circle each one.

Be sure to read all the statements in the group before making your choice.

A. (SADNESS)

0   I do not feel sad
1   I feel blue or sad
2a I am blue or sad all the time and I can't snap out of it
2b I am so sad or unhappy that it is quite painful
3   I am so sad or unhappy that I can't stand it

B. (PESSIMISM)

0   I am not particularly pessimistic or discouraged about the future
1   I feel discouraged about the future
2a I feel I have nothing to look forward to
2b I feel that I won't ever get over my troubles
3   I feel that the future is hopeless and that things cannot improve

[a] The authors wish to thank Aaron T. Beck, M.D., for granting permission to reprint the Beck Depression Inventory.

Beck Depression Inventory (*cont.*)

C. (SENSE OF FAILURE)

0   I do not feel like a failure

1   I feel I have failed more than the average person

2a I feel I have accomplished very little that is worthwhile   or   that means anything

2b As I look back on my life all I can see is a lot of failure

3   I feel I am a complete failure as a person (parent, spouse)

D. (DISSATISFACTION)

0   I am not particularly dissatisfied

1   I feel bored most of the time

2a I don't enjoy things the way I used to

2b I don't get satisfaction out of anything any more

3   I am dissatisfied with everything

E. (GUILT)

0   I don't feel particularly guilty

1   I feel bad or unworthy a good part of the time

2a I feel quite guilty

2b I feel bad or unworthy practically all the time now

3   I feel as though I am very bad or worthless

F. (EXPECTATION OF PUNISHMENT)

0   I don't feel I am being punished

1   I have a feeling that something bad may happen to me

2   I feel I am being punished or will be punished

3a I feel I deserve to be punished

3b I want to be punished

G. (SELF-DISLIKE)

0   I don't feel disappointed in myself

1a I am disappointed in myself

1b I don't like myself

2   I am disgusted with myself

3   I hate myself

H. (SELF-ACCUSATIONS)

0   I don't feel I am worse than anybody else

1   I am critical of myself for my weaknesses or mistakes

2   I blame myself for my faults

3   I blame myself for everything that happens

Beck Depression Inventory (*cont.*)

I. (SUICIDAL IDEAS)

0   I don't have any thoughts of harming myself

1   I have thoughts of harming myself but I would not carry them out

2a   I feel I would be better off dead

2b   I feel my family would be better off if I were dead

3a   I have definite plans about committing suicide

3b   I would kill myself if I could

J. (CRYING)

0   I don't cry any more than usual

1   I cry more than I used to

2   I cry all the time now. I can't stop it

3   I used to be able to cry but now I can't cry at all even though I want to

K. (IRRITABILITY)

0   I am no more irritated now than I ever am

1   I get annoyed or irritated more easily than I used to

2   I feel irritated all the time

3   I don't get irritated at all at things that used to irritate me

L. (SOCIAL WITHDRAWAL)

0   I have not lost interest in other people

1   I am less interested in other people now than I used to be

2   I have lost most of my interest in other people and have little feeling for them

3   I have lost all my interest in other people and don't care about them at all

Beck Depression Inventory (*cont.*)

M. (INDECISIVENESS)

0   I make decisions about as well as ever

1   I try to put off making decisions

2   I have great difficulty in making decisions

3   I can't make any decisions at all anymore

N. (BODY IMAGE CHANGE)

0   I don't feel I look any worse than I used to

1   I am worried that I am looking old or unattractive

2   I feel that there are permanent changes in my appearance and they make me look unattractive

3   I feel that I am ugly or repulsive looking

O. (WORK RETARDATION)

0   I can work as well as before

1a It takes extra effort to get started doing something

1b I don't work as well as I used to

2   I have to push myself very hard to do anything

3   I can't do any work at all

P. (INSOMNIA)

0   I can sleep as well as usual

1   I wake up more tired in the morning than I used to

2   I wake up 2–3 hours earlier than usual and find it hard to get back to sleep

3   I wake up early every day and can't get more than 5 hours sleep

Q. (FATIGABILITY)

0   I don't get any more tired than usual

1   I get tired more easily than I used to

2   I get tired from doing nothing

3   I get too tired to do anything

R. (ANOREXIA)

0   My appetite is not worse than usual

1   My appetite is not as good as it used to be

2   My appetite is much worse now

3   I have no appetite at all

Beck Depression Inventory (*cont.*)

S. (WEIGHT LOSS)

0 I haven't lost much weight, if any, lately
1 I have lost more than 5 pounds
2 I have lost more than 10 pounds
3 I have lost more than 15 pounds

T. (SOMATIC PREOCCUPATION)

0 I am no more concerned about my health than usual
1 I am concerned about aches and pains or upset stomach or constipation
2 I am so concerned with how I feel or what I feel that it's hard to think of much else
3 I am completely absorbed in what I feel

U. (LOSS OF LIBIDO)

0 I have not noticed any recent change in my interest in sex
1 I am less interested in sex than I used to be
2 I am much less interested in sex now
3 I have lost interest in sex completely

To score the questionnaire, just add up the points you received from your responses to each item. If you circled more than one response for an item, add *only* the points for the highest response. For example, if in answering Item G. (SELF-DISLIKE) you circled both (3) "I hate myself" and (2) "I am disgusted with myself," add 3 points for that item.

Table 1–1 presents the range of scores for each of four levels of depression. This book is designed primarily for persons whose scores on the Beck Depression Inventory are between 5 and 15.

If your score was between 0 and 4, you are probably not depressed. You may be having some real life difficulties but

Table 1-1
Beck Depression Inventory—Estimated Degree of Depression

Range of Scores	Depression Level
0–4	None or minimal
5–7	Mild
8–15	Moderate
16 or over	Potentially serious

depression may not be the best label for what you are experiencing. However, if you remain convinced that you are depressed, you may have scored low for at least three reasons:

1. Today may be an unusually good day for you.
2. The test may not include enough of the kinds of ways in which you experience depression.
3. You may not have been depressed lately but know that you have a tendency to become depressed.

If any of the above three reasons are true for you, you still may find this book helpful.

If your score was 16 or higher, we encourage you to give this book a try. If the book seems too hard to get into, then seek professional assistance as recommended in the next section.

SUGGESTIONS FOR WHEN TO SEEK PROFESSIONAL HELP

We suggest that you seek professional assistance through your community mental health clinic, a nearby university department of psychiatry or psychology, a psychologist or psychiatrist in private practice, or your physician if any of the following apply:

1. If your score on the Beck Depression Inventory was 16 or higher, indicating potentially serious depression, and if, after giving the book a try, you don't feel it's going to be helpful.

2. If you are seriously contemplating suicide.

3. If you have been experiencing wide mood swings: feeling very depressed for a while and then feeling abnormally ecstatic, flighty, and full of almost superhuman energy with virtually no "neutral" time.

4. If, as a result of reading this chapter and taking the Beck Depression Inventory, you have decided that you are not depressed but you continue to experience psychological distress of some kind.

SUMMARY

In this chapter we introduce our definition of depression—first, by saying what depression is *not* (*not* just feeling a little blue, *not* a disease, *not* being abnormal, and *not* just any upsetting feeling), and then by describing the kinds of feelings and behaviors that have been found to be characteristic of depressed persons as a group. The Beck Depression Inventory was provided so that you could measure your present level of depression. Finally, we gave some guidelines to help you decide whether you are likely to find this book helpful or whether you should also seek professional assistance.

REVIEW

———— I have a reasonably clear idea of what depression is and what it is not.

———— I have an understanding of the collection of specific feelings and behaviors that make up the depressive syndrome.

———— I have assessed the level of depression I am currently experiencing.

———— I have made a preliminary decision

———— to proceed with reading this book.

———— to seek professional assistance.

chapter 2

Social Learning: A Way to Think about People's Behavior

Human beings have tried to understand themselves and others for centuries. There is a strong desire to explain to ourselves why we like certain things and dislike or fear others, why we find it easy to do this and have so much trouble doing that, why we feel good one day and terrible on another. Some people are friendly and enthusiastic while others seem grouchy and dull most of the time. Most interestingly, some who are usually boring can suddenly blossom into "the life of the party," and some who are gruff and stingy can at times be kind, gentle, and generous.

One reason people are interested in why we do the things we do is that we like to know what makes people tick. This is pure intellectual curiosity. Another reason is that we would like to use our knowledge to influence our lives for the better. We'd like to have more of a say about how we feel and what we are likely to do. We'd like to be able to influence others to be more friendly toward us, more cooperative, more understanding. We'd like to be able to bring up our children in ways that will make them more competent in dealing with life.

Psychology is the study of behavior, mental activity, and feelings. Since human behavior is influenced by so many factors, there is, as yet, no theory that explains it completely. Different psychologists emphasize different factors, and their diverse ideas are shared by many lay people.

The approach we use in therapy is called Social Learning Theory. It is based on what is known about the *learning* process and how *social* factors influence human life.

From a social learning view, people are seen as *learning* almost everything they do. Within the limits set by our physical makeup, the way we walk, talk, eat, sleep, think, and even the way we feel is *learned*. Think, for example, of the way a sailor acquires his "sea legs," or a good mountaineer learns to have sure footing, or, for that matter, the way a baby learns to walk. The way we talk is a clear example of the learning process: Think about how easily we can distinguish a New England accent from a British accent, or a Southern drawl from a Western twang. The kinds of food we eat vary according to what we have learned to like: Some people find snails disgusting, others love them; some people think peanut butter is horrible, others enjoy it.

The way we think is a very important but neglected area of study. Some people can understand how numbers work very easily. Others have learned to think about cooking—flavors, colors, texture, nutrition—as though it were second nature to them. Still others have acquired a remarkable facility in thinking about politics, business, religion, puzzles, or mechanics. Just as we learn to do certain things, we learn to think in certain ways: Some learn to be more organized, some more intuitive, some more optimistic, some more pessimistic, some more traditional, and some more innovative.

Finally, we learn different ways of feeling. For example,

we learn to feel happy when our favorite baseball, football, or hockey team wins and disappointed when it loses, but someone who isn't interested in sports probably couldn't care less. We learn to feel sentimental about a certain song after hearing it played when we are with someone "special." We learn to feel safe in our homes and to feel loved when someone we care for smiles at us.

Knowing that people learn to act, think, and feel the way they do, we can say that depression itself is *learned*. Some individuals learn to act, think, and feel in depressing ways. Therefore, the way to control depression is for the depressed person to learn new patterns which make depression less likely. Of course, this is easier said than done! And that is what this book is designed to do—to give you step-by-step directions, which, if followed, will teach you how to change the way you think and act so that you will feel more alive and less depressed.

We will introduce here a few of the concepts we use throughout the book. The next chapter will focus on some specifics about how social learning ideas can help you deal with depression.

WHAT INFLUENCES BEHAVIOR?

Antecedents

Antecedents are situations or events that come *before* the behavior. For example, certain physical situations can increase or decrease the chances that you will feel and act depressed. You are more likely to feel sad and cry when visiting a cemetery than when visiting an amusement park.

A social situation can also act as an antecedent. You are more likely to act businesslike with your boss, happy and active with your dancing class, and sad and helpless with a friend or relative who has repeatedly served as a shoulder for you to cry on.

Places, people, or the time of the day may influence how you'll think, act, and feel. These factors are antecedents in the sense that they come before, set the stage, and bring out different behaviors from you.

Alfred, a single man who was in treatment for depression, complained that it was hard for him to meet and develop friendships with women. He said that almost every time he tried to approach a female, he became doubtful about whether he really wanted to meet her, started to act very formally, and began to think of many reasons why she was not suitable for him.

Further discussion of his problem revealed that he usually visited bars or discos when he was consciously trying to meet women. It was in these bars or discos that he suffered from his uncomfortable doubts, formal behavior, and negative thoughts about the women he saw. When he met women in other places, however, he had no such responses. The antecedents to his discomfort seemed to be the bars and discos and not the actual interactions with females.

Alfred began to keep track of places that brought out his most pleasant moods, spontaneous behavior, and positive thoughts about the women he met. He came up with the following: (1) a courtyard near his office building where many downtown workers ate their bag lunches, (2) jogging meets, especially prior to a race or a "fun run," and (3) citizen action group gatherings, especially those concerned with local issues. He found that in these places he could speak to women fairly easily and informally and that, in general, he found them interesting and easy to admire.

He wondered how he had come to associate his uncomfortable feelings with bars and discos and decided that he must have developed some sort of prejudice against them because he went there only when he felt desperate for company. He probably assumed that the women he met there were equally desperate. Whether or not this was the explanation, it was clear that he had positive biases toward the other locations, and he decided to capitalize on them to make his interactions with women more comfortable.

Consequences

Consequences are events that *follow* a behavior. There are positive, negative, and neutral consequences. Positive consequences, or rewards, make it more likely that you'll repeat a behavior. Negative consequences, sometimes called punishment, make it less likely that you'll repeat a behavior.

As you think about the behaviors and thoughts that accompany your depressed state you might think about the "payoff," that is, the positive consequences which follow from your depressive actions.

Holly's parents were very important people in their community. They cared very much for Holly, but, because of their active schedules, they usually didn't spend much time with her. She understood and even shared the excitement they felt in their roles as community leaders, but there was something nice about how they took more time to be with her when she looked sad or troubled. Holly didn't feel sad frequently, but when she did she was able to have warm, heart-to-heart talks with her parents.

Holly began to get worried when she started to have periods of sadness more often than before. At first she wondered whether it was just that she was getting older and her worries were more serious, but somehow this explanation was not satisfactory. At the suggestion of a friend of the family, Holly asked her parents to set aside a certain amount of time for her each week, at a regular time. The sad periods rapidly became less frequent.

What the friend had noticed was that, without meaning to do so, Holly's parents were *teaching* her to become sad. They were providing positive consequences each time she felt bad and showed it by her depressed expression. The irony in the situation was that, even with the best of intentions, her parents were training Holly to become sad to get attention.

Mental Factors

Your expectations, beliefs, and other thoughts can greatly influence your activities and your feelings. For example, if you strongly expect to have a "terrible time" at a school get-together, you often will, in fact, end up having a negative experience. Thoughts can act as antecedents in the sense that they can "set the stage" for feeling depressed or contented. They also can act as consequences in that you can reinforce or punish yourself with them.

Vince came to one of his therapy sessions quite excited. He had been working on his tendency to be very pessimistic and the relationship between that tendency and his recurring bouts with depression.

Today he felt he had finally found a good explanation for how pessimism helped produce depression. In his opinion, pessimism was telling yourself that something good was *not* going to happen or that something bad *would* happen. Now, if you told yourself this when you were about to begin working on something constructive, you were, in fact, punishing yourself for starting, and therefore you'd be less likely to carry out your plans. You'd get stuck at Step 1. That would mean you wouldn't accomplish what you wanted, and you'd have another reason to be depressed.

Pessimism, according to Vince, worked as a self-fulfilling prophecy, which not only helped you fail, but also increased your chances of becoming depressed because of the failure.

This was a turning point in his treatment. He began to pay

close attention to his thoughts and their influence on his behavior. Using techniques like those found in Chapters 10, 11, and 12, he began to set himself up for success, including success in managing depression.

STRATEGIES THAT HELP
SELF-CHANGE EFFORTS

1. Self-reinforcement: rewarding yourself for accomplishing what you have decided to change.
2. Step-by-step change: slow, deliberate change in an area chosen by the individual. In its most concrete form, gradual change means increasing or decreasing by *very* small steps the amount of time or the number of times that you perform the target behavior. Self-reward for each successful step is part of this process.
3. Modeling: learning by observing others. You can use people whom you like, public figures, or fictional characters as models of the kind of behavior you want to develop and use.
4. Self-observation: noticing and keeping *written* records of your behavior, thoughts, or feelings. This strategy helps you know better what you are doing *before* you start your self-change program and how much *progress* you are making as you put the program into effect.

THE QUESTION OF CONTROL

People often ask whether we have any control over our feelings or behavior. If we have learned how to act in certain ways during our childhood and if our present environment influences our behavior, how can we change anything? Aren't we at the mercy of our upbringing and our present situation? Other people ask why we have to use rewards, gradual change, self-observation, and so on. Can't we just decide to change and do it, using will power? Don't we control our environment, too?

Social Learning Theory views this problem of control as a chicken-and-egg question. It is true that our environment exerts an influence on us. It is also true that we influence our environment. The process is one of continuous interaction between a person and his or her environment. By learning what factors affect us, we can choose to change them so that they will affect us in a more desirable way.

The changes you make now will become your "past history" when you look back. You can make your history happen!

IMPORTANT IMPLICATIONS OF SOCIAL LEARNING

1. Early experiences do *not* necessarily limit your potential. You can always learn new ways of acting, thinking, and feeling.

2. You have a great deal of control over how you change because you can determine what you will and will *not* reward yourself for from now on.

3. Your expectations can influence how successful you will be in your change efforts. If you are pessimistic, every time you start to implement your change program you are, in effect, telling yourself: "What's the use, really? It's hopeless." Does that sound encouraging? On the other hand, if you are more optimistic, you are actually telling yourself: "Who knows? Maybe I *can* do it. " By being more optimistic you can increase the chances that you will continue to try and do well.

4. Social learning focuses on the present. You want to

know what factors are maintaining your behavior *now* so that you can find out how to modify them. How your behavior patterns got started may be interesting, but at this point it is *not necessary* to know that to change yourself.

Beware of avoiding this approach because it is too "mechanistic" or "not human enough." It is true that it is systematic —that is what makes it work so well. But so is language. Each letter in a word must be in *exactly* the right place, and, yet, with those words one can create beautiful poems, songs, and novels! Social learning techniques can increase your personal freedom by allowing you to have many more alternatives from which to choose.

SUMMARY

This chapter introduces the ideas used in this book to deal with depression. The ideas are known as the social learning approach. This approach focuses on how people learn to think, act, and feel. It considers antecedents, consequences, and mental factors very important influences on behavior. The chapter describes basic self-control techniques and the implications of using this approach.

REVIEW

_____ I understand what "Social Learning Theory" is.

_____ I have learned about the three main influences on behavior:

_____ antecedents

_____ consequences

_____ mental factors

_____ I know the four strategies to bring about self-change:

_____ self-reinforcement

_____ step-by-step change

_____ modeling

_____ self-observation

chapter 3

Depression
and
Social Learning

You may have been feeling depressed for a long time or for only a little while. You may feel depressed often or only occasionally. You may be able to date the onset of your depression to some specific event (your child went to college, you moved to a new city, you retired, or someone close to you died), or you may not be able to recognize any particular event that preceded your depression. Overall, the chances are good that you feel puzzled and don't feel you understand *why* you get depressed.

The major purpose of this chapter is to present a framework for understanding depression. The critical questions are: What causes people to feel depressed? What causes *you* to feel depressed? How can the social learning framework help you to identify specific behaviors and situations that contribute to your depression? How can the social learning framework help you to control your depression?

A WAY TO UNDERSTAND DEPRESSION

Except when we are sleeping, we are continuously interacting with our environment. Whether we are watching television, typing a report, talking to a salesperson, interacting with our children or spouse, talking to someone on the telephone, or just sitting and ruminating about something from the past— we are always doing something. Our interaction with our environment is continuous and reciprocal.

In a general way we can put our interactions into categories, those that lead to *positive* outcomes (you finish an assignment and your boss compliments you on it), those that have *neutral* outcomes (you drive to work in the morning), and those that have *negative* outcomes (being criticized by someone who is important to you). When too few of our interactions have positive outcomes and when too many of them have negative outcomes, we start feeling depressed. These routes to depression are shown in Figure 3–1.

Figure 3–1

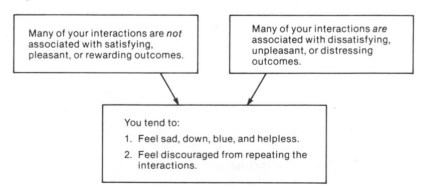

Obviously, not *all* of our interactions can be expected to lead to positive consequences; neither is it reasonable to expect that *none* of our actions will lead to negative consequences. Nevertheless, without a reasonable *balance* between positive and negative outcomes, anybody is going to feel depressed.

Here are two examples of interactions *lacking positive* outcomes:

> You spend most of your day doing the housework, preparing dinner, waiting for the plumber (who never shows up), and chauffeuring your children to their various appointments. During dinner, your family is busily engaged in talking about their school or job activities, and nobody compliments you on the dinner or inquires about your day. You feel down and begin to wonder whether your family really cares about you. You continue to feel this way for the remainder of the evening and have trouble falling asleep.

> You work hard and long on a report requested by your boss. You submit it before the due date, but you never hear about it again. You assume that your boss didn't like it and that you wasted your time.

Here are two examples of interactions associated with *negative* outcomes:

> Your wife is critical of you because you come home late from work, read the newspaper during dinner, don't spend enough time with the children, and so on. She complains to you about these things frequently.

> At a social gathering you express your opinion about a political candidate. Mrs. X points out that you are "all wrong." You feel stupid and humiliated.

Any *one* of these instances might leave you feeling a little discouraged but not necessarily depressed. But when these events are multiplied *and* when they occur over an extended

period of time, they are likely to cause you to feel quite depressed.

What determines whether an interaction is going to be
experienced positively or negatively? This always depends on
the external ("objective") situation (for example, your husband compliments you) *as well as* on your subjective interpretation and perception of the situation (for example, "He didn't
really mean it . . ."). What we say to ourselves, especially positive and negative statements, is important. Technically, we are
said to "self-reinforce" when we provide ourselves with something tangible *or* when we make a positive statement (or mental
image) *following* something we do. Self-reinforcement becomes
especially important when we are working on projects that require such long and sustained effort that we may not get any
encouraging feedback for long periods of time (working on a
term paper, doing the annual cleanup of your house, working
toward an advanced degree). The things that you say to yourself
while engaged in the activity ("I am doing a good job," "I am
making progress," "This may be hard, but the end result is
going to be worthwhile," "Why am I doing this?" play a
critical role in determining whether an interaction is going to
be experienced as rewarding or as unpleasant. People who are
depressed are prone to self-reinforce negatively rather than
positively. That is, they are less likely to compliment themselves when they do something well and are more likely to
criticize themselves during or following an interaction.

Generally, interactions with positive outcomes are those
that make us feel liked, respected, loved, useful, appreciated,
and worthwhile. Not only do these interactions make us feel
good, but they also motivate us to be more active. On the other
hand, interactions with negative outcomes make us feel bad,
unwanted, unappreciated, criticized, and humiliated. Being
depressed means that you are experiencing too few positive
outcomes and too many negative ones. This state of affairs
leads to a vicious circle: When you feel depressed you also
feel discouraged, and are thus less likely to approach situations

that might lead to satisfying outcomes. For example, the fact that your comments about a political candidate were rebuffed might make it less likely that you will be motivated to enter the same or similar social situations; the fact that you feel upset about your husband's criticism of you might make it less likely that you will be able to respond to his loving or sexual advances later on.

VICIOUS AND POSITIVE CIRCLES

Everyone knows what a vicious circle is. You are in a tight financial situation and need your car to get to work. Your car breaks down, which will cost you money and make your financial situation worse. The fact that your car needs repair causes you to miss work, which costs you money by reducing your paycheck, which makes it even more difficult for you to get your car fixed—which you need to get to work—which you need to get the money to fix the car.

With depression, it's rather easy to get into a vicious circle. Having few interactions with positive outcomes causes you to feel depressed; the more depressed we feel the less motivated we are to engage in the kinds of activities which might have positive outcomes; this causes us to feel even more depressed, which, in turn, causes us to become even less active. And so it goes on and on. This cycle continues until you feel very depressed and are very passive (see Figure 3–2).

Here is an example of depression as a vicious circle.

During the past week you have had very few interactions followed by positive outcomes. The sale on which you have been spending a lot of time and energy has fallen apart. Your wife has been preoccupied with her mother's poor health and has had little time for you. Your best friend is out of town, and

Figure 3–2

you have been spending a greater than usual amount of time by yourself. It is not surprising that you feel somewhat depressed. Consequently, you are finding it more difficult than usual to motivate yourself to do the things that you would normally enjoy: jogging in the morning, making arrangements to go fishing, setting up a luncheon appointment with an acquaintance. You are less likely, therefore, to be in situations or to engage in activities that are usually pleasant for you (that is, activities with positive outcomes). Consequently, you feel even more depressed, feel even less like doing things.

Fortunately, for every vicious circle there is a *positive* circle:

You decide to go jogging, which makes you feel better. Your wife stops worrying about her mother and returns to being her normal pleasant self in her interactions with you. Consequently, you feel less depressed and feel like making the effort to arrange for a fishing trip or calling a friend about going to lunch.

Engaging in interactions with positive outcomes leads to an improved sense of well-being, which motivates a person to engage in more activities with pleasant outcomes. A positive circle is thus set in motion.

OTHER CONSEQUENCES
OF DEPRESSION

When a person has been feeling depressed long enough and often enough, other aspects of the depressive syndrome (as discussed in Chapter 1) may occur:

1. You become pessimistic. You *correctly* perceive that your interactions are not associated with positive outcomes. You don't *expect* future interactions to lead to positive outcomes, so you become less hopeful, and eventually you feel hopeless.

2. You lose interest. You find it more and more difficult to do things, especially those requiring effort. If your efforts are not going to lead to positive outcomes, why should you even try?

3. You may begin to wonder whether there is something "wrong" with you. You may start wondering if there is something physically wrong with you, or you may start feeling that you are inferior or inadequate. You may start blaming yourself or wonder whether you are somehow being punished. It seems that there *must* be a reason for your misery.

4. Because you are doing less and less, you may not be meeting your responsibilities. You may be letting other people down. Hence, you start feeling guilty.

MULTIPLE ROADS TO DEPRESSION

How does a person get into this kind of situation? There are many different circumstances in which our interactions may not be followed by positive outcomes. We can think of these as the "causes" of depression.

Interactions that have been a source of positive outcomes for you in the past are no longer available. If you lose, through death or other forms of separation, someone who has been an important source of positive outcomes for you, then that person's departure represents a serious disruption to your interactions. Your relationship with the "departed" need not have been *all* positive. Most relationships are ambivalent; they have their positive *and* negative outcomes. Your inability to engage in interactions with that person at the level to which you have come accustomed can represent a serious reduction in the level of positive outcomes you experience. This will probably cause you to feel depressed, at least temporarily. Such things as physical disease, age-related changes, moves to a new city, and serious financial setbacks all deprive a person of interactions which have been sources of positive outcomes.

Here are some examples of circumstances leading to a reduction of positive outcomes.

You have always been a physically active person and have enjoyed participating in sports and other physically demanding activities. You have suffered a heart attack or some other physically disabling disease, and your physician forbids you to engage in many of these activities.

You move to a new city where you don't know anybody. You miss getting together with family and friends in your hometown.

With the recent birth of your first child, you are spending much more time at home, so there is a serious reduction in the number of social interactions you previously enjoyed with friends and co-workers.

You have been used to playing a lot of golf and tennis and are transferred to a part of the country where the long, hard winter prevents you from participating in these sports.

You may lack the skill to elicit positive outcomes from your interactions. The word *skill* is not easily defined because skills are specific to certain areas or situations. Someone who is an accomplished pianist may be unskilled when it comes to fixing his lawnmower. We are concerned with your skill in eliciting positive outcomes that are important to you. One particularly important skill in regard to depression is social skill. By this we mean your ability to manage your interpersonal relationships: being able to do the kinds of things that make other people treat you the way you want to be treated *and* being able to deal with people so that they don't treat you in ways that you don't want to be treated. By our definition, you might be said to lack social skill if you are unable to have social interactions which produce the kinds of positive outcomes you like. Many depressed individuals are concerned about their interpersonal relationships. They feel inadequate, uncomfortable, and sometimes disliked and rejected. In other words, social interactions usually do not have positive outcomes for them. Here is an example:

> You like talking with people. There are some people you like, and you want them to like you. However, at social gatherings involving more than one or two others, you tend to feel uncomfortable and self-conscious. You and your husband have been invited to dinner at the Franklin home. The dinner is attended by three other couples. You feel tense and ill-at-ease. Consequently, you don't participate as much as the others. Your few efforts at participation, although they are as good as those of the others, don't leave you with any feeling of satisfaction because you don't feel that you contributed enough to

the conversation. At the end of the evening you feel unhappy
and dissatisfied with yourself.

There are other, more subtle skills that influence positive
outcomes. One has to do with the standards we set for ourselves. In the previous example, if you had expected to be the
life of the party, you obviously would not have felt good about
your participation. On the other hand, if you had set a more
modest goal for yourself, you might have evaluated your own
performance more favorably. How we evaluate our own performance is determined by the standards we set for ourselves.
Getting a pay raise is "objectively" a positive outcome; however, if you expected a much more substantial reward, you may
not experience the pay raise as a positive outcome.

Job-related skills are also important. You may lack the
skills to engage in the kind of occupation you would enjoy.
You may lack the skill to make a successful career change in
mid-life. If you have recently retired from work, or if your
children have grown up and have left home, you may need
to develop new skills to allow you to replace the positive interactions that are no longer available to you.

SUBTLE WAYS OF REMAINING
DEPRESSED

Thus far, we have been discussing obvious causes of depression.
For a variety of reasons the depressed person has ended up in
circumstances in which his or her interactions lead to a relatively small number of positive outcomes and to a large number of negative outcomes. By thinking about yourself carefully,
you should be able to evaluate the degree to which your interactions are associated with positive and negative outcomes,
and have some notion about the relative importance of the

contributing factors. Look carefully at the quantity and quality of your interactions. To what extent do they lead to positive outcomes? To what extent do they lead to negative outcomes?

There is another much more subtle way in which feelings of depression may occur and continue. A person who is depressed *is* hurting for good reason. He or she is in real pain. There is a natural tendency to want to tell somebody when we hurt, undoubtedly going back to childhood when we were "reinforced" by our parents or other caring adults for telling them when and where we hurt. They wanted to know because they cared for us and needed to decide if we should see a doctor. Because they needed to know, they (our parents, our doctor, other concerned persons) usually listened to our complaints with interest, sympathy, and understanding. The chances are good that just being able to tell someone about your hurts as a child, and having them listen carefully, made you feel better. Thus, such actions often have a positive outcome. It's not too surprising therefore that an adult who is depressed and hurting would want to tell someone about it, with the expectation that the other person will listen sympathetically. Talking about your depression and being sympathetically listened to may become a positive interaction and thereby serve to *perpetuate* depression. As you remember from the previous chapter, interactions with positive outcomes are more likely to be repeated; thus you may have developed an interaction that unwittingly might serve to continue your depression. In other words, "talking depression" can become an important source of positive reinforcement.

Mary's husband, Frank, is very preoccupied with his work. At dinner, and at other times when they are together, they spend a good deal of their time talking about his problems. Mary is genuinely interested in his problems, but there are times when she would also like to discuss some of the things that happen in *her* daily life. Whenever Mary introduces a topic of interest to her, Frank shows only mild interest and quickly returns to *his* topic. In other words, Mary's efforts to have positive interactions with Frank are not very successful. At a technical level, we might also say that the interaction is not reciprocal (not in balance) since he is not willing to provide her with the interest and attention that she is providing him. Since her relationship with her husband is her major source of reinforcement (she doesn't have a job and their children have gone to college), this lack of give-and-take in their relationship is an important cause of Mary's depression. Mary begins to have trouble sleeping (she has trouble falling asleep and wakes up several times in the night), and she doesn't feel rested when she wakes up in the morning. Her interests are waning, she feels tired, and she finds that more and more it is an effort to do anything. In other words, she is beginning to feel depressed. At the dinner table, she reports her problems with sleeping and her feelings of fatigue to Frank, who becomes unusually interested and solicitous, inquires about her health, and wonders whether she should see a doctor. The next morning he may even inquire about her situation, how well she has slept, etc. Unwittingly, Mary has found a key to obtaining his interest—which she very much wants! We would predict that the frequency with which she will report her symptoms to him is going to increase.

It's easy to see how some people become "chronic depressives." The environment often unwittingly serves to reinforce talking about one's depression. As time goes on, "talking depression" becomes more frequent and assumes a more prominent role in interactions with others.

CHARTING YOUR DAILY MOOD

The purpose of this book, of course, is to help you learn how to cope with your depression and to improve the way you feel. It will be very important for you to *look carefully at your ac-*

tivities and interactions to determine which of your interactions lead to positive outcomes and which are associated with negative outcomes. In order to help you feel less depressed, the succeeding chapters will show you how to increase positive outcomes and how to decrease negative ones. To do this you will have to be able to *pinpoint* specific instances associated with positive and negative outcomes.

The general expectation is that you will feel better on days when you have a lot of positive and few negative interactions than on days when you have few positive and many negative interactions. The fact that your mood changes from day to day will be helpful, because it will allow you to become aware of the impact of specific events on your mood.

Our mood varies from day to day and also from hour to hour. Even people who say they feel depressed "all the time" find that there are days when they feel less unhappy. By keeping track of your daily mood you put yourself in a position to

1. *Identify specific interactions, activities, and situations in which you feel especially good or bad.*

2. *Evaluate your progress.*

Since your primary goal is to reduce your depression level, tracking your mood will allow you to evaluate how successful you are in improving it. The Daily Mood Rating Form (Figure 3–3) uses a 9-point scale to help you indicate how good or bad you feel. At the end of each day, about an hour before you go to bed, decide what kind of day it has been for you. If it has been a bad day, you would give it a low number; if it has been a good day, you would give it a high number. You should begin to rate your daily mood *today* and continue to make ratings at the end of each day as long as you are working on any of the chapters of this book. You may wish to monitor your mood regularly after you have succeeded in reducing your depression. In this way the mood ratings can

Figure 3–3
Daily Mood Rating Form

Please rate your mood for this day (how good or bad you felt) using the 9-point scale shown. If you felt really great (the best you have ever felt or can imagine yourself feeling), mark 9. If you felt really bad (the worst you have ever felt or can imagine yourself feeling), mark 1. If it was a "so-so" (or mixed) day, mark 5.

If you felt worse than "so-so," mark a number between 2 and 4. If you felt better than "so-so," mark a number between 6 and 9. Remember, a low number signifies that you felt bad and a high number means that you felt good.

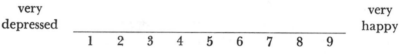

| very depressed | | | | | | | | | very happy |
| 1 | 2 | 3 | 4 | 5 | 6 | 7 | 8 | 9 | |

Enter the date on which you begin your mood ratings in Column 2 and your mood score in Column 3.

Monitoring Day	Date	Mood Score	Monitoring Day	Date	Mood Score
1			16		
2			17		
3			18		
4			19		
5			20		
6			21		
7			22		
8			23		
9			24		
10			25		
11			26		
12			27		
13			28		
14			29		
15			30		

Figure 3–4
Mary K's Daily Mood Ratings from June 10 to July 9

Monitoring Day	Date	Mood Score	Monitoring Day	Date	Mood Score
1	6–10	3	16	6–25	3
2	11	3	17	26	8
3	12	1	18	27	2
4	13	3	19	28	5
5	14	3	20	29	4
6	15	1	21	30	8
7	16	3	22	7– 1	7
8	17	4	23	2	9
9	18	6	24	3	8
10	19	3	25	4	5
11	20	7	26	5	6
12	21	9	27	6	3
13	22	6	28	7	7
14	23	3	29	8	8
15	24	2	30	9	8

serve as a warning signal if you begin to get depressed again in the future.[1]

Mary recorded her daily mood score for 30 days. Note that she felt quite depressed during the first week, her mood became more variable (she had some good and some bad days) during the second and third weeks, and she felt good on most days during the fourth week, although she still experienced an occasional bad day.

[1] A copy of the Daily Mood Rating Form is included in Appendix B. You may wish to use it to make additional copies for future daily monitoring of your mood.

SUMMARY

The social learning approach to depression attaches primary importance to the quality and quantity of our interactions. When many of our interactions are not associated with positive outcomes, we tend to feel depressed. Feeling depressed makes us feel less motivated to be active. Being passive makes it even less likely that we will have interactions with positive outcomes.

There are many reasons why you may be feeling depressed. As a result of major changes in your life situation, many interactions which had been sources of positive outcomes may no longer be available and/or you may lack the skills needed to obtain positive outcomes from your interactions. Therefore, in order for you to reduce your depression you will need to change the quality and quantity of your interactions in the direction of more positive and fewer negative outcomes. This requires that you carefully look at your activities and interactions to determine which lead to positive outcomes and which are associated with negative outcomes. The Daily Mood Rating Form will help you to become aware of the specific impact of events on your mood. The daily mood ratings will also allow you to evaluate how successful you are in improving your mood.

REVIEW

_____ I have a general understanding of the social learning approach to depression.

_____ I have begun to examine the quality and the quantity of my daily interactions to help me understand why I am feeling depressed.

_____ I have begun to think of reasons why few of my interactions have positive outcomes.

_____ I have begun to rate my daily mood using the form in Figure 3–3 and intend to continue making daily mood ratings for at least 30 days.

chapter 4

Introduction to Self-Change Methods

Many books have been written about personal adjustment. Few, however, tell how to do it or provide structured experience so you can learn how to do it. The keystone of this book is that by applying a few principles and techniques systematically, you can control your own depression. By changing your behavior and your thinking, you can reduce your depression. The chapters that follow are intended to show you how you can do it.

This chapter will explain certain basic principles and general techniques you can use to apply to your problems. The ideas and methods will be used in all of the succeeding chapters so it is important for you to master them. The key idea is that by systematically analyzing yourself—that is, your actions, your moods, your thoughts, and the quality of your interactions with others—you can formulate and successfully implement your own plan for self-change.

People who are depressed often feel or believe that they cannot change. The control of their own behavior or the events in their lives seems out of their hands. They feel helplessly caught in a set of circumstances, unable to see how they can change the situation through their own actions. The obstacles to change seem immense. The feeling of powerlessness pervades their lives. They may see how changing their own behavior might improve things, but the amount of effort required seems beyond their resources. Since so many of their previous social experiences often have been associated with negative outcomes, disappointments, rejections, and failures, this feeling of powerlessness or lack of belief in their ability to change is, of course, quite reasonable and understandable.

There are three critical ingredients for self-change:

1. The belief that one can change and influence one's own behavior.

2. The recognition that self-change is a skill that is gradually mastered and learned from experience.

3. The development of an action plan.

BELIEVING IS SEEING
(THE POSSIBILITIES)

The belief that people *can* change is, of course, a basic assumption in psychology and the other social sciences as well. Among all living creatures, human beings have the greatest potential for change. We get "hung up" if we expect unrealistically large changes. We can't all become concert pianists no matter how much we practice; we can't all become professional mathematicians no matter how many math classes we take. But there is no question that, with systematic effort, everyone can improve his or her musical or mathematical ability.

The changes needed for you to overcome your depression are all quite within your capabilities: learning how to relax (Chapter 6), how to increase the number of your pleasant activities (Chapter 7), how to change your behavior in social situations (Chapters 8 and 9), how to change the "quality" of your thinking (Chapter 10), and how to approach your problems more constructively (Chapter 11).

SLOW BUT SURE

Self-change is a gradually acquired skill. Like all other skills it requires effort, practice, and knowledge. Much of psychology is concerned with the study of the conditions that help people learn new skills, including the skills required to change their own behavior. Making use of this knowledge vastly increases our chances of being successful.

PLANNING FOR ACTION

It is not enough to know. One needs to formulate a plan that is reasonable, based on sound knowledge, can be implemented and, therefore, has a very good chance of success.

In this chapter we will describe the basic steps one needs to go through in order to develop *any* systematic self-change plan. It is intended to prepare you for the specific self-change plans suggested in Chapters 6–12. These steps can also be applied to other problems as well.

The steps to be described are:

1. Specifying the problem and deciding what to change.
2. Self-observing and gathering base-line data on the problematic behavior.
3. Discovering antecedents (events that occur before the problematic behavior happens).
4. Discovering consequences (events that occur after the problematic behavior happens).
5. Setting a helpful goal for change.
6. Contracting or rewarding yourself for accomplishing your goal.
7. Putting the finishing touches on your self-change plan and implementing it.
8. Evaluating your progress.
9. Stopping the program.

**Step 1: Specifying the Problem
and Deciding What to Change**

To use our approach, you must begin by selecting some *particular problem* as the target for your self-change plan. The first thing to do is decide *what* to change. Deciding which of several problems to work on is not an easy task for many people. Since it will take time and effort on your part to develop and implement your plan, you ought to pick a problem that is reasonably important to you and one with which you have a good chance of success. The problem you choose should be something you want to increase ("I want to have lunch with my friends more often"), something you wish to decrease ("I want to spend less time on my housework"), or some new skill you wish to learn ("I want to learn how to develop a self-change plan").

In specifying a problem you will typically move from a *general* or more abstract statement of the problem ("I want to become more active") to *specifics* ("I want to do physical exercises for 10 minutes every day before breakfast"). This process of moving from generalizations to specifics is called *pinpointing*. It requires that you narrow things down. A problem is said to be "pinpointed" if another person (or you) can tell by watching whether you have performed the behavior. This requires a somewhat detailed description of what is to be done. Pinpointing may also include a description of the situation in which the behavior will occur ("I want to feel more relaxed when talking with Mrs. Miller").

Useful pinpointing often includes numbers. "I would like to watch at least 30 minutes of television every night" is better than "I would like to watch some TV every night." "I would like to read one chapter of this book every day" is better than "I would like to do some reading every day."

The importance of good pinpointing cannot be overemphasized. Without it, you will be much less able to assess your progress, and you will find it difficult to apply the methods we are suggesting. Chapters 6–12 will assist you in moving from a general statement of a problem to specifically pinpointed target behaviors.

Step 2: Self-Observing and "Base-Lining"

Let's assume that you have pinpointed a specific problem (for example, you want to worry *less* often about what your child is doing when he is away from home). In order to establish a *reasonable* goal for change ("I will not worry more than 5, 8, or 10 times a day") and in order to be able to judge whether you are accomplishing your goal, you need to gather *base-line data.* This means that you want to *count* all occurrences of the pinpointed target behavior (every time you worry about him) for a specified period of time (for example, 1 week). As a result of doing this, you might discover that you worry about him, on the average, 10 times per day. You might then decide that a reasonable goal would be to reduce your worrying to 8 times per day during the next week. By *self-observing* the number of times the pinpointed behavior occurs *before, during,* and *after* you begin your self-change program, you will be better able to evaluate whether your self-change program is helpful.

There are many relatively simple ways people have found useful in observing and recording their actions. The important thing is to keep accurate records of the pinpointed behavior. Ideally, you should be able to record the behavior right when it occurs in natural situations. Therefore, it helps if your recording system is portable. If this is not feasible, you might want to do your counting at the end of the day at a regularly scheduled time. Keep in mind that you *must* be accurate.

Here are two examples of methods clients have developed for self-observing:

> *Example 1:* Margaret decides to focus on her self-deprecatory thoughts. She strongly suspects that she is contributing to her own depression by "putting herself down" frequently. By way of pinpointing the problem, Margaret has made a list of 10 of her typical self-deprecatory thoughts ("I am unattractive, clumsy, stupid," "I am a lousy housekeeper," "I have no will power," "I have been a bad mother," "I am not doing enough for my own mother," "I have let other people down," "Things will always be bad for me," "Nobody really cares whether I am dead or alive"). As a result of her careful pinpointing, Margaret is able to tell accurately when she is experiencing a self-deprecatory thought.
>
> To collect base-line data, Margaret designs a daily chart (Figure 4–1) on which to enter the number of self-deprecatory thoughts experienced during each hour of the day and to jot

Figure 4–1

Margaret's Daily Chart for Self-Observing Self-Deprecatory Thoughts

---

Date: *5-31-78*

Target Behavior: *Self Deprecatory Thoughts*

Time of Day	No. of Negative Thoughts	Comments
8– 9	*2*	*Was busy fixing breakfast, getting kids off to school*
9–10	*12*	*Had trouble getting started with housework*
10–11	*5*	*Busy shopping*
11–12	*2*	*Getting food stored in refrigerator, preparing lunch*
12– 1	*15*	*Lunch by myself*
1– 2	*2*	*Watched news and soap opera on TV*
2– 3	*8*	*Watched TV*
3– 4	*12*	*Started on preparing dinner*
4– 5	*8*	*Getting dinner ready*
5– 6	*2*	*Busy serving and eating dinner*
6– 7	*15*	*Doing the dishes, nobody helped*
7– 8	*12*	*Watching TV; other family members doing various things*
8– 9	*15*	*" " " " " " " "*
9–10	*8*	*Getting ready for bed*
10–11	*2*	*Read interesting and absorbing novel*
Daily Total	*120*	

---

down her observations. To count the target behaviors as they happen, Margaret purchased a wrist counter.[1] (An acceptable alternative would be making a mark on a small piece of paper every time a negative thought occurs.)

For each day she computes a daily total, and the results for 1 week are shown in Table 4–1.

---

[1] A mechanical device worn on the wrist. The "Response Counter" is available for $5.95 from Behaviordelia, Inc., P. O. Box 1044, Kalamazoo, Michigan 49005.

Table 4–1
Margaret's Daily Totals for a Week of Base-Lining

Mon.	Tues.	Wed.	Thurs.	Fri.	Sat.	Sun.
120	144	101	108	98	100	62

Example 2: Bill decides that he wants to increase his pleasant activities because he thinks this may help him to feel less depressed. To pinpoint the target behavior, Bill has written down a list of 10 activities he has enjoyed in the past and could do now: going to a basketball game, listening to one of his records, playing poker with his friends, reading a good novel, planning a trip, having a lively talk with a friend, attending church services, having free time all by himself, jogging, preparing breakfast for the family. Bill relied on his memory to generate his list, but he also found looking at the items on the Pleasant Events Schedule (Table 7–1) helpful.

Figure 4–2
Bill's Self-Observation Card

Number of Pleasant Activities

Date: *10-22-78 (Sunday)*

1. *Watched a football game on T.V. in afternoon – not very enjoyable because of interruptions and kids' chatter.*

2. *Managed to get in an hour of reading before dinner – interesting novel.*

3. *Had good conversation with neighbor about upcoming election after dinner.*

TOTAL = 3

To record and count pleasant activities Bill makes up 3″ × 5″ index cards for each day of the week, as shown in Figure 4–2. He continues self-observing for 1 week, with the daily totals shown in Table 4–2.

Table 4–2
Bill's Daily Total of Pleasant Activities during Base-Line Observation Week

Sun.	Mon.	Tues.	Wed.	Thurs.	Fri.	Sat.
3	1	0	1	1	1	4

Small booklets of 3″ × 5″ cards are adequate for counting many target behaviors. They are especially useful if you want to record not just the occurrence of the behavior but also what the situation was like, what happened before, and what happened after. Wrist counters and pocket counters will be useful for behaviors that are fleeting, occur with high frequency, and are difficult to remember.

For most target behaviors (such as the number of negative thoughts, social contacts, and pleasant activities), counting will be sufficient. When the amount of time spent on the pinpointed behavior is important (for example, if pinpointed behavior is exercising or reading your favorite kind of novel), you may also want to record the amount of time spent in the behavior. Using a stopwatch can be helpful.

While we recommend that base-line data be collected for at least a week, there is no absolute rule for how long you should self-observe before implementing your self-change plan. Since feelings of depression often cycle over time, it might help to take the time *now* to get a thorough picture of what you experience. Weekends, for example, may vary from weekdays, but not always. The purpose of base-line data is to establish how often the behavior is happening and in what situations. At the end of the base-line period you should be fairly confident that you know how often you experience the behavior(s) you wish to change.

Obtaining self-observation data is tedious and takes time. Be patient with yourself. Take the time now to "get the facts" before jumping ahead. A fringe benefit of self-observation is that just becoming more aware of our own behavior sometimes reduces negative and increases positive behaviors.

A graph is often useful for analyzing your base-line data. In the graph shown in Figure 4–3, days (the time unit) are marked off on the horizontal axis, and the numbers of pleasant activities (the pinpointed behavior) are marked off on the vertical axis. The graph shows that during the first week this cli-

Figure 4–3

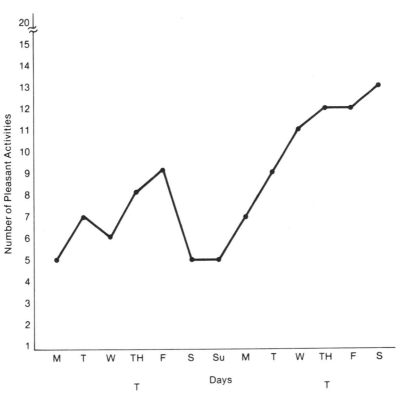

ent's number of daily pleasant activities was low and there was relatively little variation from day to day during the first week. During the second week, when treatment began, there was a small but noticeable increase.

Step 3: Discovering Antecedents

Discovering antecedents can be a big help as you formulate your self-change plan. There are two general factors that influence much of our behavior: What happens *before* the behavior happens (*antecedents*) and what happens *afterward* (*consequences*). Discovering antecedents can be a challenging and interesting process. Think of it as sleuthing, a type of detective work. You are on the lookout for as many clues as possible, thinking about them, trying out a few hunches to see if they make a difference, and continuing until you have gained a better understanding of how certain antecedents may be influencing your behavior. Let us look at a few examples:

> *Example 1.* Your pinpointed behavior is self-deprecatory or put-down thoughts ("I am not doing this well," "I know I am going to blow it," "Nobody likes me," "I am dumb, ugly, awkward"). You would like to think these thoughts less often, and, as part of collecting base-line data, you have been counting how often they occur for the past week. You discover that they mainly happen in two types of situations: when you are by yourself with nothing particularly to do and when you are with people you consider to be "superior" to yourself. Being by yourself and being with "superior" people are antecedents for your self-critical thoughts.

> *Example 2.* Initiating conversations with people you know but would like to get to know better is your focus. Through self-observation you discover that you always feel more tense and anxious just before initiating a conversation with people you would like to know better. Your feelings of tenseness probably interfere with your ability to engage in conversations with these people.

Example 3. You would like to lose weight and have decided to observe your eating habits. During self-observation you discover that you do most of your snacking in the kitchen, especially while preparing meals. Being in the kitchen is an antecedent for your problem eating.

Example 4. You are interested in reducing the number of times you feel anxious and upset. You discover through self-observation that you always feel upset when your mother-in-law "drops in" on you. Your mother-in-law's unexpected presence is an antecedent to your feeling upset.

In each of the examples the objective was to discover events or situations which may influence the behavior of concern to you. There are four kinds of antecedents for which you will be searching: *social settings* (Example 1), *your own feelings and thoughts* (Example 2), *physical circumstances* (Example 3), and the *behavior of other people* (Example 4).

There is nothing mysterious about discovering antecedents, but it takes a conscious effort and some careful attention. This is best accomplished through self-observing in a systematic fashion, because we typically fail to notice antecedents and often "forget" about what leads up to our experience of depression. The antecedents have been "automatic" in that we don't notice them. One technique that is helpful in dealing with this automatic quality of antecedents is to pause before responding.

You can control antecedents by avoiding them, by changing them, or by not responding to them. Avoiding antecedents entirely may not always be practical, but you might be able to cut down. Thus, in Example 3 you can probably spend less time in the kitchen, and in Example 4 you might try to arrange for your mother-in-law to visit less often and at pre-arranged times. For Example 1, your self-change plan might include spending less time by yourself without anything to do, and in Example 2 your plan might include making an active effort to relax yourself (Chapter 6) prior to initiating conversations.

You should try to discover antecedents during the base-line period. This will allow you to use your information about the antecedents in your self-change plan. List what you consider to be relevant antecedents and consider possible ways of controlling them. The following example illustrates how discovering antecedents can be helpful in developing a self-change plan:

> Eileen feels concerned about the deterioration of her relationship with her husband, Stuart. Up until a year ago Eileen felt happy and satisfied with her marriage and optimistic about their future together. Over the past year the number of arguments between them has risen sharply, and things have gotten to a point where they both feel angry and hurt a lot. Eileen feels that their arguments contribute to her feeling depressed so she would like to design a self-change program aimed at reducing the number of arguments.
>
> Eileen designs the self-observation chart shown in Figure 4–4. In addition to obtaining base-line data, Eileen is also interested in discovering what specific conditions and events precede their arguments. Note that Eileen has decided to enter her daily mood score on the chart, to make it easier for her to determine the influence of the arguments on her mood. (As it turned out, Eileen felt considerably more depressed on days when they had many arguments.)
>
> After self-observing for 1 week, Eileen concludes that the majority of their arguments are stimulated by disagreements about finances and the children's behavior. She decides to concentrate first on finances. In order to reduce financial matters as an antecedent for arguments, Eileen proposes to Stu that they set aside regular times every week when they can work on reaching agreement on nonroutine purchases.

Step 4: Discovering Consequences

Consequences are "events" which happen *after* we engage in behavior. They affect how we feel about the behavior and influence the likelihood that we will engage in the behavior in the future. There are basically two kinds of consequences that

Figure 4–4

Eileen's Self-Observation Chart

Date: 2-12-78

Target Behavior: *Number of arguments with Stu*

Mood Score for this day: 3

Number of Arguments: 5

Behavior	Antecedents
7:30 Stu criticizes me for not having his breakfast ready. I tell him that maybe he should fix it himself.	Children slow in getting ready. Need to be nagged to get dressed, etc.
7:45 I tell Stu that we could save money if he gave up smoking, and didn't spend so much on the car.	Stu lets me know that he doesn't like the new drapes I bought and that the old ones were OK as far as he was concerned.
7:50 I tell Stu to try to be home on time.	Stu gets ready to leave looking angry and upset.
5:00 Stu criticizes me for being too harsh on the children. I tell him that he is too lenient.	My son, Bill, drops food on the floor. I criticize his table manners.
7:00 I tell Stu that I want to keep the drapes and that he is generally uncaring about the appearance of the house.	Stu wants me to see about returning the new drapes.

we need to be concerned about: (1) reactions from other people, and (2) our own reactions (that is, the things we say to ourselves as we evaluate our performance).

In general, consequences may be positive, neutral, or negative. Positive consequences, by definition, make us feel good and make it more likely (perhaps easier) that we will repeat the behavior in the future. Negative consequences, of course, make us feel bad and make it less likely (more difficult) to do certain things in the future. Neutral consequences are in between; since they are not as good as positive consequences and not as bad as negative ones, they do not have as much influence on us.

What relevance does all of this have to formulating a self-change plan? Let's look at a few examples:

> *Worrying about Health:* You have decided to worry less often about your health. During self-observation you discover that your worrying is often followed by one of two events: (1) when you share your concerns with your husband, he sympathetically listens to you and offers suggestions (thus showing more interest in you than he usually does), and (2) when you are alone and worrying, you are likely to have a snack to calm yourself. In both instances, your worrying has been followed by a positive consequence (having your husband show interest or having a snack), which is—you guessed it—going to make it *more* likely that you will continue to worry.

> *Learning about Real Estate:* To know more about real estate you have enrolled in a course. Your target behavior is working on your assignments, so you are self-observing the frequency and duration of your studying. You find that quite often your studying is interrupted by demands from members of your family, the phone, and so on. These interruptions act as a kind of negative consequence for your studying, which—you guessed right again—is not helping you to accomplish your goal.

> *Starting Conversations:* Initiating social contacts is your focus. You discover during self-observing that after you have started a conversation, you find yourself thinking about making a fool of yourself, that you should have said this or that differently,

or that the other person probably didn't enjoy talking with you. This self-criticism acts as a negative consequence, which discourages your efforts to become more socially active.

When you want to *decrease* a behavior, you don't want it to be followed by positive consequences. When you want to *increase* a behavior, you don't want it to be followed by negative consequences. Instead you want just the opposite. How to develop a structured *plan* to have your target behavior followed by the desired kind of consequence will be discussed in Step 6 (Contracting).

As part of your efforts to gather base-line information, try to identify *consequences* that follow certain behavior. List consequences that you think may interfere with achieving your goal, and consider some possible ways of controlling them.

Step 5: Setting a Helpful Goal

Begin with a modest goal. If your concern is initiating conversations with people and your base-line data indicates that you haven't been engaging in the behavior at all, your initial goal might be one conversation per week. If your goal is to increase physical exercise and you have been exercising at a low and irregular rate, your goal might be 5 minutes of exercise per day. *No step is too small.* You *want* to select a relatively *easy* goal in order to make it more likely that you will be successful in your self-change program. Increase your goals *slowly,* and only *after* you have accomplished your previous goal.

Step 6: Contracting

Contracting means making a specific agreement with yourself to reward yourself *if and only if* you do certain things. The purpose of the contract is to arrange in advance a specific, posi-

tive consequence (reinforcement) to *follow* the achievement of
a goal. For example, your contract might state that you will
have dinner at your favorite restaurant *if and only if* you complete base-line observations for 1 week.

Why are rewards so important? First, any self-change plan
is tedious and difficult to develop and carry out. Second, meaningful change takes effort. Therefore, it is highly desirable for
you to incorporate a contract in which you arrange to reinforce
yourself for accomplishing your goals.[2]

Reinforcers may involve material rewards, time, or mental
events. Examples of material rewards include food, magazines
or books, clothes, records, and other objects requiring money.
Time could involve earning time to do things you like to do
but rarely have time for, such as taking a relaxing bath, sleeping late, sunbathing, talking on the phone, "wasting time," and
so on. Mental rewards can be self-generated "pats on the back"
(such as thinking about your good points, your accomplishments, good relations with others) or mental "treats" (such as
daydreaming about pleasurable things, meditating or listening
to music). The items on the Pleasant Events Schedule (Table
7–1) might suggest other reinforcers.

There are four important considerations in selecting a reinforcer.

1. It must be something that is going to make you feel
good.

2. It must be accessible to you. You can't go skiing in the
summer, and you may not be able to afford a trip to Hawaii.

3. You should be concerned about the strength of the
reinforcer. Will you gain enough from the reward to compen-
sate you for the time and effort that it will take to achieve your

---

[2] Some people find contracting objectionable because it makes them feel
they are rewarding themselves for something they should be doing anyway. If,
for this or other reasons, you find contracting aversive, omit it from your self-
change plan. It is an optional component. We recommend the inclusion of contracting because it has been our experience that it makes the accomplishment
of goals easier for many people.

goal? You should think of the reinforcement as not only rewarding the target behavior but as offering enough reinforcement for your *total* effort, including such things as self-observing.

4. It must be something that you can definitely control. Thus, having your husband take you out to dinner is a reinforcer you might want to select *if* you can count on him to deliver the goods. If you involve other people in your contract, you will probably want to discuss it with them beforehand. There are advantages to involving another person because it mobilizes another motivational factor: social pressure.

You also need to be concerned about the time relationship in writing your contract. Try to make the reinforcement take place *as close in time* to the achievement of a goal as possible; the sooner the better (see Figure 4–5). You don't want to reinforce yourself 2 weeks later. Of course, it may not be practical for you to reinforce yourself immediately, but it's better to do

Figure 4–5
Model Contract

Required Behavior	If I, *Eleanor Jacobsen,* *go to the Bridge Club on Monday afternoon and to the Obsidian Club on Tuesday evening and if I initiate a conversation at each of these gatherings with someone whom I had not met before,*
Reward	I will reward myself *by spending Wednesday afternoon at the Valley River Shopping Center and try to find and buy a dress I really like.*

Signed,

Eleanor Jacobsen

so, especially in the beginning. Perhaps you should reconsider your choice of rewarding events if there is a time delay.

Step 7: Finishing Touches and Action

You are now ready to put the finishing touches on your self-change plan. Let us briefly review what you have accomplished thus far:

You began with a general problem (for example, you feel lonely) and you were able to make it more specific through pinpointing (for example, you want to increase the number of social contacts you have with people you like who are approximately your age). You wrote out a contract in the notebook you are using for developing your plan: "If I develop a self-observation system and collect base-line data for 2 weeks I will buy *War and Peace* by Tolstoy, which I really would like to have." By using a 4″ × 5″ index card for each day you were able to collect accurate data on the target behavior. You did this by taking a few minutes at midday, at 5 P.M., and at 10 P.M. to record the number of social contacts you had had until then, and to enter a few comments about each with the goal of discovering relevant antecedents and consequences. At the end of 1 week of self-observation you buy *War and Peace*. Looking over your data you learn that:

1. During the week you had a total of four social contacts all of which were initiated by acquaintances who phoned you. You went out to lunch with one of them and had a good time (positive consequence).

2. You considered calling some of your friends, but the thought made you feel apprehensive. You guessed that they were probably busy and worried that they wouldn't enjoy being with you (negative antecedent).

3. When you went out to lunch, your husband was upset

because he didn't know you had gone and no one was home when your child came home from school (negative consequence).

On the basis of your self-observations you decide that:

1. Your goal will be to increase your number of social contacts to three per week for 2 weeks.

2. If no one has called you by 11 A.M. you will call one of your friends and suggest that you and she do something together.

3. Prior to calling one of your friends you will make an active effort to relax yourself and to rehearse the first three statements you will make.

4. You will advise your husband of your plans ahead of time and get a babysitter or make some other arrangements for your child.

5. You will make a contract with your husband: "If I, Eleanor Jacobsen, achieve my goal of three social contacts per week, you, Larry Jacobsen, will accompany me to the shopping center and help me select a new dress."

You are now ready to put your plan into action.

Sounds too simple? The plan assumes that you have friends you can call and that your husband, while perhaps somewhat jealous and overprotective, is basically a helpful man. The plan may seem easy because the target behavior doesn't require developing new skills on your part. The plan might have been more difficult to develop if the target behavior had involved improving the quality of your social interactions, reducing negative and worrisome thoughts, or reducing the discomfort you feel in a specific situation. That's what the succeeding chapters are all about.

Step 8: Evaluating Your Progress

Your major goal, of course, is to reduce your depression. You are evaluating this goal through the daily mood ratings you began in Chapter 3 and which you are continuing as long as you are using this book. If you haven't been completing these daily mood ratings, be sure to start now! (Check back to Figure 3–3 if necessary).

Are you achieving the specific goal of your plan? Self-change plans can't influence your depression unless you are able to increase, or to decrease, the target behaviors you have selected to change. If the plan is working, you might want to increase your goals gradually until you get to a level with which *you* feel satisfied. Increase your goal *gradually*, and don't increase just for the sake of increasing. If your program is *not* working, re-evaluate your whole program and consider what changes to make.

To illustrate, let's take another look at Eileen's progress:

Eileen's target was to reduce the number of arguments with her husband. Her theory was that by reducing their arguments she could improve the quality of their relationship and that this, in turn, would result in her feeling less depressed. From base-lining she had learned that they were averaging five arguments per day and that many of these arguments were preceded by Stu's critical comments about Eileen's spending habits. Eileen's self-change plan involved setting up regular times when she and her husband would, uninterrupted by the children, try to agree on nonroutine purchases desired by either of them. Eileen's goal was to reduce the number of their arguments to no more than three per day. In order to evaluate the effectiveness of the plan she needed to know whether: the intervention (regular meeting to talk about finances) actually decreased their arguments, and whether a reduction in arguments resulted in an improvement in her depression.

Eileen continued to count their arguments and to record her

daily mood on her self-observation chart. At the end of 3 weeks she summarized her data (Table 4–3). As can be seen, Eileen

Table 4–3
Summary of Eileen's Self-Observation

	Base-line	Intervention
Day	1 2 3 4 5 6 7 8	9 10 11 12 13 14 15 16 17 18 19 20 21
No. of Arguments	5 6 4 7 3 4 5 3	2 4 0 2 1 1 0 3 0 1 2 1 1
Daily Mood Score	3 2 5 2 6 5 2 5	6 4 8 6 7 6 7 5 7 6 5 6 7

Average No. of Arguments: 4.8
Average Mood Score: 3.6

Average No. of Arguments: 1.5
Average Mood Score: 6.1

had good reason to feel pleased with her self-change plan. Not only had it drastically reduced their arguments, but Eileen was also feeling much less depressed.

Common sources of difficulty are:

1. Poor pinpointing—target behaviors too vaguely defined.

2. Faulty record keeping that results in spotty or incomplete data.

3. Reinforcing yourself even when you have not completely fulfilled your end of the contract.

4. Reinforcement too weak.

5. Reinforcement delayed too long.

6. Goal too broad or ambitious.

Step 9: Stopping the Program

When you feel you have achieved satisfactory results, there will be a strong temptation to discontinue a specific self-change program. There is nothing wrong with this. However, you need to be concerned about whether the goals you have achieved are going to be maintained. Your best bet is to use a "fading out" procedure. Let's say that after 4 weeks you are satisfied with the results of your program (for example, you have one really pleasant social contact per day, and that feels about right to you). You might decide to stop reinforcing yourself (you cancel the contract), *but* you continue to self-observe for another 2 weeks. If your self-observation shows that the target behavior is dropping off, put the reinforcement back in your program. If the behavior is maintained at the level you are satisfied with, you stop self-observing.

A piece of advice: Save your self-change plan, your data, and your notes. If you should get depressed again in the future, you won't have to start from scratch.

A final piece of advice: Work on *one* self-change plan (never more than two) at a time. It gets too confusing otherwise.

REVIEW

You may feel a little overwhelmed at this point and uncertain about whether you can put all the steps together into a meaningful self-change plan. This has indeed been a difficult chapter—not because any one of the steps are particularly complex but because there are so many of them. Keep in mind that our intent is to provide you with the general skills you will need in order to execute any self-change plan. You will be provided with additional suggestions and instructions in Chapters 6–12.

At this point it may be useful to review the steps in designing a self-change plan. You may want to re-read specific sections of this chapter as needed. We also urge you to go through the motions of actually designing a *complete* hypothetical self-change plan starting with a problematic behavior chosen from one of the examples or making up one.

1. The first thing you must decide is which problem to work on. *Suggestion*: Try to start with as concrete and specific a problem as you can. It is easier to pinpoint from "I want to have more fun when my wife and I are together" than from "I want to feel less depressed."

The problem I have chosen to work on for this exercise is:

_____

_____

2. After you have selected a problem, you move on to *pinpointing* the problem. This involves listing as many specific instances of the problem behavior as you can think of (approximately 10). The purpose of pinpointing is to allow you to recognize when the behavior occurs.

Now try to pinpoint your problem: _____

_____

_____

_____

_____

_____

_____

_____

_____

_____

_____

Question: Is your pinpointing specific enough so that someone else, but at least you, can clearly observe and count occurrences of the target behavior?

3. You are now ready to design a self-observation chart and a method for collecting base-line data. The main considerations here are simplicity and accuracy. Your system should allow you to collect information about antecedents and consequences.

For example, if the target was to increase the number of pleasant interactions between you and your wife, there is no need for a counter. You can probably remember the times the pinpointed behavior occurred during the previous day. The self-observation chart might look like Figure 4–6.

If the pinpointed behaviors occur often (for example, experiencing negative thoughts, smoking cigarettes, talking about depression with acquaintances) you might need to use a mechanical counter (or some other systematic way of counting) rather than rely on your memory. If the pinpointed behaviors involve activities which go on for longer periods of time (for example, doing housework, studying, reading a book) the self-observation method would need to include measuring the length of time the behavior occurred.

Figure 4–6
Self-Observation Chart

Date:	2-28-77
Mood Score:	8
Number of occurrences:	2

Behaviors	Antecedents	Consequences
1. Talked about our vacation plans	Bill was off today	We agreed on camping trip. Both looking forward to it.
2. Went out to dinner	I didn't have enough time to fix dinner	Bill upset because of high cost of restaurant. Both of us felt upset.

Now try to develop a self-observation method and chart for your pinpointed behaviors.

4. You are now ready to collect base-line data. This should go on for about one week—during which you make no effort to increase or decrease the behavior(s). You just do what you have been doing all along.

5. Using Table 4–3 as a possible model, make a systematic effort to summarize your base-line data. (For this exercise, make up imaginary data.) Decide on a reasonable (modest) goal for change.

On the basis of what you have learned about antecedents and consequences, what interventions can you think of to facilitate your ability to accomplish your goal? Remember that if your goal is to *decrease* a behavior, you want to avoid antecedents that stimulate the behavior and to avoid positive consequences for the behavior. On the other hand if you want to *increase* a behavior, you want to avoid or minimize antecedents which interfere with the behavior and to avoid negative consequences. Fixing a goal for change *and* making a systematic effort in planning and doing the things that will maximize the changes of accomplishing your goal are at the heart of your self-change plan.

6. You may now want to draw up a *contract* to reward yourself for accomplishing your goal. In drawing up the contract (for example, see Figure 4–5), you need to specify the reinforcer and the exact conditions under which it will be awarded.

7. You are now ready to implement your plan. You will now want to stick with the plan as much as possible and give it a chance to work. A 2-week period is usually sufficient time to see if something is working or not. During this time you are, of course, continuing to collect self-observation data. Without it you have no systematic way of evaluating the effectiveness of your plan.

8. You now come to the moment of truth. Did your plan work? The first thing you want to know is whether you accomplished your goal. Did the pinpointed behaviors increase, or decrease, as you had intended? If not, you need to go back and revise your plan. If you accomplished your goal, or there was at least some noticeable change in the target behavior, are you now feeling less depressed, or are you feeling less often depressed, than when you began your self-change plan? The daily mood scores should help you to determine whether there has been any reduction in your depression. If you accomplished your goal for change but there has been no change in your depression, it means that the problem you selected and pinpointed (Steps 1 and 2) is not related to your depression. In that case you will need to select another problem to work on.

Example: Myron, who has been feeling quite depressed, decides to work on cutting down on smoking cigarettes. He has been smoking two packs a day. His self-change program is very successful in bringing down his smoking to five cigarettes per day within 4 weeks. Unfortunately, there is no corresponding change in his depression level. Myron concludes that his smoking is not an influential factor in his depression. He decides next to work on the quality and quantity of his social interactions. This time his self-change plan succeeds not only in regard to the target behavior but also is accompanied by a significant reduction of his depression.

Chapter 5 presents some useful guidelines to help you select particular problems that may be related to your depression. You can then use the basic principles introduced in this chapter, along with specific suggestions contained in subsequent chapters, to plan and implement your own self-change program.

part II

The
Strategies

chapter 5

Creating a Personal Plan to Overcome Depression

Thus far, you probably have been reading straight through this book. The chapters up to now have been general background, and are needed in order to understand and use the rest of this book. But from here on you may not need to read each chapter. Instead, you may need to skip around and read chapters out of order to get the best results from this book. There are two reasons for this: First, some of the chapters deal with specific problems of much greater importance to *your* depression; other chapters may not. Second, we want you to tackle no more than one or two problems at a time. After finishing this chapter you should have a good overview of what is available in the following chapters. In addition, you will have *set priorities* in such a way that you will be able to decide which problems you should work on first.

In Chapter 1 you learned that not everyone experiences

depression in the same way. Some people will feel guilty and have trouble sleeping and eating when depressed; others will isolate themselves and feel lonely and friendless; still others will cry often and give up their usual pleasant activities.

Every depressed person has a unique set of specific problems. You need to evaluate how *you* experience depression and to use the parts of this book which can be of most help to *you*. At this point you may feel eager to read and use everything you can. Every problem we suggest may sound familiar, and you may feel like changing everything at once. Your enthusiasm is fine, but we urge you to slow down. There is a natural tendency for all of us to want many things to change quickly. Unfortunately, this is not realistic. If you try to do too much, you're likely to end up confused, discouraged, and more depressed than ever. You're much more likely to be successful if you focus on a small number of problems that are very important to you. If you do one or two things at a time, you can make progress and feel more self-confident. Then you can try one or two more things, if you wish, and continue to improve yourself. Take it slow; set yourself up for success, not for failure.

This chapter will help you identify the problems you have and determine which are related to your depression, and it will help you decide how important each one is. Then you can concentrate on the sections of the book related to those problems. Not every problem experienced by people in life is covered in this book. Instead, we have tried to focus on those problems that seem to be most related to depression. We will, however, make suggestions for how you can get help with other problems.

SELF-ASSESSMENT: TAKING STOCK
OF YOUR PROBLEMS

Relaxation

Do you think of yourself as a relaxed person or a tense, anxious person? Try to answer not just in terms of whether you know how to relax, but also in terms of whether you actually *feel relaxed* most of the time. If you are experiencing any of the following problems, you are probably not feeling relaxed most of the time:

1. If your muscles feel tight, tense, or cramped during the day, or if you wake up with muscle cramps during the night, you may be experiencing muscle tension.

2. If you feel tired a lot, and there is no major physical reason for it, it may be that you are wasting energy because your muscles are tight and tense.

3. If you have frequent headaches (more than one or two a week), or if your headaches are very intense, you are probably tensing your facial muscles or the muscles in your neck and shoulders.

4. If you have trouble sleeping, you are probably not relaxing at night. If you regularly take more than an hour to go to sleep, or if you wake up in the night or early morning more than once or twice a week, then you may want to learn how to relax.

5. If you have painful stomach aches more than once or twice a week it is possible that they are caused by tension (obviously, you should also check out such symptoms with a medical doctor).

6. If you often feel jittery or shaky, then you should learn to relax.

If any of the problems mentioned sounds like yours, then learning to relax could be helpful. However, it still may *not* be the most important problem for you. On page 89 there is a place to list all of the problems on which you *could* work; later in this chapter you will decide, working from that list, which *one* or *two* problems you will work on first. For now, if you are experiencing any of the difficulties just described, go to page 89 and write "Relaxation" on the first line under the *Problem* heading. Next to the problem, write "Chapter 6" under the *Chapter* heading. That is the section in this book which describes how to relax and how to use relaxation to solve specific problems like insomnia, headaches, nervous stomach, etc. Ignore the *Importance* heading for now, and continue evaluating your own depression-related problems.

Pleasant Activities

Many people who are depressed have drastically cut down or have stopped doing things which are enjoyable for them. They may be busy doing what they *have* to do but have given up the things they *want* to do just for enjoyment. Consequently, they feel that the fun has gone out of life. Sometimes they also stop feeling like anything *could* be much fun or enjoyable. Nothing sounds very pleasant, so there seems to be no reason to try and get busy again.

Think about whether these things have happened to you. Are you doing as many pleasant things as you used to be before you became depressed? Compared with other people your age, are you doing as many pleasant, enjoyable things as they seem to be doing? If you answered "no" to either of these questions, this area is another on which you might choose to work. If so, turn to page 89 and write "Pleasant Activities" under the

Problem heading and "Chapter 7" under the Chapter heading. Later you will decide whether this is one of the most important problems for you.

Problems with People

Evaluating your own social behavior with others is a difficult task. If you are like most people, it is hard to be objective or accurate about your personal attractiveness and social appeal. It may help to talk over the following questions with someone whom you know well and trust, rather than just trying to judge yourself. If no one like that is available, do the best you can on your own.

Consider the following:

1. Do you have trouble behaving in an assertive manner? All of these skills are part of being appropriately assertive:

- Giving praise or compliments sincerely.

- Saying "no" when you mean it.

- Speaking up when asked for your opinion.

- Offering constructive criticism when it would be useful.

- Being able to express anger without blowing up at others.

- Being able to tell others about your feelings of love or friendship for them.

Being assertive is a broad category; it includes all of these things and more. In general, we would say that assertion is the ability to express your own thoughts and feelings without *imposing* them on others or making others uncomfortable. If you lack that skill, turn to page 89 and write "Social skill: Assertion" under the *Problem* heading and "Chapter 8" under the *Chapter* heading.

2. Is your personal style pleasant or unpleasant for those around you? Are people comfortable with you, or do you have mannerisms and behavior habits that make others uncomfortable? Some unpleasant mannerisms that depressed people often develop are the following:

- Slow, halting speech.

- Criticizing others.

- Lack of responsiveness (not answering questions, not taking your turn in a conversation, etc.).

- Ignoring others.

- Not showing interest in what others say.

- Lack of eye contact while talking to others.

- Focusing on negative things in your speech, complaining, brooding out loud, etc.

- Lack of good grooming ("letting yourself go").

- Unpleasant facial expression (frowns, scowls).

If you have acquired any of these negative personal habits, you may find that people are avoiding you or enjoying your company less. That may make you even more depressed than you already are. If you have some of these problems write "Social skills: Personal style" under the *Problem* heading and "Chapter 8" under the *Chapter* heading on page 89.

3. Do you spend very little of your time doing things with other people? Often people who are depressed tend to be socially isolated or to lose interest in being with friends. Even if they are around people, they often stop interacting with others, getting to know others better, or making plans to do pleasant things with others.

Think about yourself: Are you spending less time with

people than you did before you became depressed? Are you spending less time with people than most others seem to spend? Have you stopped getting together with friends? Have you started sitting by yourself quietly when with a group of friends, rather than talking to them? If any of these things are happening to you, this is likely to be a significant problem area. If so, write "Social skills: Isolation" under the *Problem* heading on page 89 and "Chapter 9" under the *Chapter* heading.

There are many kinds of social problems. If you feel this is a problem area for you, but none of the specific problems described above seem to fit, there are several things you can do. You might skim Chapters 8 and 9 to see whether the material covered there seems to address your particular problem. If so, enter "Social skill" under the *Problem* heading on page 89 and write the appropriate chapter number next to it. Later you can decide whether to start with that problem or whether it is less important for now.

If the problems you have are not covered in Chapters 8 or 9, or if they seem to be related to interpersonal problems in your marriage or at work, keep reading this chapter. The evaluation of marital and vocational problems will be discussed toward the end of this chapter. Some social problems may not be covered in this book at all, such as severe conflicts with one particular person (e.g., a neighbor or a parent), or problems with impulsive or explosive anger. If one of these is an important problem for you, it might be a good idea to talk to a counselor. Such a talk may help you decide whether you need to seek help for your social problems or whether there are other life problems which need to be tackled first.

Troublesome Thoughts

Often people who are depressed have a number of negative, self-critical, or pessimistic thoughts. In fact, it is hard to imagine that anyone who is usually thinking about happy or pleasant things could be depressed. Think about the following questions:

1. Do you have unpleasant negative thoughts whenever your attention is not completely directed?

2. Do you find yourself expecting negative outcomes and thinking about them even when there's no good reason to think something bad might happen?

3. Do you sometimes (as often as once a day) think about something that seems really horrible to you?

4. Are you upset because you don't seem able to turn off your negative, self-critical, or pessimistic thoughts?

If you answered "yes" to any of these questions, then learning how to control your thoughts might be helpful to you. If so, write "Controlling thoughts" under the *Problem* heading on page 89 and "Chapter 10" next to it.

Approaching Your Problems Constructively

Another problem depressed people may face is an inability to react in a reasonable or constructive way when they run into a problem. Think about your own reaction to difficulties. Do you overreact to upsetting events and find it hard to cope with problems? Do you tend to think of yourself as a victim of problems, rather than tackling them and trying to solve them? Do you feel that it is shameful to have problems or that you are worthless if you run into a difficulty?

If you recognize yourself in these statements, or if they sound familiar (although not exactly the way you might express them), then you may not know how to approach your problem constructively. If so, on page 89 you should write "Constructive approach" under the *Problem* heading and "Chapter 11"

Importance	Problem	Chapter

under the *Chapter* heading next to it. Later you will decide
whether this is one of the most important problems you face
right now.

Self-Control Problems

Helping yourself is difficult. This book assumes that you
are able and willing to work on your own to change some of
your life problems. You may be *willing;* the fact that you have
gotten this far shows that you are interested. However, you will
soon have to start working fairly hard and following through
on your plans. For depressed people this is often a difficult
thing to do. When people get depressed, they often feel tired,
passive, easily discouraged and ready to quit. It's not easy to
keep going when you feel lousy. But you will need to keep
going, even when it's hard, in order to start feeling good about
yourself. In order to tell whether you might find it especially
difficult to keep working on your problems, think about the
following questions:

1. Have you tried a self-help program before and then
   given up on it?

2. Do you "freeze" in difficult situations and let things get
   out of hand? That is, do you find that you know what
   you should do but wind up not doing it for some
   reason?

3. Do you start things—like dieting, giving up smoking—
   and then drop it because you have lost interest?

4. Do you have a number of half-finished projects sitting
   around at home or at work?

If you answered "yes" to any of these questions, you may
need to master self-control skills before you begin to work on

other specific problems. If so, write "Self-Control" under the *Problem* heading on page 89 and "Chapter 12" under the *Chapter* heading. If you list this particular problem, you should *immediately* put the number 1 in the left-hand column titled *Importance*. You will need to be able to make a sustained effort in order to solve any other problems you have already listed.

PROBLEMS RELATED TO DEPRESSION
BUT NOT COVERED IN THIS BOOK

Marital Problems

This book will *not* try to help you resolve major marital problems. Some of your difficulties may be helped by this book; for instance, if your mate wants you to be more active and do more things that are enjoyable, rather than sitting around so much, then working on Chapter 7 (*Pleasant Activities*) may help your marriage at the same time that it helps you personally. However, most serious marital problems are more complex, and you should think about getting professional help for them.

There are four qualities we feel a good marriage should have. If your marriage does not provide the satisfactions discussed in the following list, you may want to talk with your mate about marital counseling. The next section, *Seeking Help for Marital Problems*, will describe some procedures for finding a counselor in your area. (By counselor we mean a counseling or clinical psychologist, marriage and family counselor, clinical social worker, or other trained professional.)

1. In a good marriage, partners share pleasant activities together. They don't spend *all* their time together, of course, but they do take time often to do things that are mutually pleasurable. If you and your spouse spend very little time to-

gether, or if all your time together is spent on daily, routine chores, you might want to explore together what activities you could begin sharing. You might be able to do this on your own, but you might also consider looking for a counselor who could help you.

2. In a good marriage, there is a reasonable level of conflict. Disagreements occur, of course, but they can be worked out in a good marriage without extreme anger or prolonged conflict. If you fight frequently or fight with great bitterness, you might want to seek help from a marriage counselor.

3. In a good marriage, mutual satisfaction is derived from the couple's sexual relationship. Sex may be frequent or infrequent, partners may be creative or satisfied with a routine, orgasm may occur every time or it may not. The specific details of the sexual relationship vary tremendously among good marriages, but in good relationships, the partners agree about sex and enjoy the sexual relationship they have worked out together. If this is not true of your marriage, then you may wish to seek help for this problem. Be sure to read the next section, *Seeking Help for Marital Problems*, carefully if you are selecting a counselor for help with sexual problems; not all counselors are trained to deal with sexual difficulties.

4. In a good marriage, there is almost always a close, intimate relationship in which partners have mutual goals and plans. Marriage partners can let each other know very private, personal thoughts and feelings. They can seek help from each other, share their fears and disappointments, and decide together about how to handle problems that come up. We are not saying that you have to share everything with your partner or reveal all your private thoughts, but a good marriage is usually an intimate relationship, and marital intimacy arises out of willingness to reveal oneself to one's partner. If this is not true in your marriage, you may wish to seek help in order to change your relationship.

Seeking Help for Marital Problems. We suggested in Chapter 1 that professional help could be sought through your community mental health clinic, a nearby university department of psychiatry or psychology, a psychologist or psychiatrist in private practice, or your personal physician. Those suggestions also apply to seeking help for marital problems, but a few additional suggestions may be helpful. First, you might begin by calling your local mental health center and asking whether they have a family counseling service division. Second, when contacting any of these resources, be sure to specify that you want help for *marital problems* and that you would like help *as a couple,* rather than individual therapy. Third, some competent counselors may be available in your area who do not fit into the above categories. For instance, there might be a good counseling department at a university close to you with counselors available who specialize in family problems. Some universities train social workers and offer family counseling as part of that training, or there might be social workers at a state or local agency who could help you.

If you and your partner have sexual problems, you need to be *especially* careful in selecting a professional therapist. Sexual counseling is a relatively new field, and there are a number of unqualfied people calling themselves sex therapists who have "jumped on the bandwagon" without adequate training. To receive qualified sexual counseling, you should probably follow the recommendations of your community mental health center or contact a nearby university with a department of psychiatry or a graduate department of psychology.

Appendix A lists additional self-help books that might supplement this one. Included are several books dealing with marital and sexual problems; one of these may be useful to you.

Vocational Problems

Many people become depressed because they are experiencing great dissatisfaction with their jobs or educational plans. Dissatisfaction can be caused by any number of problems, ranging from dislike of a particular co-worker to boredom and frustration about the meaning or importance of one's work. Women who have been housewives may feel frustrated or bored. Many men and women in midlife (40s and 50s) experience a "letdown" when they feel that their work is no longer as challenging or interesting as it was. Dissatisfaction is often increased by the feeling that there are no alternatives, that nothing will ever change. If you don't know what other job options you have, don't know about training programs available, or don't realize what skills you might already have, it is hard to know what choices you might make to achieve greater satisfaction with your work.

Luckily, there are things you can do to find out about work alternatives. Most community or junior colleges have vocational counseling available to anyone in the area; usually this is provided free or for a minimal charge. You can easily call and find out whether such a service is available in your area. In addition, many communities have vocational rehabilitation programs available; your local mental health center would know about programs in your area. If you check into these resources, you will discover that there are *always* alternatives to an unsatisfying job. That discovery may be the first step to overcoming your depression. It may be that just *considering* alternatives and knowing you have choices will help. This can give you a greater sense of control, and you may decide that what you have is better than the alternatives, or that you can make changes within your present job. Or you may decide that you really do need a change. Either way, the fact that you have considered alternatives may give you a new sense of freedom and responsibility.

Alcohol and Drug Problems

It is not at all uncommon for people who are depressed to have problems with alcohol or other drugs. The problems can be related in numerous ways. Sometimes people begin using alcohol or other drugs when they become depressed because they want to feel better. Others may become depressed as a result of their problems with alcohol or other drugs. Undoubtedly there are also cases where the two problems (depression and drug use) develop independently, but having both of these problems makes it very difficult to solve either one.

Most people whose use of alcohol or other drugs interferes with their lives are unwilling to admit that they *have* a problem. Thus, your own self-evaluation of whether you have a drug or alcohol problem is unlikely to be accurate or objective. If you are depressed and you drink or use drugs, you should seek out someone you know who will be honest with you, and talk to them about your use of alcohol or other drugs. Then make a decision about whether you need to seek professional help. One book which may be helpful to you if you have a drinking problem is *How to Control Your Drinking* by William R. Miller and Ricardo F. Muñoz.[1] Alcohol and drug problems can be helped, and there is nothing shameful about admitting your need for help. If you are depressed and abusing alcohol or other drugs, it is *essential* that you find the strength to seek the help you need.

Physical Problems

People who are depressed often have physical problems as well. Some of these have been mentioned already (feeling tired all the time, having headaches or bad stomachaches). If you have these physical problems—or any others—you definitely should see a physician and *listen* to the advice given. Depression can be the first sign that you are ill, and you almost certainly cannot make good diagnoses about your own health. If medical treatment is advised, follow through on it and see what effect the treatment will have on your depression. If your doctor says you are healthy and that your physical problems are caused by your depression, then listen to that advice, too. Some-

---

[1] Miller, W. R., and Muñoz, R. F. *How to Control Your Drinking.* Englewood Cliffs, N.J.: Prentice-Hall, 1976.

times it's hard to believe that stomachaches, headaches, and the like are caused by your behavior and emotions, but they can be. If this is the case for you, we urge you to keep working on overcoming your depression, either by using this book or by seeking a counselor. Chapter 6, *Learning to Relax*, may be particularly helpful in dealing with many of your physical complaints.

Sleep Problems

Problems in sleeping deserve special attention because so many depressed people have trouble sleeping. Some have difficulty getting to sleep, others wake up too early in the morning, and still others want to sleep all the time during the day but can't go to sleep at night. Our advice for these problems is the same as that for other physical ones. First, see a physician to find out whether you have a medical problem. Be careful, however, that you do not automatically accept sleeping medication as the answer. Sometimes physicians prescribe sleeping pills without clearly establishing that a medical or physiological problem exists and without realizing that almost all medication actually disturbs sleep. If you do have a sleeping problem, you probably will want to work on it as part of overcoming your depression. Chapter 6 may be helpful. You may also want to read *How to Sleep Better* by Thomas Coates and Carl Thoresen.[2]

WHERE SHOULD YOU START?

On page 89 you now have a list of problems to pursue. To that list, add any major problems you have identified which

[2] Coates, T. J., and Thoresen, C. E., *How to Sleep Better*. Englewood Cliffs, N.J.: Prentice-Hall, 1977.

are not covered in the subsequent chapters of this book. If relevant, be sure to include marital problems, work or school problems, and alcohol or other drug problems as one of these additional major problems. Next to each, under the *Chapter* heading, write "Professional help" or "Other self-help book," since those problems will not be covered by this book.

The next step is to decide where to begin; remember that you should only work on one or two problems at a time. If self-control is on your list, you already know the first problem you must pursue. Similarly, if you have indicated that you have a problem with alcohol or other drugs, you might be wise to pursue it first and return to this book when that problem is under control. In all other cases, you will have to make up your own mind where to start.

Under the *Importance* heading, number the problems you have, beginning with number 1 for the most important and working through the entire list. The following guidelines may help if you are having a lot of trouble making decisions about each problem's relative importance:

1. Try not to equate "Importance" entirely with "Difficulty of Changing." That is, don't put all the hardest problems first just because you know how difficult they are to change. For instance, learning to relax or finding an hour a day to do more pleasant activities may be relatively *easy* changes for you, but they may be very *important* to overcoming your depression. In fact, you will feel much better *if you start with some problems that are relatively easy to solve and really matter to you.* Then, when you are feeling better, you can tackle some of the more complex or difficult problems. On the other hand, don't start with easy problems if you know they are trivial; if you do, you will use up your initial enthusiasm about changing before you really get to anything important.

2. If nothing stands out as more important than other problems, we suggest that you begin with Chapter 7, *Pleasant Activities.* This is almost always an important problem for de-

pressed people, and increasing pleasant activities usually leads to a positive change in mood.

3. You can always change your mind, so don't get too worried about which problems are most important. If you start on a problem and find that you can't resolve it until you work on something else, just change your plan. For example, imagine that you started out by trying to work on increasing pleasant activities but found you were always tired because you weren't sleeping at night. In this case you would just switch the problem order, work on relaxation and sleep, and then return to pleasant activities when you find you are getting more rest. Allow yourself to experiment a little; you can always change your plan!

After you have numbered the problems, you are ready to go. Now you can start working on the first one or two problems, using either this book, professional help, or some other self-help book. Once you have made significant progress on the first problems, you can work down the list, in order of importance. Thus, occasionally you may set this book aside for a while to work on problems using a different resource, but you can always return to this book when you are ready to tackle a problem that is included here. Keep working down your problem list as far as you want. If you feel fine after solving the first two, that's wonderful! You may not want to go further. Most people, however, will probably need to work out several problems before they feel satisfied with the positive changes in their depression. *You* are the best judge of how much *you* will need to do.

After you have worked on the problems, we urge you to finish by reading all of the final section of the book, Part III, which gives you some ideas about how to *maintain* your gains, how to *adapt* to future changes, and how to *plan* a self-determined purpose for your own life. Part III should be helpful to you regardless of what problems you now have on your problem list.

SUMMARY

You are now facing a major, and exciting, task. You began this book feeling depressed and probably confused about your feelings of depression. Now you understand more about depression and social learning. You also have pinpointed some specific problems related to your feelings of depression. Finally, you have a tentative plan for tackling those problems, and you are about to begin carrying out that plan.

You have already made considerable progress! You should be very pleased with the effort you have made thus far. You will still need to work hard to keep making progress, but you are off to a good start. We hope you continue to be successful. If you are not, remember that failure with this book does not mean you are a hopeless case. It only means that this method did not work for you, and you will need to find another kind of help in order to overcome your depression.

REVIEW

_____ I now know that I should tackle only one or two problems at a time in order to overcome my depression.

_____ I have listed the problems which seem to be most clearly related to my depression.

———— I have decided on the order in which I will work on my problems.

———— I have decided which chapters to use.

———— I have decided to seek a counselor or use another self-help book for help with problems that are not covered in this book.

chapter 6

Learning to Relax

Malcolm is a 45-year-old man who has been depressed for the last 5 or 6 weeks. He also has been feeling very tense much of the time and, for the first time in his life, has consistently had trouble falling asleep at night. It used to take him only 10 or 15 minutes to fall asleep, but lately he tosses and turns for at least 2 hours before finally drifting off.

Malcolm blames his tension and sleeping problems on his increased job responsibilities. He was promoted to the position of office manager at his company a couple of months ago. He was very happy to receive this promotion and wants to prove that he can do a good job. But the new position is full of pressures, and he finds himself worrying about it most of the time. When he first began having trouble falling asleep, Malcolm went to see his physician. The doctor said his physical health was good and, fortunately, discouraged him from taking any sleeping pills, urging him instead to find ways to relax more. Unfortunately, however, his doctor didn't offer any specific suggestions on how Malcolm could relax more; hence, Malcolm has continued his daily routine of intense work, worrying about his performance, and feeling more and more tense and discouraged.

Barbara is a 36-year-old woman who, since adolescence, has had a problem with frequent headaches. Lately her headaches have been more frequent and more severe. Like Malcolm, Barbara consulted her physician; he pronounced her to be in good physical health. When the headaches occur, Barbara takes aspirin but it doesn't seem to help very much. When Barbara gets a headache, the only thing she feels like doing is taking a nap or watching TV. Therefore, she has been spending more and more time at home and is doing fewer of the things she used to find enjoyable.

Phyllis is a 38-year-old woman who, with her husband and two young children, recently moved to a new community. Phyllis feels lonely and isolated in her new community; she misses her old friends. She has always been able to get along well with other people. In her former job she enjoyed comfortable friendships with several of her co-workers, and in the community she was an active, well-liked member of several social and service clubs. At her new job and in her new neighborhood, Phylllis initially was friendly and warm toward a number of people, but was disappointed that her attempts at friendship were not more successful. As time went on, Phyllis found that she was often nervous when talking with others, especially if she was in a group of people. She joined a service club in the new town, but at the first meeting was so tense and fearful that she hardly said anything. She didn't go back to the service club and persuaded her husband to turn down some social invitations from people at his job. Phyllis couldn't understand why she was so anxious when she had always been relaxed and easygoing in social situations before. She knew her social isolation and loneliness were part of the reason for feeling so depressed, but somehow she couldn't force herself to relate to people in her new community.

Malcolm, Barbara, and Phyllis, despite their different situations, have one thing in common: All three are experiencing some tension-related problems along with depression. As we pointed out in Chapter 1, people who are depressed often also have problems with anxiety or tension. For many, the anxiety or tension contributes directly or indirectly to their feelings of depression. Phyllis, for example, knows her depression is due, in part, to her feelings of social isolation in her new community. Yet because she feels so fearful and tense in social situations, she avoids them and has become even more socially isolated. Malcolm worries a lot about his new job responsibilities; his tension makes it more difficult to fall asleep at night. Getting less sleep and feeling tense so much of the time probably makes him feel quite fatigued and, therefore, less effective in his job. Like Malcolm, Barbara, and Phyllis, you may find yourself caught in this kind of vicious circle where tension-related problems are not only problems in their own right (like Malcolm's sleep problems and Barbara's headaches) but also make it more difficult to do the kinds of things that might help you overcome your depression.

COLLECTING SOME INFORMATION FIRST

In this chapter we will present a well-tested and quite simple method for learning to relax. First, though, it will be helpful to collect some base-line data on how tense you are each day and how frequently you experience tension-related symptoms. By keeping records each day *for 1 week*, you will be able to accomplish two important steps:

1. You will have a base level against which you can compare your progress as you learn to relax more.

2. You, can identify particular situations and/or times of the day when you are most tense.

First, you need to establish a scale to measure how tense you are. We suggest that you use the scale on the Daily Monitoring-Relaxation Form (Figure 6–1). On this scale, a 10 equals the most tense or anxious you have been, and 0 equals the most relaxed you have ever been. Malcolm decided that, for him, 10 (the most tense he could remember being) was when he was being interviewed for his new job and 0 was how relaxed he felt after swimming while on vacation the previous summer. For Barbara, 10 was a few years ago when her young son failed to return home and she was afraid he had been injured or was lost; 0 was how she felt while sunbathing at her family's beach cabin. Write down at the top of Figure 6–1 what 10 and 0 are for you, and then for practice rate how relaxed you are *right now*.

Each day you should write three scores on Figure 6–1:

1. Your average relaxation score for the day (how relaxed you felt most of the day that day)

2. The relaxation score for when you felt the *least* relaxed during the day. Also, be sure to note the time, where you were, and a brief description of what you were doing.

3. The relaxation score for when you felt the *most* relaxed during the day. Again, be sure to record the time, location, and a brief description of what you were doing when you felt this relaxed.

In addition to recording these three scores each day, you should keep track of any specific tension-related symptom you might have each time it occurs. (Figure 6–1 lists some symbols you can use.) If you have a tension-related physical problem like headaches or stomachaches, it will also be helpful to note

Figure 6–1 Daily Monitoring–Relaxation

Date: _____ to _____

Relaxation Rating: 0 = Most relaxed you have ever been
10 = Most tense you have ever been

	Monday	Tuesday	Wednesday	Thursday	Friday	Saturday	Sunday	Average Score (add your scores and divide by 7)
Average Score for the Day								
Least Relaxed Time								
Score								
When								
Where								
Situation								
Most Relaxed Time								
Score								
When								
Where								
Situation								
Occurrence of Tension Symptoms								
H = Headache								
SA = Stomachache								
SP = Sleep problem								
Relaxation Practice								
When								
For how long								
Score before								
Score after								

the time at which they occurred, where you were, and what
you were doing. For the first week, just leave the section labeled
Relaxation Practice blank.

Shown in Figure 6–2 are samples from Malcolm's and
Barbara's daily monitoring for a single day.

One word of caution: Don't expect ‹this method—or *any*
method—to result in your getting an average rating of 0 or 1
every day or even to attain a 0 as your most relaxed rating
most days. That would be an unrealistic goal for anyone.
Furthermore, it wouldn't be desirable for most people to be
that totally relaxed all day every day. Studies have shown that
for many kinds of tasks there is a desirable level of tension
somewhere between total relaxation and high tension. If Malcolm became so relaxed that he consistently rated himself 0
or 1 while on the job, he probably would get fired because
he wouldn't be very productive. A more appropriate goal for
Malcolm might be somewhere between 3 and 6 while he is
at work. At that level, Malcolm would feel considerably calmer
than he does now and would be able to work quite effectively.
When he is not working, it would be good if he could average around 2 or 3 with an occasional 0 and 1 for his most
relaxed times.

LEARNING TO RELAX

After a week of collecting base-level data, you should begin
practicing the relaxation method we will describe in this section.

Learning to relax is similar, in some ways, to learning any
new skill—like tennis, cooking, or oil painting. It takes regular
practice, patience, and time. With regular practice, you can
soon control your bodily tension and experience a greater
degree of relaxation more of the time. While there are many

Figure 6–2
Samples

Malcolm	Barbara
Average Score 7	Average Score 6
Least Relaxed	Least Relaxed
Score 8	Score 7
When .... *Late morning*	When .... *8-9 A.M.*
Where .... *Office*	Where .... *Home*
Situation .... *Turning down Joe's request for salary increase*	Situation .... *Trying to settle kid's argument*
Most Relaxed	Most Relaxed
Score 4	Score 3
When .... *5-6 P.M.*	When .... *Early evening*
Where .... *Home*	Where .... *Park*
Situation .... *Having drink and reading newspaper*	Situation .... *Taking dog for walk*
Occurrence of Tension	Occurrence of Tension
Symptoms .... *(SP)*	Symptoms ...... *(H) In morning when kids were bickering (H) In late afternoon cooking dinner*

Symbols for tension-related symptoms: (SP) — sleep problem
(SA) — stomachache
(H) — headache

effective ways to learn to relax (for example, strenuous exercise, deep muscle relaxation, yoga, and transcendental meditation), we believe that the simplest method, and the one that seems to be suited to nearly any kind of person, is the relaxation technique developed by Dr. Herbert Benson. His book, *The Relaxation Response,* is well worth reading, particularly if you are interested in learning about the physiologic changes that occur in conjunction with relaxation.[1] The method described here is based upon Dr. Benson's technique. There are five preliminary steps:

1. Choose a quiet, comfortable environment where there are few distractions and where you won't be disturbed by other people.

2. Choose a time of the day when you are least likely to be disturbed by others and when you won't be worried about having to get somewhere or about doing something right after your practice session. Dr. Benson suggests that practice sessions *not* be held within 2 hours after a meal since the digestive processes apparently interfere with the relaxation response.

3. Choose a word or phrase to repeat, either silently or aloud, while you are practicing your relaxation. Repeating the word or phrase is important because it is a way to help keep your mind from wandering during the practice session. Dr. Benson suggests using the word *"one."* Any simple word or phrase will do, and we recommend that you choose one that is pleasing to you.

4. Develop a passive attitude while practicing. Don't worry about how well you are performing because that kind of self-evaluation will prevent the relaxation response from occurring. Also, don't worry when distracting thoughts occur to you. They will occur for almost everybody. When you become aware of distracting thoughts, simply return to repeating your special word or phrase. Dr. Benson writes that keeping a passive or

[1] Benson, H. *The Relaxation Response.* New York: Avon Books, 1975.

"let-it-happen" attitude seems to be the most important element in being able to get deeply relaxed.

5. Select a comfortable position. This is important in order to prevent undue muscular tension. Sitting in a comfortable position on your bed or in a soft chair is probably best. Lying down is another good position and one you might like to try later on. However, when people lie down to practice relaxation, they tend to fall asleep. If you fall asleep during a practice session, that certainly shows you are relaxed! But it's impossible to practice while you are asleep! Therefore, we recommend that at first you find a comfortable sitting position.

Those are the preliminaries. The procedure itself is very simple. There are five steps:

1. Sit quietly in a comfortable position.
2. Close your eyes.
3. Relax all your muscles as fully and deeply as possible. You can start with your foot muscles and progress up to your facial muscles. Or start with relaxing your facial muscles and then relax your shoulder and arm muscles, your chest and stomach muscles, your leg muscles, and end with your foot muscles.[2]
4. Breathe easily and naturally through your nose. *Become aware of your breathing.* As you breathe out, say "one" or *your* special word or phrase, either silently to yourself or aloud. For example, breathe *in* . . . then *out,* "one," *in* . . . *out,* "one," etc.
5. Continue for 10 to 20 minutes. Open your eyes to check the time, if you wish, but do not use an alarm. When you finish, sit quietly for several minutes, at first with your eyes closed and, later, with your eyes open. Do not stand up for a few minutes.

---

[2] *The Relaxation Book* by Gerald Rosen (Englewood Cliffs, N.J.: Prentice-Hall, 1977) presents an easy-to-follow procedure for systematically reducing muscle tension.

We recommend that you practice this method from 10 to 20 minutes *once or twice each day*, preferably at a regular time and place. Don't worry if your progress seems slow; getting tense or concerned about relaxing is, of course, not very relaxing! As long as you work at the procedure and practice conscientiously, you will gradually experience an enjoyable state of relaxation. The secret is *not* to try too hard!

COMMON PROBLEMS

One of the most frequent problems people have with this procedure is the occurrence of distracting thoughts. As we noted previously, don't worry if your mind wanders during your practice sessions, and don't feel that having distracting thoughts means that you have failed. Instead, simply redirect your attention to your breathing and to repeating your word or phrase.

Another problem is external distractions. As far as possible, avoid this problem by carefully selecting a time and place where you won't be disturbed. After a while you will be able to tolerate some distractions. In the beginning, though, try to find a time that is quiet for you.

Some people feel that they are losing control as they "float" into a state of relaxation. If you experience this feeling as a problem, you might want to approach the practice sessions at a slower pace, simply sitting quietly for several minutes before you begin repeating your special word or phrase and concentrating on your breathing. With practice, you will come to see that *you* are the real director of what you feel, and that you can *control* how relaxed you want to be. If you doubt this, try the following experiment in one of your practice sessions. During the middle portion of your session, purposely open your eyes and tense up your muscles. Doing this should convince you that you are in charge!

A number of miscellaneous physical reactions or sensations may occur while you practice relaxation. At times, you may experience small muscle spasms or jerks while you relax. Or you may experience tingling sensations in your muscles or a feeling of floating in your head. These reactions are not unusual and, in fact, are signals that you are *succeeding* in relaxing. With further practice, these reactions either will diminish or will become very familiar and not bothersome to you.

Finally, as is true for learning any new skill, consistent practice is very important. Most people who have learned to relax using this method look forward to their relaxation sessions each day. But at first, practicing may seem like a chore, and you might find yourself coming up with all sorts of excuses for skipping a practice session. If this is true for you, we suggest that you refer back to Chapter 4, *Introduction to Self-Change Methods*. Read carefully the section on contracting and rewarding yourself (step 6), and use the suggestions there to set up a self-reward plan for regularly practicing the relaxation method.

RECORDING YOUR PRACTICE SESSIONS

You should continue to complete Figure 6–1 each day. You may wish to use the Daily Monitoring–Relaxation Form in Appendix B to make additional copies for your use in successive weeks. At the bottom of the form is a place for you to record your daily relaxation practice sessions. For each session, you should note the time and how long you practiced. Then, using the same relaxation scales as before (0, very relaxed; 10 very tense), rate how relaxed you were immediately *before* the practice session and immediately *after* the session. At the end of each week, look back over your ratings to see if your practice sessions have improved your relaxation. Again, don't worry if your progress seems slow at first. If you continue to be dissatisfied, experiment by choosing a different time or place for your practice sessions, or try a different position.

APPLYING THE RELAXATION PROCEDURE TO SPECIFIC SITUATIONS

After you have practiced the relaxation technique for at least a week or 10 sessions, you can begin adapting it to your particular problem situation. This step will require some creativity on your part. While you are experimenting, be sure to continue your regular practice sessions at your usual time in your usual place.

The first step in making specific applications is to decide when might be the most effective time to use the relaxation technique. For some people, this decision will be relatively simple. Malcolm, for example, has problems falling asleep at night, and a logical time for him to use the relaxation technique would be when he goes to bed. For other kinds of problems, the decision may be more difficult. One aid in making this decision is to examine your daily monitoring forms to see if there is a clear pattern to your tension. Try to identify particular times of the day or particular situations when you feel most tense. Then try to schedule practice sessions *before* these high-tension times. It may not be possible to hold your usual practice sessions at these times, but see if you can use some modified version of the technique to do then *in addition to* your regular relaxation sessions. Some examples will help illustrate alternatives.

Malcolm: In addition to his problem in falling asleep, Malcolm initially felt quite tense most of the time. Practicing relaxation each evening had helped him reduce his tension level, and he was able to fall asleep more easily. However, he realized that he was still feeling quite tense at work. His daily monitoring record showed that for the past 3 weeks his "least relaxed" time on most days had occurred at work. Malcolm decided to get up 20 minutes earlier on weekday mornings in order to have a regular practice session before going to work. After several days of doing this, he was pleased that he felt much calmer at work, especially in the morning. To extend this calmness, Malcolm decided to try a modified version of the technique at lunchtime. In his office it wasn't possible to get the kind of privacy and quiet he needed, so he started delaying his lunch by 15 minutes and using the first part of his lunch hour to go sit in his car and practice the relaxation method for 10 minutes. He found he was not able to get as completely relaxed as he did during his regular relaxation sessions, but he still found that 5 or 10 minutes of relaxing in his car helped him to be less tense during the afternoon. Later on, Malcolm found he didn't have to retreat to his car. He was able to relax adequately in his office by simply closing his door and asking not to be disturbed for 5 minutes. Then, even though there were more distractions and less time, he could regain some of the calm sense of relaxation that he felt during his regular sessions.

Barbara: Having faithfully practiced her relaxation each morning before the rest of her family got up, Barbara found that she was more relaxed and had fewer headaches. Sometimes, though, she still developed headaches in the late afternoon as she began preparing dinner for the family. With the children around and because she needed to begin cooking dinner at that hour, it was not practical for Barbara to take twenty minutes for relaxation. However, she *could* take 10 or 15 minutes right before the children got home from school to practice the relaxation technique. She began to schedule two relaxation sessions each day: her usual pre-breakfast sessions and a shorter mid-afternoon session.

Phyllis: Phyllis had been faithfully practicing the relaxation method for about 3 weeks. She usually practiced in the morning before breakfast and had found that she felt calmer going to work in the mornings. She had begun to feel somewhat more comfortable chatting with people at work, especially when she talked with just one other person. Phyllis still felt quite fearful and jittery at coffee break time because then people talked with one another in a small group. Phyllis wanted to join the coffee break group but was afraid she'd get nervous and wouldn't be able to join in on the conversation without feeling ill-at-ease. Since the coffee break lasted only 15 minutes, there was not enough time to have a regular relaxation session before attempting to join the group. So Phyllis decided to use the first 5 minutes of her coffee break to have a modified version of the relaxation procedure in the relative privacy of the restroom. She was not able to get as deeply relaxed as she did at home during her regular relaxation sessions, but, after a few days' practice, she found her tension lowered to a point where she could approach and begin to interact with the coffee break group.

Much later, she worked up her courage and returned to the service club. Before leaving for the meeting, she held a special relaxation session at home and found that she was reasonably relaxed going to the meeting. About halfway through the meeting, she noticed that she was beginning to tense up. She knew she could get even more tense if she stood up and excused herself. So she stayed where she was, took a deep breath, and relaxed her muscles the way she did at the beginning of her relaxation sessions. She also repeated her special word to herself a couple of times. She was happy to find that doing this helped her feel calmer and that she could do it without anyone noticing her.

These examples are intended to show the need for being flexible and creative in applying the relaxation procedure to your specific situation. Again, it is important not to stop your usual relaxation sessions while doing this kind of experimentation. It is unlikely that modified versions will produce the same degree of relaxation that you can achieve—with practice—in your regular relaxation sessions. Creative use of modified versions, however, can help you be less tense at those times when you particularly need to feel more relaxed.

We have stressed the importance of scheduling your regular relaxation sessions or doing modified versions of the relaxation method immediately before tension-producing situations occur. We think this is the most effective approach because you can get more relaxed before your tension builds up too much. Sometimes, though, you may not be able to have a relaxation session right before a tension-producing situation occurs. Or, even if you did, perhaps you still will find yourself getting tense once you're in the situation. If and when this happens, we suggest that you try a trick like Phyllis used. There are all kinds of things people can do to help reduce their tension without anyone else noticing. Here are some suggestions:

1. Take a deep breath and focus on your breathing for a couple of minutes.

2. Say "one" or your special word to yourself for a couple of minutes.

3. Picture yourself relaxing in your favorite place.

4. Relax the muscles that feel the most tense. People vary in terms of which muscles they typically feel are the most tense or tightest; for some, it's the hands; others, the shoulders or back; and still others, the facial muscles. You probably are aware of where you feel the most tense. Purposely relax those muscles.

Try one of these methods or a combination of them and see if they help you reduce your tension. Experiment to see what works best for you, and then use that method the next time you find yourself becoming tense.

EVALUATING YOUR PROGRESS

At this point you should have at least 2 weeks of daily monitoring data on Figure 6–1. In the previous section we suggested that you examine your daily monitoring forms in order to identify particular times in your day or particular situations that seem to produce the most tension. When you have identified these situations, write them down on Figure 6–3. When you write them down, try to make them neither too specific (for example, turning down Joe's request for a salary increase) nor too general (for example, turning down requests). Ideally, the problem situations you list should strike a good balance between being too specific and too general (for example, dealing with employees' requests). To broaden your list or to get some ideas on describing situations that are problems for you, you may want to refer to the Pleasant Events Schedule (Table 7–1), the Assertion Questionnaire (Table 8–1), or the Social Activity Questionnaire (Table 9–1). Again, you will probably want to make copies of Figure 6–3 after you have listed the situations that are tension-producing for you. Then, each day for each situation that occurred, rate the degree of your relaxation in that situation. Be sure to rate every occasion on which the situation occurred; that may be more than once on some days. A rating of 10 should indicate that you were very uncomfortable and tense. A rating of 0 should indicate that you were completely relaxed and comfortable.

Figure 6–4 is a sample sheet from Phyllis' daily monitoring for a single day.

Note that Phyllis jotted down the names of people or brief comments for some of her activities. She did this so she could better remember the situations. You may also find this helpful.

From now on, complete *both* Figure 6–1 *and* Figure 6–3 every day.[3] You can change your list of problem situations on

[3] These forms are included in Appendix B so that you can make additional copies of them.

Figure 6-3 Daily Monitoring–Relaxation in Problem Situations

Relaxation Rating: 0 = Most relaxed you have ever been
10 = Most tense you have ever been

Dates: _____ to _____

Problem Situations	Monday	Tuesday	Wednesday	Thursday	Friday	Saturday	Sunday
1.							
2.							
3.							
4.							
5.							
6.							
7.							
8.							
9.							
10.							

Figure 6–4
Phyllis' Daily Monitoring

Problem Situations

1. Initiating a conversation with a stranger .... 5 *(man at store)*

2. Talking with a co-worker .... 4 *(Sam)*

3. Joining the rest of the group at coffee break .. 8 *(Judi)*

4. Introducing myself to someone .... 7 *(new girl at office)*

5. Inviting an acquaintance to join me for some
   social activity ....

6. Accepting a social invitation ....

7. Going to a service or social club meeting ....

8. Inviting a neighbor over for coffee .... 6 *(Sally)*

Figure 6–3 as time goes by. In fact, you should review it each week to make sure it includes the situations that are *currently* the most tension-producing for you. At the end of each week, compute the average relaxation scores on Figure 6–1 and compare them with the previous week's *and* with your base-level data (your first week of self-monitoring on Figure 6–1). Also, compare your scores on Figure 6–3 with those from the previous week. If you are dissatisfied with your progress, consider how you are applying the relaxation procedure. Are you still having a regular relaxation session at least once a day? Would it be a good idea to change the time and/or the place of this session? Are there some new ways you could apply modified versions of the relaxation method immediately before the situations that are still tension-producing for you? How about trying some of the "on-the-spot" techniques we suggested? Equally important, are you expecting too much too fast? Remember that changing the way you respond in some problem situations is going to take some time, lots of patience, and faithful practice.

Remember to continue having regular relaxation sessions in addition to any tension-reducing modifications you have found useful. Learning to stay more relaxed can make a big difference in overcoming your depression!

SUMMARY

This chapter was written especially for people whose tension-related problems (such as feeling very anxious in certain social situations, having frequent headaches, or having trouble sleeping) may contribute to their depression. A method of learning the skill of relaxation was presented along with suggestions for applying the relaxation technique in specific problem situations.

REVIEW

_____ In order to collect base-line information on my tension level, I filled out Figure 6–1 every day for 1 week and then continued to complete this daily monitoring form so I could evaluate my progress.

_____ I learned the relaxation technique presented in this chapter (*or* another technique that I have found helpful) and have been practicing relaxation in regular sessions each day.

_____ On the basis of my daily monitoring on Figure 6–1, I identified the kinds of situations or times of day when I felt most tense, and, using Figure 6–3, have kept track of how relaxed I felt in these situations each day.

_____ I have developed a modified version of the relaxation technique and have been using it to help me feel more relaxed in tension-producing situations.

_____ I have evaluated my progress (at least once) by:

    _____ Figuring my average relaxation score on Figure 6–1 for each week and comparing it with my average score for the previous week.

    _____ Comparing my ratings (on Figure 6–3) how relaxed I am in my particular problem situations each week with my ratings from the previous week.

_____ On the basis of my evaluation I have decided I am:

    _____ Not presently satisfied with my progress and need to:

        _____ Continue holding regular practice sessions at least once a day (perhaps finding a better time and place).

        _____ Develop or change my modified versions of the relaxation technique to use immediately before tension-producing situations occur.

_____ Try some of the "on-the-spot" techniques suggested for reducing tension once I am in a tension-producing situation.

_____ Satisfied with the progress I am making so I will go on to a different chapter but will:

_____ Continue to practice relaxing each day.

_____ Continue to use the modified versions of the relaxation method and "on-the-spot" techniques that I've found helpful in reducing my tension.

chapter 7

Pleasant
Activities

It is very likely that your rate of pleasant activities (events you used to experience as enjoyable) is low. You are not doing many of them and/or you don't derive much pleasure when you do them. The purpose of this chapter is to assist you in

1. Assessing the degree to which your frequency of pleasant activities and the extent to which you are enjoying them may be contributing to your depression.

2. Developing and implementing a self-change plan aimed at increasing pleasant activities.

RELATIONSHIP BETWEEN PLEASANT
ACTIVITIES AND DEPRESSION

When we engage in very few activities which we experience as pleasant, we feel depressed. Also, when we feel depressed, we don't feel like engaging in the kinds of activities which are likely to be a source of pleasure and satisfaction for us. These are very important facts, and, because of their simplicity, they are not often given the emphasis they deserve.

There is a chicken-and-egg problem that intrigues scientists. Does a *low rate* of pleasant activities *cause* us to feel depressed, or does *feeling depressed* cause us to do little? The answer is likely to be that it works both ways—doing few pleasant activities causes us to feel depressed *and* being depressed causes us to do little. One can think of this as a vicious circle. The less we do, the more depressed we feel; the more depressed we feel, the less we feel like doing anything. We feel trapped in a downward spiral. Fortunately, there is also a positive circle. The more we do, the less depressed we feel; and the less depressed we feel, the more we will like doing things.

The fact that there is a relationship between the number of pleasant activities we engage in and our mood provides us with a potential "handle" on depression. By increasing pleasant experiences, we can make ourselves feel better. Similarly, by maintaining a reasonable level of pleasant activity, we can avoid becoming depressed. In other words, we shift from being controlled *by* our depression to being able to control *it*.

Before addressing ourselves to the practical application of this relationship between pleasant activities and our mood, we need to clarify several questions: (1) What types of activities or events are likely to be experienced as pleasant? (2) What is a reasonable level of engagement in pleasant activities?

WHAT KINDS OF ACTIVITIES ARE LIKELY
TO BE EXPERIENCED AS PLEASANT?

Several years ago, we began a series of studies aimed at identifying a comprehensive list of activities experienced as pleasant by many people. We were interested in learning something
about the nature of such activities and the degree to which
people resemble each other in the kinds of activities they
enjoy. Perhaps most importantly, we were looking for activities which had the greatest impact on mood level.

We began by asking persons of all ages to list 10 activities or events which they had experienced as pleasant. This
resulted in the "Pleasant Events Schedule" (PES), a list of 320
potentially pleasant activities, reproduced here as Table 7–1.
Inspection of this list reveals the wide range of activities that
are potentially pleasant for many people. Since then, we have
had literally thousands of persons tell us how often they engage in these activities during a 30-day period, and how much
enjoyment they derive from them. Along with monitoring
their daily rate of these activities, our participants have also
monitored their daily mood. From these studies, we have been
able to draw the following conclusions:

*People differ markedly in regard to the specific kinds of
activities they experience as pleasant.* Every one of us has his
or her own set of potentially pleasant activities. In a very real
sense, each of us must discover for ourselves which activities
are pleasant for us. In order to identify activities that are
potentially pleasant, relevant, and meaningful to a particular
person, the first step consists of having the person identify
and pinpoint them. Fortunately, the nature of the activities
that are a source of pleasure for us tends to remain fairly stable
over time. So, to the extent to which we know what kinds of

activities are pleasant for us, we have discovered something very basic about ourselves.

A subset of pleasant activities exists which is especially important in regard to depression. When our participants engaged in certain activities, they felt good; when they did not, they were more likely to feel depressed. For this reason, these activities have been *starred* in Table 7–1. We refer to them as "mood-related activities," and they fall into three basic groups:

1. Social interactions in which the person feels wanted, liked, respected, understood, appreciated, and accepted (for example, being with happy people, having people show interest in what you have said, thinking about people you like, being with friends).

2. Activities associated with feelings of adequacy, competence, and independence (for example, doing a project in your own way, planning or organizing something, doing a job well, learning to do something new).

3. Activities that are "intrinsically pleasant" (for example, laughing, being relaxed, eating good meals, thinking about something good in the future, seeing beautiful scenery, having peace and quiet, sleeping soundly at night). These kinds of activities are usually associated with emotions that are incompatible with being depressed. For example, it is impossible to laugh and to be depressed at the same time.

In general, there are three kinds of activities that are especially important in combatting depression: (1) those that involve us in pleasant and meaningful interactions with other people; (2) those that make us feel more competent and adequate and give us a sense of direction and purpose; and (3) those involving emotional states that are incompatible with being depressed.

DEVELOPING A SELF-CHANGE PLAN

How can you use this relationship between mood and pleasant activities to work for you in combatting your depression and in preventing the occurrence of depression in the future?

The remainder of this chapter will show you

1. How to assess your own rate of pleasant activities.

2. How you can determine the degree of association between your activities and your mood.

3. How you can become aware of the importance of specific activities that are especially important for your mood.

4. How you can go about designing and implementing a self-change plan.

The goal of your plan will be to reduce your depression by improving the quantity and quality of your pleasant activities.

SELF-ASSESSMENT

By rating yourself on the Pleasant Events Schedule in Table 7-1 you can evaluate your current level of pleasant activities. This will also assist you in pinpointing specific activities you want to increase as part of your self-change plan. Answering the questions will also make you more aware of the many potentially pleasant activities available to you which you may not have thought of.

Reminder—This would be a good time to review briefly

the section on contracting and rewarding yourself in Chapter 4 (Step 6).

Taking and scoring this test will take you approximately 2 hours. You should plan to take it in a quiet place and at a time when you will not be interrupted. Since it will take considerable effort on your part, you should plan to reward yourself. Decide *now* what kind of a reward you are going to give to yourself when you have finished taking and scoring this test.

How often have these events happened in your life in the past month?

Please answer this question by rating each item on the Frequency Scale (Column *F*):

0—This has *not* happened in the past 30 days.

1—This has happened *a few times* (1–6 times) in the past 30 days.

2—This has happened *often* (7 times or more) in the past 30 days.

Place your rating for each item in Column *F*. Here is an example:

Item 1 is *being in the country.* Suppose you have been in the country 3 times during the past 30 days. Then you would mark a 1 in Column *F* next to Item 1.

Some items will list *more than one event;* for these items, mark how often you have done *any* of the listed events. For example, Item 12 is *Doing artwork (painting, sculpture, drawing, movie-making, etc.).* You should rate Item 12 on how often you have done *any* form of artwork in the past month.

Since this list contains events that might happen to a wide variety of people, you may find that many of the events have not happened to you in the past 30 days. It is not expected that anyone will have done all of these things in a single month.

Begin now and put your frequency rating for each of the 320 items in Column *F*.

Table 7-1
Pleasant Events Schedule

	F	P	F × P	√ [a]
*1. Being in the country				
2. Wearing expensive or formal clothes				
3. Making contributions to religious, charitable, or other groups				
4. Talking about sports				
*5. Meeting someone new of the same sex				
6. Taking tests when well prepared				
7. Going to a rock concert				
8. Playing baseball or softball				
*9. Planning trips or vacations				
10. Buying things for myself				
11. Being at the beach				
12. Doing art work (painting, sculpture, drawing, movie-making, etc.)				
13. Rock climbing or mountaineering				
14. Reading the Scriptures or other sacred works				
15. Playing golf				
16. Taking part in military activities				
17. Rearranging or redecorating my room or house				

[a] Use this column to check items for your Activity Schedule.
* Starred items are mood-related activities.

Pleasant Events Schedule (*cont.*)

	F	P	F × P	√[a]
18. Going naked				
19. Going to a sports event				
20. Reading a "How to Do It" book or article				
21. Going to the races (horse, car, boat, etc.)				
*22. Reading stories, novels, poems, or plays				
23. Going to a bar, tavern, club, etc.				
24. Going to lectures or hearing speakers				
*25. Driving skillfully				
*26. Breathing clean air				
27. Thinking up or arranging a song or music				
28. Getting drunk				
*29. Saying something clearly				
30. Boating (canoeing, kyaking, motor-boating, sailing, etc.)				
31. Pleasing my parents				
32. Restoring antiques, refinishing furniture, etc.				
33. Watching TV				
34. Talking to myself				
35. Camping				

a Use this column to check items for your Activity Schedule.
* Starred items are mood-related activities.

Pleasant Events Schedule (*cont.*)

	F	P	F × P	√ [a]
36. Working in politics				
37. Working on machines (cars, bikes, motorcycles, tractors, etc.)				
*38. Thinking about something good in the future				
39. Playing cards				
40. Completing a difficult task				
*41. Laughing				
42. Solving a problem, puzzle, crossword, etc.				
43. Being at weddings, baptisms, confirmations, etc.				
44. Criticizing someone				
45. Shaving				
46. Having lunch with friends or associates				
47. Taking powerful drugs				
48. Playing tennis				
49. Taking a shower				
50. Driving long distances				
51. Woodworking, carpentry				
52. Writing stories, novels, plays, or poetry				
*53. Being with animals				

[a] Use this column to check items for your Activity Schedule.
* Starred items are mood-related activities.

Pleasant Events Schedule (*cont.*)

	F	P	F × P	√ [a]
54. Riding in an airplane				
55. Exploring (hiking away from known routes, spelunking, etc.)				
*56. Having a frank and open conversation				
57. Singing in a group				
58. Thinking about myself or my problems				
59. Working on my job				
*60. Going to a party				
61. Going to church functions (socials, classes, bazaars, etc.)				
62. Speaking a foreign language				
63. Going to service, civic, or social club meetings				
64. Going to a business meeting or a convention				
65. Being in a sporty or expensive car				
66. Playing a musical instrument				
67. Making snacks				
68. Snow skiing				
69. Being helped				
*70. Wearing informal clothes				
71. Combing or brushing my hair				

[a] Use this column to check items for your Activity Schedule.
* Starred items are mood-related activities.

131

Pleasant Events Schedule (*cont.*)

	F	P	F × P	√ [a]
72. Acting				
73. Taking a nap				
*74. Being with friends				
75. Canning, freezing, making preserves, etc.				
76. Driving fast				
77. Solving a personal problem				
78. Being in a city				
79. Taking a bath				
80. Singing to myself				
81. Making food or crafts to sell or give away				
82. Playing pool or billiards				
83. Being with my grandchildren				
84. Playing chess or checkers				
85. Doing craft work (pottery, jewelry, leather, beads, weaving, etc.)				
86. Weighing myself				
87. Scratching myself				
88. Putting on makeup, fixing my hair, etc.				
89. Designing or drafting				
90. Visiting people who are sick, shut in, or in trouble				

[a] Use this column to check items for your Activity Schedule.
* Starred items are mood-related activities.

Pleasant Events Schedule (*cont.*)

	F	P	F × P	√ [a]
91. Cheering, rooting				
92. Bowling				
*93. Being popular at a gathering				
*94. Watching wild animals				
95. Having an original idea				
96. Gardening, landscaping, or doing yard work				
97. Shoplifting				
98. Reading essays or technical, academic, or professional literature				
99. Wearing new clothes				
100. Dancing				
*101. Sitting in the sun				
102. Riding a motorcycle				
103. Just sitting and thinking				
104. Social drinking				
*105. Seeing good things happen to my family or friends				
106. Going to a fair, carnival, circus, zoo, or amusement park				
107. Talking about philosophy or religion				
108. Gambling				
*109. Planning or organizing something				

a Use this column to check items for your Activity Schedule.
* Starred items are mood-related activities.

133

Pleasant Events Schedule (*cont.*)

	F	P	F × P	√ [a]
110. Smoking marijuana				
111. Having a drink by myself				
112. Listening to the sounds of nature				
113. Dating, courting, etc.				
*114. Having a lively talk				
115. Racing in a car, motorcycle, boat, etc.				
116. Listening to the radio				
*117. Having friends come to visit				
118. Playing in a sporting competition				
119. Introducing people I think would like each other				
120. Giving gifts				
121. Going to school or government meetings, court sessions, etc.				
122. Getting massages or backrubs				
123. Getting letters, cards, or notes				
124. Watching the sky, clouds, or a storm				
125. Going on outings (to the park, a picnic, a barbecue, etc.)				
126. Playing basketball				
127. Buying something for my family				
128. Photography				

[a] Use this column to check items for your Activity Schedule.
* Starred items are mood-related activities.

Pleasant Events Schedule (*cont.*)

	F	P	F × P	√ [a]
129. Giving a speech or lecture				
130. Reading maps				
131. Gathering natural objects (wild foods or fruit, rocks, driftwood, etc.)				
132. Working on my finances				
*133. Wearing clean clothes				
134. Making a major purchase or investment (car, appliance, house, stocks, etc.)				
135. Helping someone				
136. Being in the mountains				
137. Getting a job advancement (being promoted, given a raise or, offered a better job; getting accepted to a better school, etc.)				
138. Hearing jokes				
139. Winning a bet				
140. Talking about my children or grandchildren				
141. Meeting someone new of the opposite sex				
142. Going to a revival or crusade				
143. Talking about my health				
*144. Seeing beautiful scenery				
*145. Eating good meals				

[a] Use this column to check items for your Activity Schedule.
* Starred items are mood-related activities.

Pleasant Events Schedule (*cont.*)

	F	P	F × P	√ [a]
146. Improving my health (having my teeth fixed, getting new glasses, changing my diet, etc.)				
147. Being downtown				
148. Wrestling or boxing				
149. Hunting or shooting				
150. Playing in a musical group				
151. Hiking				
152. Going to a museum or exhibit				
153. Writing papers, essays, articles, reports, memos, etc.				
*154. Doing a job well				
*155. Having spare time				
156. Fishing				
157. Loaning something				
*158. Being noticed as sexually attractive				
159. Pleasing employers, teachers, etc.				
160. Counseling someone				
161. Going to a health club, sauna bath, etc.				
162. Having someone criticize me				
*163. Learning to do something new				
164. Going to a "Drive-in" (Dairy Queen, McDonald's, etc.)				
*165. Complimenting or praising someone				

[a] Use this column to check items for your Activity Schedule.
* Starred items are mood-related activities.

Pleasant Events Schedule (*cont.*)

	F	P	F × P	√ [a]
*166. Thinking about people I like				
167. Being at a fraternity or sorority				
168. Taking revenge on someone				
169. Being with my parents				
170. Horseback riding				
171. Protesting social, political, or environmental conditions				
172. Talking on the telephone				
173. Having daydreams				
174. Kicking leaves, sand, pebbles, etc.				
175. Playing lawn sports (badminton, croquet, shuffleboard, horseshoes, etc.)				
176. Going to school reunions, alumni meetings, etc.				
177. Seeing famous people				
178. Going to the movies				
*179. Kissing				
180. Being alone				
181. Budgeting my time				
182. Cooking meals				
183. Being praised by people I admire				
184. Outwitting a "superior"				
*185. Feeling the presence of the Lord in my life				

a Use this column to check items for your Activity Schedule.
* Starred items are mood-related activities.

Pleasant Events Schedule (*cont.*)

	F	P	F × P	√ [a]
*186. Doing a project in my own way				
187. Doing "odd jobs" around the house				
188. Crying				
189. Being told I am needed				
190. Being at a family reunion or get-together				
191. Giving a party or get-together				
192. Washing my hair				
193. Coaching someone				
194. Going to a restaurant				
195. Seeing or smelling a flower or plant				
196. Being invited out				
197. Receiving honors (civic, military, etc.)				
198. Using cologne, perfume, or aftershave				
199. Having someone agree with me				
200. Reminiscing, talking about old times				
201. Getting up early in the morning				
*202. Having peace and quiet				
203. Doing experiments or other scientific work				
204. Visiting friends				
205. Writing in a diary				
206. Playing football				
207. Being counseled				

[a] Use this column to check items for your Activity Schedule.
* Starred items are mood-related activities.

Pleasant Events Schedule (*cont.*)

	F	P	F × P	√ [a]
208. Saying prayers				
209. Giving massages or backrubs				
210. Hitchhiking				
211. Meditating or doing yoga				
212. Seeing a fight				
213. Doing favors for people				
214. Talking with people on the job or in class				
*215. Being relaxed				
216. Being asked for my help or advice				
217. Thinking about other people's problems				
218. Playing board games (Monopoly, Scrabble, etc.)				
*219. Sleeping soundly at night				
220. Doing heavy outdoor work (cutting or chopping wood, clearing land, farm work, etc.)				
221. Reading the newspaper				
222. Shocking people, swearing, making obscene gestures, etc.				
223. Snowmobiling or dune-buggy riding				
224. Being in a body-awareness, sensitivity, encounter, therapy, or "rap" group				
225. Dreaming at night				

[a] Use this column to check items for your Activity Schedule.
* Starred items are mood-related activities.

Pleasant Events Schedule (*cont.*)

	F	P	F × P	√ [a]
226. Playing ping-pong				
227. Brushing my teeth				
228. Swimming				
229. Being in a fight				
230. Running, jogging, or doing gymnastics, fitness, or field exercises				
231. Walking barefoot				
232. Playing frisbee or catch				
233. Doing housework or laundry; cleaning things				
234. Being with my roommate				
235. Listening to music				
236. Arguing				
237. Knitting, crocheting, embroidery, or fancy needlework				
*238. Petting, necking				
*239. Amusing people				
240. Talking about sex				
241. Going to a barber or beautician				
242. Having house guests				
*243. Being with someone I love				
244. Reading magazines				
245. Sleeping late				

[a] Use this column to check items for your Activity Schedule.
* Starred items are mood-related activities.

Pleasant Events Schedule (*cont.*)

	F	P	F × P	√ [a]
246. Starting a new project				
247. Being stubborn				
*248. Having sexual relations				
249. Having other sexual satisfactions				
250. Going to the library				
251. Playing soccer, rugby, hockey, lacrosse, etc.				
252. Preparing a new or special food				
253. Birdwatching				
254. Shopping				
*255. Watching people				
256. Building or watching a fire				
257. Winning an argument				
258. Selling or trading something				
259. Finishing a project or task				
260. Confessing or apologizing				
261. Repairing things				
262. Working with others as a team				
263. Bicycling				
264. Telling people what to do				
*265. Being with happy people				
266. Playing party games				

a Use this column to check items for your Activity Schedule.
* Starred items are mood-related activities.

Pleasant Events Schedule (*cont.*)

	F	P	F × P	√ [a]
267. Writing letters, cards, or notes				
268. Talking about politics or public affairs				
269. Asking for help or advice				
270. Going to banquets, luncheons, potlucks, etc.				
271. Talking about my hobby or special interest				
272. Watching attractive women or men				
*273. Smiling at people				
274. Playing in sand, a stream, the grass, etc.				
275. Talking about other people				
276. Being with my husband or wife				
*277. Having people show interest in what I have said				
278. Going on field trips, nature walks, etc.				
*279. Expressing my love to someone				
280. Smoking tobacco				
281. Caring for houseplants				
*282. Having coffee, tea, a coke, etc., with friends				
283. Taking a walk				

a Use this column to check items for your Activity Schedule.
* Starred items are mood-related activities.

Pleasant Events Schedule (*cont.*)

	F	P	F × P	√ [a]
284. Collecting things				
285. Playing handball, paddleball, squash, etc.				
286. Sewing				
287. Suffering for a good cause				
288. Remembering a departed friend or loved one, visiting the cemetery				
289. Doing things with children				
290. Beachcombing				
*291. Being complimented or told I have done well				
*292. Being told I am loved				
293. Eating snacks				
294. Staying up late				
295. Having family members or friends do something that makes me proud of them				
296. Being with my children				
297. Going to auctions, garage sales, etc.				
298. Thinking about an interesting question				
299. Doing volunteer work, working on community service projects				
300. Water skiing, surfing, scuba diving				
301. Receiving money				

[a] Use this column to check items for your Activity Schedule.
* Starred items are mood-related activities.

Pleasant Events Schedule (*cont.*)

	F	P	F × P	√ a
302. Defending or protecting someone; stopping fraud or abuse				
303. Hearing a good sermon				
304. Picking up a hitchhiker				
305. Winning a competition				
306. Making a new friend				
307. Talking about my job or school				
308. Reading cartoons, comic strips, or comic books				
309. Borrowing something				
310. Traveling with a group				
*311. Seeing old friends				
312. Teaching someone				
313. Using my strength				
314. Traveling				
315. Going to office parties or departmental get-togethers				
316. Attending a concert, opera, or ballet				
317. Playing with pets				
318. Going to a play				
319. Looking at the stars or moon				
320. Being coached				

a Use this column to check items for your Activity Schedule.
* Starred items are mood-related activities.

After you have gone through the list for the first time and have assigned a frequency rating to each of the 320 items, go over the list once again. This time ask yourself this question:

How pleasant, enjoyable, or rewarding was each event during the past month?

Please answer this question by rating each event on the Pleasantness Scale (Column *P*).

0—This was *not* pleasant (use this rating for events which were either neutral or unpleasant).

1—This was *somewhat* pleasant (use this rating for events that were mildly or moderately pleasant).

2—This was *very* pleasant (use this rating for events that were strongly or extremely pleasant).

If an event has happened to you *more than once* in the past month, try to rate roughly how pleasant it was *on the average*.

If an event has not happened to you during the past month, then rate it according to how much fun you think it would have been.

When an item lists more than one event, rate it on the events *you have actually done* (if you haven't done any of the events in such an item, give it the average rating of the events in that item which you would have liked to have done).

Place your rating for each event in Column *P* (pleasantness).

Example: Item 1 is *Being in the country.* Suppose that each time you were in the country in the past 30 days you enjoyed it a great deal. Then you would rate this event 2 since it was very pleasant.

The list of items may have some events which you would not enjoy. The list was made for a wide variety of people, and it is not expected that one person would enjoy all of them. Go through the entire list rating each event on *roughly how pleasant it was* (or would have been) *during the past 30 days*. Please be sure that you rate each item.

After you have rated each item on frequency and pleasantness, you are ready to do some easy computations that will allow you to assess your rate of pleasant activities.

1. Add the frequency ratings (Column *F*) and divide by 320. This is your *mean frequency score*. For example, adding all your frequency ratings gives you a total of 176. Dividing this total by 320 equals 0.55. Your mean frequency score tells you something about how much (or how little) you engage in the activities on the list. It reflects your overall activity level. By comparing your score with the average range for persons your age given in Table 7–2, you can evaluate yourself. If

Table 7–2

	Average Ranges		
Age Group	*Mean Frequency Score*	*Mean Pleasantness Score*	*Mean Cross Product Score*
20–39	0.63–1.03	0.86–1.26	0.99–1.19
40–59	0.57–0.97	0.82–1.22	0.92–1.12
60 or older	0.50–0.90	0.78–1.18	0.86–1.06

your score is equal to or lower than the low end of the average range, you are definitely low. You are not engaging in the activities to the extent that people your age do.

2. Add the pleasantness ratings (Column *P*) and divide by 320. Thus, if your rating total was 256 you would obtain 0.80. This is your *mean pleasantness rating*. The mean pleas-

antness rating tells you something about your current *potential* for pleasurable experiences. If it is low (equal to or lower than the low end of the average range shown in Table 7–2), it means that, at present, there are relatively few activities that are likely to be sources of satisfaction and pleasure for you. If the score is high, it means that potentially you have a large number of activities and events from which you could derive satisfaction.

3. Compute a cross product score for each item and enter it in the column marked *F* × *P*. For example, if you were not in the country during the past 30 days (marked 0) but being in the country is a very pleasant activity for you (marked 2), then the product score would be $0 \times 2 = 0$, and you would enter 0; if you have been watching television (Item 33) a great deal and you have therefore assigned it a frequency rating of 2, but you don't enjoy watching television and have, therefore, assigned it a pleasantness rating of 0, the product score would be $2 \times 0 = 0$. You are now ready to compute your *mean cross product score* by adding the *F* × *P* scores of all 320 items and dividing this total by 320. The cross product score is probably the most important score because it is a measure of how much satisfaction and pleasure you derived from your activities during the past month. If it is high, it means that you are deriving considerable pleasure and satisfaction from your activities, and the remainder of this chapter may not be particularly useful to you.

My Mean PES Frequency Score is _____.

My Mean PES Pleasantness Score is _____.

My Mean PES Cross Product Score is _____.

If your cross product score is low, you can derive one more useful bit of diagnostic information by examining your score pattern. There are three possible patterns that can produce a low cross product score.

Pattern 1—Low frequency/low pleasantness: You are not engaging in many of the activities on the list *and* you are not deriving much pleasure from the ones that you do engage in.

Pattern 2—Low frequency/average or above average pleasantness: You are not engaging in the kinds of activities which are potentially enjoyable for you.

Pattern 3—Average or above average frequency/low pleasantness: You are doing many things but are not deriving much enjoyment from your activities.

Your score pattern can assist you later on in designing your self-change plan. If you show Pattern 1, your first goal might be to enhance the pleasure you derive from your activities, and then, after you have accomplished this goal, aim to increase the number of pleasant activities. If your scores match Pattern 2, your goal can simply be to increase pleasant activities. If you show Pattern 3, you might want to concentrate on increasing your enjoyment of the activities you are already doing.

Check which of the three patterns fits your PES scores.

GATHERING BASE-LINE DATA

The purpose of this section is

1. To allow you to observe for yourself the degree to which your daily mood is related to your pleasant activities.

2. To assist you in setting a goal and in pinpointing specific pleasant activities to be increased.

The development and complete execution of a self-change plan to increase pleasant activities requires from 4 to 6 weeks, with time needed in between steps. For example, it requires 2 weeks of base-lining prior to setting a goal for increase. Your best bet is to read the remainder of this chapter to give you an overview. Then return to Step 1 and allow the time needed to complete each step before moving to the next one.

You will self-observe on an individualized *Activity Schedule*. Your Activity Schedule will consist of 100 activities that are potentially pleasant for you. You construct an Activity Schedule by following these steps:

Step 1

Using the cross product scores for individual items in Table 7–1, place a check mark in the *Check Items* column next to those activities with a cross product score of 4. These are very pleasant activities, and you have been engaging in them during the past month. How many do you count? _____

Go back to the beginning of Table 7–1 and place a check mark in the same column next to activities with a cross product score of 2. How many check marks do you have now? _____

If your total is less than 100, continue to add activities from those with a *pleasantness* rating of 2 and a *frequency* rating of 0. These should have a cross product score of 0. They are potentially pleasant activities, but you have not done them during the past 30 days. How many do you have now? _____ If you are still short of 100, add some of the starred activities. These are the mood-related items. As you will recall, they have been found to be associated with mood for a fairly substantial proportion of the people who have taken our test. You should now have 100 activities, all of which are potentially pleasant for you.

Step 2

This step will take more time and effort, and you should plan to reward yourself for completing it. Using the 100 items you have checked off in Step 1, write your own Activity Schedule on the form provided in Appendix B. This form will allow you to monitor your pleasant activities *and* your daily mood for 30 days. (Use Figure 7–1 as a model.) Since it is likely that you will want to monitor through more than a single month, make several copies of your Activity Schedule so that you will not have to write it again.

You are now ready to collect base-line data on your pleasant activities and to study its association with mood as follows:

At the end of each day (select a regular time to do this, like right after the 10 P.M. news), go down the Activity Schedule and place a check mark next to those activities or events which occurred during that day *and* which you experienced as pleasant. Since you are trying to monitor your *pleasant* activity level, do not check an activity if it was not at least somewhat pleasant. Compute your total pleasant activity score by *adding* all the check marks for that day. Using the instructions given in Chapter 3, you should also rate your mood level for that day. Using the graph provided in Appendix B and the example shown in Figure 7–2 as a model, plot your pleasant activity score and mood score for each day. Graphing will allow you to see the relationship between your activity level and your mood.

Self-observe your mood and your rate of engagement in pleasant activities of a period of 2 weeks.

In doing the self-observing it is helpful to keep an "objective" attitude. The goal is for you to learn something about yourself. You are not trying to prove anything to anybody. You are not trying to change at this point. You are merely

Figure 7-1 Sample Activity Schedule (Mrs. B)

Activity	|1	2	3	4	5	6	7	8	9	10	11	12	13	14	15	16	17	18	19	20	21	22	23	24	25	26	27	28	29	30
																					Day										
1. Reading stories, novels, or plays		✓	✓	✓			✓																								✓
2. Breathing clean air																														✓	
3. Saying something clearly			✓							✓													✓			✓					
4. Having daydreams																								✓	✓						
5. Writing stories, novels, plays, or poetry																															
6. Being with animals	✓							✓	✓	✓	✓	✓	✓	✓	✓	✓	✓	✓	✓											
7. Having a frank and open conversation						✓													✓	✓	✓	✓	✓	✓	✓					✓
8. Working on my job																				✓	✓									
9. Playing a musical instrument																														
10. Making food or crafts to sell or give away																										✓				
11. Watching wild animals													✓																	
12. Having an original idea																														
13. Talking about philosophy or religion						✓	✓																							
14. Listening to the radio		✓							✓						✓	✓	✓	✓							✓			✓		
15. Giving gifts									✓		✓																	✓		
...and so on through 100 items.																															
Total for Day	11	8	8	8	10	9	14	10	15	21	22	17	14	15	16	9	18	18	7	20	25	8	22	8	26	16	17	13	18	24
Mood Score	3	2	1	6	6	1	6	4	8	5	6	4	2	4	7	3	2	6	1	6	6	4	7	3	8	4	6	7	7	8

151

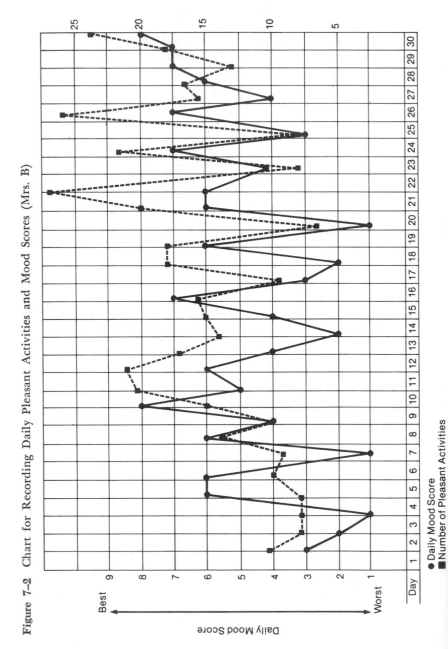

Figure 7–2 Chart for Recording Daily Pleasant Activities and Mood Scores (Mrs. B)

Number of Pleasant Activities

Daily Mood Score

● Daily Mood Score
■ Number of Pleasant Activities

studying your own behavior and trying to see what relationships there may be between it and your depression.

After you have been self-observing for 2 weeks (you should definitely reward yourself for having mastered and completed this fairly difficult and new task), you are ready to begin using your "data."

The really important question you want to answer at this point is this: Is there an association (a correlation) between your rate of pleasant activities and your mood level? In the example shown in Figure 7–2, there clearly is a strong correlation; Mrs. B feels much better on days when she engages in many pleasant activities than she does on days when she engages in very few of them. An easy way to determine whether there is an association between your pleasant activities and your mood is to compute your average activity score for your 3 most depressed days and for your 3 best days. Is there a difference? As you can see from the example shown in Figure 7–1, Mrs. B's average pleasant activity score on her 3 best days (Days 9, 25, 30) was 22 compared with 8 on her 3 worst days (Days 3, 6, 19).

To the extent that there is a positive correlation (association) between your pleasant activities and your mood, it makes good sense to try to increase your pleasant activities if you want to feel better.

There is other useful information that one can sometimes derive from the self-observation data. For example, you might discover that you always feel worse on Mondays (when you have to return to work) or on weekends (when you don't have a regular routine). These kinds of clues might be useful when it comes to formulating your plan.

DISCOVERING ANTECEDENTS

Before formulating a specific self-change plan, you may find it useful to spend a little time identifying the reasons for your low rate of pleasant activities. In this section we will list and describe some *general* conditions that can produce a low rate of pleasant activities. Typically, there is more than one reason. All (or none) of the examples we will cite may be applicable to you. You will have to decide on their relative importance. The idea is to assist you in pinpointing specific antecedents and to lay the groundwork for defining specific target behaviors for change. These "targets" will be needed later in formulating your plan.

Pressure from activities which are not pleasant but must be performed. There are many things most of us do that we may not experience as pleasant. Some of them may be downright unpleasant. Mothers often derive little satisfaction from housework or from catering to the needs of their children. Many people do not enjoy some aspects of their work. Neglecting these responsibilities causes us to feel guilt because we are letting other people down. But doing these things leaves us feeling resentful and frustrated. This is a fairly common problem. Part of the solution requires trying to achieve a better *balance* between unpleasant but necessary activities (*Type A* activities) and those activities a person would really like to do (*Type B* activities). Careful planning of one's time may be a useful component of a self-change plan aimed at increasing pleasant activities in the face of strong pressure from Type A activities.

Lack of care in choosing activities with high pleasantness potential. To maintain our well-being it is not necessary to engage in a *large* number of pleasant activities *if* we carefully choose activities to maximize their potential for enjoyment. We allow ourselves to drift into activities and hence spend a good bit of our time on things that don't have much enjoyment potential for us. This might be especially critical for people who are very busy (for example, those whose job demands leave very little time for Type B activities), and for those individuals whose range of potential activities is limited for reasons of health, age, and financial ability. If this fits you, careful attention to selecting *really* enjoyable activities may be useful.

Many major changes in a person's life situation have the effect of removing the necessity or the availability for potentially enjoyable, pleasant activities that have been extremely important to the person in the past. This is a very important cause for a low rate of pleasant activities. It affects many people. Some examples may help to illustrate the frequency and the variegation of this antecedent condition.

> *Example 1:* Mary used to derive a great deal of satisfaction from planning and cooking meals and otherwise taking care of her family. Her children have left home, and her husband has died. Many of the potentially pleasant activities which played such a very important role in her previous life are no longer needed.
>
> *Example 2:* Bill, who enjoyed his work and the opportunities it provided him for social interaction, retired when he was 55 on an early retirement plan and is finding it difficult to fill his time.
>
> *Example 3:* John recently graduated from college. He had enjoyed most related activities (preparing for exams, writing papers, reading course-related books) because he was doing them well. However, such activities are not required by his present job.

We could multiply these examples indefinitely. What they all have in common is that the person's life situation has changed in such a way that the environment (family, school, job, etc.) no longer provides the positive outcomes that had previously been so important for the person. A self-change plan to cope with this kind of antecedent should include the substitution of activities to replace those which have been lost because the environment no longer requires or needs them.

Anxiety and discomfort interferes with enjoyment. Your ability to derive enjoyment from your activities may be reduced by the fact that you experience anxiety and tension in the situation.

> *Example 1:* You are invited to a bridge party. You enjoy playing bridge, but you worry all the time about making mistakes.
>
> *Example 2:* You are at a social gathering where you know many of the people. Nevertheless, you feel very uncomfortable and self-conscious.

If you see this as an important reason for your not deriving much enjoyment from your activities, your plan should include learning how to relax (Chapter 6) and practicing relaxation in the situations in which you feel tense.

Relaxation may be a useful component of your self-change plan if tension interferes with your enjoyment of activities that would otherwise be pleasant for you. Tension may come about in three ways:

1. There is something about the potentially pleasant situation that makes you feel tense. For example, you enjoy playing bridge, but Mr. X is very critical of players who make mistakes, and you feel tense in his presence. Or, perhaps you enjoy being in small social gatherings, but after a while you start worrying about saying enough or saying the right things or what other people are thinking about you.

2. Something has happened which has left you feeling distressed, and consequently you derive little enjoyment from subsequent potentially pleasurable experiences. For example, you have just received some distressing news, and you are unable to enjoy social interactions because you are still feeling upset. Or, you had an argument with your spouse which has left you feeling upset and which threatens to ruin the rest of your day.

3. You are generally tense and given to worrying a lot, and this interferes with your ability to enjoy yourself.

If you have learned how to relax yourself in Chapter 6, you have acquired a very useful skill for increasing the quality of your pleasant experiences. If anxiety is a problem, you should include in your self-change plan making an active effort to relax yourself in situations in which you experience anxiety and tension.

To help you use what you have learned about the reasons for your low rate of pleasant activities, try to summarize your conclusions.

The reasons I am not deriving any pleasure from my activities are:

_____ Too much pressure from competing Type A activities;

_____ Activities I like to do are not needed by anyone;

_____ Poor match between what I do and what I really like to do;

_____ I feel too anxious and tense in situations which I might enjoy otherwise.

Comments

_____

_____

_____

You should try to be as specific as possible (e.g., I can't plan my activities because I never know when my husband is going to be home), and write out your conclusions. You will find it helpful in formulating your plan.

FORMULATING YOUR PLAN

The objective of your plan is to accomplish a *modest* increase in your pleasant activity level from your base level. This may involve an increase in activities that you have done and found pleasant in the past, or it may involve engaging in activities that you have never done before but which you think might be pleasant.

It is very important that you set aside a specific time and place to develop (in writing) your plan. Be sure that you will not be interrupted or disturbed while you are doing it. The first step in planning is to set aside a specific time and place to formulate and later to examine and to revise your plan.

We see planning as a very important component in your ability to implement any self-change procedure for the following reasons:

1. *Commitment*—By formulating a plan for the coming week, you are making an explicit statement or commitment as to how you would like to spend the next 7 days. You are forced to make choices, to establish priorities, and to put things in perspective.

2. *Balance*—Having a plan allows you to examine the balance between activities that must be performed (Type A) and activities you really want to do (Type B). This, as you will recall, constitutes a very important goal in regard to combatting depression.

3. *Anticipate*—Having an explicit plan forces you to anticipate problems that might interfere with implementation of the plan. For example, if you want to attend an interesting auction on Wednesday afternoon, you may have to get a baby-

sitter, arrange to have access to the family car, or make other preparations for transportation, make a reservation, etc. A very important part of planning is looking ahead and then making whatever arrangements need to be made in order to be able to follow through.

4. Be prepared to *resist demands*—Since you know what you want to do and when you want to do it, you will be in a much better position to resist demands on your time that might disrupt your plan.

5. *Control*—To the extent that you are able to stick with your plan, you will achieve a *feeling of control*. This is a very important by-product. It will make you feel that you are able to give active direction to your life, that you are not at the mercy of external forces, that you are in control of your own life. By controlling your time, you are able to control your life.

In making a practical plan, it is useful to distinguish between Type A and Type B activities. You are already familiar with this distinction. Let us try to clarify it further:

Type A activities are either neutral or unpleasant. They are activities we feel obligated to perform. Examples might be appointments with lawyers or dentists, cleaning the house, reminding someone that they owe us money, collecting debts, paying the bills, doing yard work (unless you enjoy doing yard work), taking exams, applying for a job, being in a situation that makes you physically uncomfortable, and being in a social situation you don't want to be in. They are activities you experience as neutral or unpleasant but which you nevertheless feel need to be done and which you would feel guilty not doing.

Type B activities by definition must be pleasant. They are the activities you wish to do whether anybody expects it of you or not. To say that Type A activities involve "work" while Type B activities involve recreation and fun is only partially correct, since some people enjoy at least some of their work-related activities. For example, a student may look forward to reading a certain book that is relevant to a course he/she is taking, and a musician may look forward to practicing or rehearsal. Thus, the distinction between Type A and Type B is determined by your subjective feeling about the activities. Is it something that you feel obligated to do even though you don't enjoy it (Type A), or is it something that you want to do because you expect to enjoy it (Type B)? Your activity schedule should consist *only* of Type B activities, and you should select from that list in making up your weekly plan. If a Type B activity is *not* on your list, add it to your list and cross out something that you feel could very easily be omitted. Keep the number of activities at 100.

Plan your time efficiently. Be concerned with using your time *efficiently*. There are some Type A activities (like cleaning the house, writing a term paper, reading a book for an exam) that are done most efficiently if you allow a single chunk of time for them, at a time and place when you will not be interrupted or disturbed. On the other hand, there are some Type A activities (like making a phone call, writing short letters, paying bills) that can be squeezed into nooks and crannies where they don't tie up too much time.

Anticipate. Be sure to include arrangements that have to be made in preparation for engaging in the planned activity. You may have to arrange for a babysitter, get tickets, get your cooking done early in the day, buy a fishing license, or purchase supplies for a backpacking trip.

You are now ready to formulate a specific self-change plan for yourself.

Setting a Specific Goal

Example: To obtain base-line data, Mike has been self-observing his daily mood and his pleasant activities for 2 weeks. Dividing his activity total for the 2-week period (42) by the number of observation days (14), he figured his average pleasant activities at 3 per day. Mike was struck by the fact that his daily totals were quite variable. On some days he didn't have any, and on 1 day he had 7.

From the graphing of his daily mood and pleasant activities scores (for which he used the graph in Appendix B) Mike concluded that there was indeed a correlation between his mood and his pleasant activities level. He had felt more depressed on days when his pleasant activity score was 0. On the basis of his base-lining, Mike set the following goals for the next 2 weeks:

1. He would not let his daily pleasant activities drop below 4. Mike saw this as very important.

2. Mike also committed himself to increasing his average daily pleasant activities to 4 for the following week. This meant that his total for the next 2 weeks would have to add up to 28.

Using *your* base-line data, set a specific goal for yourself:

My goal for the next week is to increase my average pleasant activities score by _____. To do this I must bring my weekly total to _____ (add 7 to weekly total). I will also try to keep my pleasant activity level from falling below _____ on any day (select a minimum you feel is realistic).

Be modest in setting your goal. Remember it is more important for you to be successful than to try for a large increase and fail.

To implement your plan you will find it useful to *plan ahead* for each coming week by using a weekly plan (Figure 7–3).[1]

Label each activity Type A or Type B by putting an A or a B after the activity. Are there too many As? If so, is it

[1] A copy of the weekly plan form is included in Appendix B so that you can make additional copies for future use.

162

Figure 7–3 Weekly Plan

Date:	Monday	Tuesday	Wednesday	Thursday	Friday	Saturday	Sunday
Time							
8:00							
9:00							
10:00							
11:00							
12:00							
1:00							
2:00							
3:00							
4:00							
5:00							
6:00							
7:00							
8:00							
9:00							
10:00							

necessary that you do all of them next week? Are there some that you could transfer to the next week? What sort of balance do you have between the As and the Bs? How many hours each day are you devoting to each? Will this plan for the coming week allow you to obtain your goal for increase? Make changes in your weekly schedule as needed.

To help you evaluate this part of your plan, you should plan to check off with a red pen activities and events that you were not able to carry out as per your plan. Do this at the end of each day as part of your self-observing. This will give you feedback on how realistic your scheduling is. Carefully review your weekly plan at regular intervals to help you evaluate how realistic it is and to identify reasons why you are unable to stick with it. Don't worry about having a lot of red marks. It isn't easy to anticipate the week ahead, and unexpected things *will* happen. It takes practice. What *is* important is that, as you continue to do this over the weeks ahead, the number of red marks go down. If you feel so inclined, you might actually count the number of red marks. They will go down as you get more proficient at being able to plan your time.

In formulating your plan you should be explicit about the arrangements you will have to make to accomplish it (getting a babysitter, etc.). Another important part of your plan might call for you to make an active effort to be relaxed in certain situations to increase your enjoyment of them.

Reward Yourself for Attaining Your Goals

It is useful to include in your plan a contract (see Chapter 4, *Step 6)* for rewarding yourself. What you are trying to do is not easy. In Chapter 4 you read about the importance of re-inforcing yourself. The chances of your being able to carry out your plan successfully and to accomplish your goals are going to be substantially increased if you plan to reward yourself.

We suggest that you construct a *reward menu*: a list of

events and objects you would like to have and you are able to give to yourself. You should include rewards that are dependent upon somebody else's behavior (for example, your husband taking you out to dinner) only if you can be sure that you can count on the other person to keep his/her end of the agreement.

Attach a point value to each of these events and objects, giving 100 points to the biggest reward. Thus, for example, getting a new car or taking a vacation in Hawaii might be rated 100 points; buying your favorite magazine might be worth 5 points. In assigning points to rewards you should take cost and availability into consideration. For example, people don't buy new cars very often, and the chances are that you could only use that once in your program, if at all. On the other hand, you may very well be able to buy a new magazine once a week and enjoy it. The 100s, therefore, should be the really big rewards.

Now attach points for specific accomplishments, making them "contingent," that is, you will give yourself (or be given) a reward very shortly, but only after you have accomplished a specific goal. For example, buying a new outfit might be made contingent upon your keeping your pleasant activity level at, or above, a certain average for 4 weeks, but you might give yourself a new magazine for every day that you keep your pleasant activity level above a minimum. The important thing is to make these "contingencies" explicit. Don't leave things to chance. They should definitely be part of your overall plan.

EVALUATION

You have two ways of deciding how you are doing. One is in terms of the self-observing data you will be gathering during all this. Are you accomplishing your goal of achieving the kinds of increases you set out for yourself at the beginning of each week? Is your mood level getting better?

The second way is in terms of using your weekly plan. Are you planning realistically? Are you making the arrangements that are necessary for you to stick with your schedule?

It is very important not to give up if things aren't perfect right away. Rome was not built in a day. It is very unlikely that you can immediately formulate a plan that is perfect. You should not expect to. The idea is to use the feedback that you will get from regularly evaluating your program. If something didn't work, try to make changes.

GETTING STARTED

You now have a self-help plan designed to increase your pleasant activity level and thereby improve your mood. You have "diagnosed" yourself during the self-assessment part. You have used this information to define a specific goal for change, and you have designed a specific plan for accomplishing this goal. Congratulations! You should have rewarded yourself with at least 50 points for having gotten this far!

Now you need to begin implementing the plan. The suggestions in this chapter may have made good sense to you and you would like to follow through, but perhaps you feel pessimistic. You may not be sure whether it is worth the effort.

If you are finding it difficult to get started, it may be because

1. You have tried various treatments and self-help procedures in the past which did not work. Understandably, you feel pessimistic about this one.
2. You feel that you don't have enough education to follow the procedures described in this chapter.

3. You are feeling too depressed to make the effort.
4. You are afraid to try this procedure because it might fail, and in that case you might feel even more discouraged.

One or more of the above may very well apply to you. There is no doubt that you are going to have to make a *concerted effort* to get started, that it is going to be difficult in the beginning, and that there are going to be failures and setbacks. You can maximize the chances of being successful if you set modest goals and reward yourself for progress. Also, you should be prepared for setbacks and be willing to revise and improve your plan as you get more experience with it.

REVIEW

_____ I assessed my pleasant activities by completing the Pleasant Events Schedule in Table 2–1.

My mean frequency score was _____.

My mean pleasantness score was _____.

My mean cross product score was _____.

_____ I compared my mean cross product score with the average scores for people my age and decided

_____ A low number of pleasant activities is not one of my problems. I decided to start working on a different chapter.

_____ My level of pleasant activities is low in comparison to people my age.

_____ By examining my PES scores, I gained some additional information. Specifically, my score pattern suggests that

_____ I am not engaging in many pleasant activities, and I don't enjoy them when I do them (Pattern 1). An appropriate goal for me would be to focus on enhancing the pleasantness of my activities and then aim to increase the number of these activities.

_____ I am not engaging in activities that are potentially enjoyable for me (Pattern 2). An appropriate goal for me would be to increase my pleasant activities by doing more of the things I really enjoy doing.

_____ I am doing many things, but I'm not getting much pleasure or enjoyment from my activities (Pattern 3). An appropriate goal for me would be to increase my enjoyment of activities I am already doing.

_____ I constructed an Activity Schedule for myself by identifying 100 activities (on the PES) with the highest cross product scores and writing them on the Activity Schedule form in Appendix B.

_____ I rewarded myself by _____ for getting this far.

_____ Since I was still doing my daily mood ratings, I was ready to begin base-line observations.

_____ At the end of each day, for the next 2 weeks, I self-observed my mood and my pleasant activities and entered the scores on my Activity Schedule.

_____ During the base-line period I also identified "reasons" (antecedents) for my low rate of pleasant activities. I gained some definite ideas and formulated them in concrete terms.

_____ I decided that feelings of tension and worrying seriously interfere with my being able to enjoy many of my activities. *I plan to take this into consideration in formulating my self-change plan.*

———— Fortunately, I already know how to relax myself using the methods in Chapter 6 (or some other method).

———— I decided that before proceeding with my pleasant activities self-change plan, I would need to learn how to reduce my feelings of tenseness in specific situations. I have gone to Chapter 6 and will return to this chapter when I am able to achieve a level of relaxation satisfactory to me.

———— I completed 2 weeks of base-line self-observations.

———— At the end of the base-line period, I figured out my pleasant activities average, noting the lowest and the highest number.

———— I also graphed my daily pleasant activities and mood scores. Inspecting my graph convinced me that

———— There is a definite correlation between what I do and my mood.

———— There is no correlation between my activities and how I feel.

———— I am not sure.

———— When ready to formulate my self-change plan, the first thing I did was to set a specific goal for change. To help me achieve this goal I incorporated the following features into my self-change plan.

———— I planned ahead for each coming week using the Weekly Plan shown in Figure 7–3.

_____ In planning ahead I tried to achieve a balance between Type A and Type B activities.

_____ I made arrangements ahead of time so that I could do the activities I planned.

_____ I planned to make an active effort to feel relaxed in situations that tend to make me feel anxious.

_____ I wrote out my self-change plan so that I could more easily revise it, or use it again in the future, if needed.

_____ I wrote a contract to reward myself for achieving my goal.

_____ I implemented my plan for increasing pleasant activities.

_____ I continued to self-observe my pleasant activities and daily mood during the implementation period.

_____ After 1 or 2 weeks of implementation I evaluated my progress by

_____ Determining whether I was accomplishing my goal for increasing pleasant activities. I did this by figuring my daily pleasant activities totals and comparing them with my goal.

_____ Determining whether my depression was diminishing. I did this by inspecting my daily mood scores.

_____ Seeing how realistic my planning ahead had been. I did this by seeing how many red marks there were on my weekly plan (Figure 7–3).

_____ On the basis of my evaluation, I decided that

———— I was satisfied with my progress and would

  ———— Continue to use my self-change plan for another 1 or 2 weeks.

  ———— Increase my goal.

———— I was not satisfied with my progress and would

  ———— Change my goal.

  ———— Change other aspects of my self-change plan.

chapter 8

Learning How to Be Socially Skillful

You probably recall from the last chapter that many of the mood-related pleasant activities involve social interactions. We think these activities are often of central importance in depression. For many people, depression level seems to parallel the ups and downs of the quality and quantity of their social relationships. Therefore this chapter and the next one will be devoted specifically to social behavior.

We think about social skill as the ability to behave in ways that lead to reinforcement from other people, rather than punishment. In less psychological language social skill is the ability to make people respond warmly and with interest to you and the ability to avoid making people ignore you or get upset with you.

There are a number of ways to be socially skillful. If you

think about the people you enjoy, they are probably different from each other—some are quiet and gentle, some are funny and energetic, some are helpful and reliable, and so on. There is no *right* way to be or to get people to like and respect you; instead, there are all kinds of different socially skillful behaviors. Therefore, this chapter *won't* tell you how to walk, talk, and smile— you won't have a script to learn. This chapter *will* try to suggest techniques you can use to change your behavior so that people will respond more positively to you. But you will have to use the suggestions in your own way, and you will have to decide on many of the specific details to flesh out the techniques we suggest.

Because of studies done by psychologists, we know quite a bit about the social skill problems of depressed people. We know, for example, that depressed people are less active in many social situations. They find it hard to initiate contact with new people, and they seem to give and receive fewer positive statements than others do. In addition, depressed people are rated as less socially skillful than others by people who observe them in social interactions. Depressed people are less comfortable in social situations, and they are especially sensitive to being ignored or rejected. Depressed people lack assertiveness; they don't stick up for themselves, and they don't say what they are thinking (whether it is good or bad).

These are just some of the social skill problems that depressed people may have; yours may have been mentioned or you may have a somewhat different problem that causes your interactions with others to fail to be a source of pleasure for you. For each of your problems you should ask a very important question: Does the problem exist because you never learned a better approach, or does the problem exist because you have stopped using skills you once had? This is important, because it is harder to learn new skills than it is to begin using again skills that you have let slide. This chapter will be devoted especially to helping people learn new skills. The next chapter is for those who aren't presently using skills they once did use.

ASSERTION

Jack grew up in a home where his parents talked very little and almost never asked his opinion. Jack is 24 now, but he still hesitates to let others know how he feels. Yesterday, Jack went out to dinner with a business acquaintance and the following things happened:

1. Jack's steak was tough and overcooked; he ate it without complaining and told the waitress everything was fine.

2. Jack had admired his friend's behavior during a conference that afternoon, but Jack was afraid to praise his friend.

3. Jack had hoped to get to know this friend better during dinner, but he didn't know how to talk about himself and ended up discussing the weather and local politics.

4. At one point, Jack disagreed with his friend's political views, but he was afraid to say so and pretended to agree.

5. When dinner was over, Jack wanted to suggest going into the bar to listen to a good folksinger who was performing, but he didn't. Instead, Jack went home and felt depressed, lonely, and discouraged.

Some people take a negative view of assertion. To them, being assertive means being loud, demanding, or obnoxious. Others view assertion more acceptingly, but still think mainly of its negative side. In this view, assertion mainly consists of things like frankly expressing one's complaints, being insistent in demanding service, and refusing inconvenient requests from others.

Our view of assertion is much broader; we see it as the ability to express one's own thoughts and feelings openly, whatever they may be. Certainly that includes things like voicing complaints, but it also includes things like expressing growing feelings of warmth and affection, inviting others to share an activity, and letting others know about one's hopes and fears. To us, being assertive means being willing to share oneself with others, rather than holding everything inside. Thus, it is a very important part of close, warm relationships. For most of us, such relationships are important, and we feel depressed when we don't have at least one or two of these positive, warm relationships. Without being assertive in the way we define the term, a person has very little chance of developing or maintaining the closeness and warmth that are so important for preventing or overcoming depression.

At a less philosophical and more practical level, we think it is important for people to learn to be assertive for other reasons as well. First, it helps avoid or prevent aversive encounters with others; no one can take advantage of someone who is appropriately assertive. Second, those who are appropriately assertive are likely to get more positive responses from other people; they express more positive feelings, and they receive them in return. Assertive people say more, thus providing a chance for others to express their positive feelings in response. Finally, those who are more appropriately assertive feel better understood by others. You probably have noticed yourself that when you are depressed, you often feel isolated and cut off from others; no one else seems to understand what you are feeling or wanting—and sometimes no one really seems to care. But people can't know how you feel and show their caring unless you take the first step of expressing your own thoughts and feelings.

How assertive are you? The questions listed in Table 8-1 are designed to help you decide whether you are assertive and how comfortable you are with assertion. They will also help you pinpoint situations which call for assertion. You should go over the list of questions twice. The first time you should rate each item on how often it has occurred in the past month. The second time you should rate how comfortable you were (or, if it did not happen, how comfortable you *would be* if it

Table 8–1

Assertion Questionnaire

Rating frequency of assertion

Indicate how often each of these events occurred by marking Column A, using the following scale:

1 . . . This has *not* happened in the past 30 days.
2 . . . This has happened *a few times* (1 to 6 times) in the past 30 days.
3 . . . This has happened *often* (7 times or more) in the past 30 days.

Rating how you feel about assertion

Indicate how you feel about each of these events by marking Column B, using the following scale:

1 . . . I felt *very uncomfortable or upset* when this happened.
2 . . . I felt *somewhat uncomfortable or upset* when this happened.
3 . . . I felt *neutral* when this happened (neither comfortable nor uncomfortable; neither good nor upset).
4 . . . I felt *fairly comfortable or good* when this happened.
5 . . . I felt *very comfortable or good* when this happened.

Important: If an event has not happened during the past month, then rate it according to how you *think you would feel if it happened.* If an event happened more than once in the past month, rate roughly how you felt about it *on the average.*

$$A \quad B$$

1. Turning down a person's request to borrow my car
2. Asking a favor of someone
3. Resisting sales pressure
4. Admitting fear and requesting consideration
5. Telling a person I am intimately involved with that he/she has said or done something that bothers me
6. Admitting ignorance in an area being discussed
7. Turning down a friend's request to borrow money

A   B

8. Turning off a talkative friend
9. Asking for constructive criticism
10. Asking for clarification when I am confused about what someone has said
11. Asking whether I have offended someone
12. Telling a person of the opposite sex that I like him/her
13. Telling a person of the same sex that I like him/her
14. Requesting expected service when it hasn't been offered (e.g., in a restaurant)
15. Discussing openly with a person his/her criticism of my behavior
16. Returning defective items (e.g., at a store or restaurant)
17. Expressing an opinion that differs from that of a person I am talking with
18. Resisting sexual overtures when I am not interested
19. Telling someone how I feel if he/she has done something that is unfair to me
20. Turning down a social invitation from someone I don't particularly like
21. Resisting pressure to drink
22. Resisting an unfair demand from a person who is important to me
23. Requesting the return of borrowed items
24. Telling a friend or co-worker when he/she says or does something that bothers me
25. Asking a person who is annoying me in a public situation to stop (e.g., smoking on a bus)
26. Criticizing a friend
27. Criticizing my spouse
28. Asking someone for help or advice
29. Expressing my love to someone

A   *B*

30. Asking to borrow something

31. Giving my opinion when a group is discussing an important matter

32. Taking a definite stand on a controversial issue

33. When two friends are arguing, supporting the one I agree with

34. Expressing my opinion to someone I don't know very well

35. Interrupting someone to ask him/her to repeat something I didn't hear clearly

36. Contradicting someone when I think I might hurt him/her by doing so

37. Telling someone that he/she has disappointed me or let me down

38. Asking someone to leave me alone

39. Telling a friend or co-worker that he/she has done a good job

40. Telling someone he/she has made a good point in a discussion

41. Telling someone I have enjoyed talking with him/her

42. Complimenting someone on his/her skill or creativity

were to happen). There are no right or wrong answers to these questions; their purpose is to provide you with information about yourself. Please read over the instructions at the start of the questionnaire, then work quickly, making two ratings for every item.

To score the questionnaire, add up all the frequency ratings and then add up all the comfort ratings. Compare your scores to those in Table 8–1. If you find that either of your scores is lower than the score at the lower end of the range in Table 8–2, you may want to become more assertive. The next

Table 8–2

Assertion Scores: Frequency and Comfort Ratings

Frequency	61– 81
Comfort	102–137

part of this chapter is written to help you with that goal. If your scores are higher than the averages shown in the table, you probably are appropriately assertive. In this case, you may want to skip ahead to page 188 in this chapter.

Let's go through a few examples to make sure this is clear. Let's assume Jack, the man described at the start of this section, answered these questions. When he added up his scores he had a total of 12 for frequency and a total of 46 for comfort. These scores are clearly below the ranges given in the table, so Jack should conclude that he is less often assertive than average and less comfortable than average about being assertive. Next, let's assume that Jack answered the questions again after working on becoming more assertive. This time his frequency score was 25 and his comfort score was 58. This would mean that he is now assertive about as often as others, but he is still a little uncomfortable about it. Finally, let's assume that Jack keeps working at it and is quite successful. This time his scores are 35 for frequency and 100 for comfort. This would mean that he is assertive about as often as others—but clearly on the upper end of the distribution—and that he is more comfortable about being assertive than the average person.

LEARNING HOW TO BE ASSERTIVE

Now that you are familiar with the concept of assertion, it is time to begin applying it directly to your own life. At this point, you may feel convinced that you would like to be more assertive but baffled about how to begin. The rest of this section will describe a method for you to use to learn to be more assertive in your everyday life.

The next step is to develop a Personal Problem List. This should be a list of from 5 to 10 situations which meet all of the following criteria:

1. You currently are handling the situation in a nonassertive way.

2. The situation occurs regularly in your life (at *least* once a month).

3. The situation is troubling to you.

4. The situation strikes a good balance between being too specific ("My mother complaining about the pot roast I cooked last night") and too general ("Anyone complaining to me about anything"). A good balance might be: "My family complaining to me about my behavior." If the item is too specific it may never occur again, and if it is too general it may be hard to find a way of dealing with it that will fit all the possible situations.

5. The different situations on the list should be reasonably different from each other; if they are too similar, merge the items.

6. The different situations should cover a diverse number of areas (home, school, work, shopping, dining out, etc.), and types of behavior (resisting pressure, expressing warmth, making requests, handling disagreements, etc.), unless you have difficulty in only one area.

As you write your list, be sure to consider items from the assessment you just completed. The following sample list may help as you prepare your own.

Personal Problem List

1. Telling Jack that I am bothered by something he did.

2. Letting Theresa know that I would like to have her for a friend.

3. Expressing my preference to my husband about how we spend our free time together.

4. Asking my supervisor at work for more feedback about how I am doing.

5. Calling to cancel an appointment.

6. Apologizing to my family when I let them down.

7. Walking out of a store without buying things when a salesperson gets pushy.

8. Telling the neighbors about my complaints (about their noise, letting dogs run loose, etc.).

9. Telling my husband I need more time with him.

10. Introducing myself to new people at parties.

KEEPING TRACK OF YOUR ASSERTION

When you have completed your list, turn to the Self-Monitoring of Assertion Form in Figure 8–1. On this form, write in the 10 situations on your Personal Problem List; add more lines if you have a few more items than 10. You should begin keeping track *every day* of your assertiveness in all 10 of the situations. To do this, follow these instructions:

Each day, fill out a copy of the personalized form. For each situation, rate how comfortable you were (from 0 to 10) and how skillful you were in asserting yourself (from 0 to 10) *each time it occurred.* Be sure to rate every occasion on which the situation occurred; that may be more than once on some days. A 0 rate should indicate totally unsatisfactory performance (you were completely uncomfortable, or you were completely non-assertive). You would also rate 0 if you *avoided* the situation when it came up. A rating of 10 should indicate near perfection in performance (you were completely relaxed and comfortable, or you were extremely skillful in your assertive behavior). Most ratings, of course, will fall between these two extremes and should reflect *your own feelings* about your comfort and assertion in the situations.

The reason we want you to keep track of your behavior is so that you can see how it changes over time as you use the suggested techniques.[1] You should keep all of your rating forms so that you can look back later and see your progress. Also, each week it would be a good idea to figure out your average comfort and skill ratings for each situation. Your day-to-day ratings will probably vary a lot, but the weekly averages should show fairly steady progress.

PRACTICING ASSERTIVE IMAGERY

After a week of self-monitoring, you will be ready to begin practicing assertion in your own imagination. This procedure, which will be explained in detail, will give you maximum flexibility because you can practice as often as you want, wherever you want. In the privacy of your own mind, you can try out numerous responses and refine your own personal style without making your mistakes out loud. You can practice handling situations that vary in small, but important ways (for instance, whether you are asking a request of a male or a fe-

[1] The Self-Monitoring of Assertion Form is included in Appendix B so that you can make additional copies for use in subsequent weeks.

Figure 8–1
Self-Monitoring of Assertion Form

Situation	Comfort	*Skill in Asserting Myself*
1.		
2.		
3.		
4.		
5.		
6.		
7.		
8.		
9.		
10.		

male) because you create the situation in your head. In general, you will be entirely in control until you feel ready to try out your new skill in reality, with other people. Anticipating situations in this way makes it more likely that they will go better when they occur.

Begin your sessions by focusing on 1 or 2 of the 10 situations on your personalized list. There are three basic strategies for choosing where to start. You can pick the 2 situations which seem easiest to you so that you are assured of some success at the start. Or, you can pick the 2 situations that are most likely to come up soon so that you will be prepared for them. Or, you can pick any 2 at random and just get started. Any of these strategies can work; use the one that appeals to you the most.

For the first few sessions you should practice at least 15 minutes every day, and you should have most of your practice sessions in a place where you can concentrate well and will not be interrupted, for instance in your bedroom or lying down on the living room couch. Later on, you can be more flexible about where, when, and how often you can practice, but at the start you should take extra care to create a good practice environment for yourself.

CREATING VIVID IMAGES

In each session, you should follow these steps. First, select one of your situations and imagine a concrete example of that situation. Close your eyes and imagine the scene; try to vividly imagine where it occurs, who is there, where you are in the scene, etc. Get a real picture of the scene in your imagination, as if you could see a photograph of it, and then start the action and turn the photograph into a movie. In the movie, imagine what each person is saying and doing, and picture the events leading up to the moment when you will want to assert yourself. Then imagine, as clearly as you can, your own behavior; imagine yourself saying something which you would feel very good about in that situation. It should be assertive, not passive or aggressive. It should please you; you should feel that you would be satisfied with yourself if you really handled the situation that way. It doesn't have to be witty, charming, earth-shattering, or the ultimate assertive act. It should simply be a way to handle the situation that pleases you. Then imagine what would happen after that; what would the other people say and do? Usually, you should imagine the positive effects of your behavior; in fact, most assertion will be received well.

However, it won't always be, and you should occasionally imagine that others do not react positively. In that case, remember that the *goal is to handle the situation as well as you can*, not to manipulate, control, or predict other people's actions.

After running through a scene completely once, go back and do the same scene again, but change some of the details. Change one of the people, or change what is said that leads up to your assertion, or change slightly the content of your assertive behavior. Continue this sequence several times; each time follow the complete sequence, but change it in some way from the last time through. The sequence should always contain the following:

A *vivid image* of the scene—as if it were a *photograph*, which turns into

A *movie* that shows what leads up to your

Assertive statement, which should be satisfying to you and which creates a

Response, usually positive, from the other people in the scene.

The following are examples of such an imagery sequence; obviously you will have to embellish the relevant visual images in your own mind. In the following example, the situation on the personalized monitoring list was "Expressing my preference to my husband about how we should spend our free time together."

First Sequence:

Photograph: You are with your husband; you have both gotten home from work on Friday afternoon and are sitting in the living room playing with the dogs and having a drink. You are a little tired and would like to go out to dinner and then go for a walk by the river.

Movie: The dogs are playing a little bit, but are not too distracting. Your husband sits up, scratching one dog's head. He looks across the room and says, "I've been thinking, and I'm not really sure what we should do tonight. There's a good movie on, but maybe we should play racquetball and get some exercise."

You start to feel a little anxious, but the dog looks up at you and licks your hand, so you decide to be brave in your reply.

Assertion: "Both of those would be all right with me, but I would *really* like to do something else. I'd like it if we could go out for dinner and then take a walk by the river. It's a lovely evening, and I think it would be relaxing for us both to be outside for a while after working inside all day."

Response: Your husband looks a little reluctant, but thoughtfully replies, "I guess that sounds OK to me. Maybe we could play racquetball tomorrow morning when we're rested. How about if we go to the Excelsior for dinner? Does that sound good?"

Second Sequence:

Photograph: Same scene as before, except that it is winter instead of summer. It is dark outside, and there is a fire burning in the fireplace. You would like to spend the evening at home, talking and planning your weekend trip to the coast.

Movie: You chat for awhile about the day; you feel relaxed. You get up and poke the fire, then throw on another log. Turning away from the fire, your husband says, "Do you think we should call some friends and go out to a tavern?" You consider your reply.

Assertion: "That sounds like we would be up pretty late, and we wanted to get an early start tomorrow. Maybe we should stay home and plan whether to go to Cascade Head or Cape Perpetua tomorrow. Then we could get ready, get to bed early, and get started early in the morning."

Response: "Sounds like a good idea to me. I'm kind of tired tonight anyway."

CREATING YOUR OWN EXAMPLES FOR
YOUR PERSONALIZED PROBLEM LIST

Now try out a few examples using one of your own situations; then write out the essential elements, as in the examples above. You can be brief and just capture the major images and words. Check to make sure that all four components are there. Especially check to make sure that you are satisfied with your assertion. If you feel you need help at this stage, try asking a friend or relative to go over the scenes with you and make helpful suggestions.

Once you are satisfied with your ability to produce appropriate scenes, set up a schedule for this week's practice; try to schedule a regular time and place. Remember, you should practice at least 15 minutes every day, using 2 of the situations on your personalized list. Be sure to continue monitoring your behavior in all 10 of the situations every time they occur.

TRANSFERRING FROM IMAGERY
TO REAL LIFE

After a week of imagery practice, you should be ready to begin trying out your skills in the real world. Remember that at first you will be a little awkward, but every time you try it, assertion will feel a little more natural. At first you should try to plan the situations for trying out your skills, rather than waiting and hoping that a good chance will come along. Try to plan situations that are most likely to be successful. For example, if making a request is one of your items, try to ask a kind, helpful person for help rather than choosing someone who is usually

186

grouchy. Or, if offering a compliment is an item, try to do it casually and privately, rather than putting someone else in an awkward position. Rehearse as explicitly as you can the real life situation before you try it. Be sure to rate the situations you plan, along with the naturally occurring ones, on your self-monitoring forms.

EVALUATING YOUR PROGRESS

After 10 days of practicing assertions you should evaluate your progress. Go back over the rating forms and your average scores. Are they improving? If you have successfully practiced the imagery and used it in a real life situation, you are well on the way to becoming an appropriately assertive person. All that remains is to repeat exactly the same sequence of steps using the other items on your personalized list. Choose about 2 at a time to work on, first in imagery and then in real life. You can begin to make your schedule more flexible. Try the imagery while waiting for service, riding the bus, or taking a coffee break. Just be sure to continue doing it *regularly*—at least 10 minutes every day. You can also begin to be more flexible about the real life use of the technique. You might start taking advantage of naturally occurring situations, as well as setting up optimal situations for yourself. You now have the basic tools you need to improve your skill at being assertive. Hold on to the basic tool, but also begin to explore its possibilities while you improve.

If you are not making progress yet, you should try to understand why and to make some changes. Here are some possibilities:

1. You may have a long history of being very nonassertive. If so, you probably need more time using this technique; you should stick with it for another few weeks.

2. You may not be practicing as often as you need, or you may be taking "shortcuts" with the techniques. Make sure that you are practicing regularly, that you are creating good, vivid images, and that you are taking time to go through the whole scene carefully.

3. You may be setting very high standards for yourself and not admitting progress in your ratings if your images or behavior are not perfect. Use the whole scale from 0 to 10; don't wait to upgrade your ratings until you can give yourself a perfect 10!

4. If you have tried these suggestions and are still not making progress, this may not be the technique for you. Not everyone improves with the same method, and you may respond beautifully to another method. There are a number of books on the market designed to help people increase their assertive behavior. Probably the best one is *Your Perfect Right* by Alberti and Emmons.[2] Other books you might find helpful are listed in the Appendix of this book. Or you might want to seek out a counselor rather than trying self-help.

HOW DO YOU APPEAR TO OTHERS?

Gloria is a depressed, 38-year-old woman. Watching Gloria while she sits with a group of acquaintances is very informative. The group is sitting in a circle, but Gloria's chair is 3 feet further back than any of the others. Figure 8–2 shows a diagram of the seating arrangement. Gloria is sitting in chair 1; she could pull up to be a part of the group, but she has not done that. Gloria is looking down at the floor while she sits. Her hands are in her lap, her right hand fidgeting with a ring on her left hand. When she looks up occasionally, her face

2 Alberti, R. E., and Emmons, M. *Your Perfect Right* (2nd ed.). San Luis Obispo, Calif.: Impact, 1974.

Figure 8–2

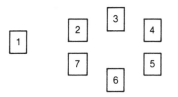

appears nervous and unhappy; she never smiles. Others in the group ask her questions from time to time; her answers are halting and there are long pauses between words. Sometimes she doesn't answer at all, so the conversation eventually goes on without her. When Gloria does talk, she usually complains about how bad she feels; she says nothing positive to anyone in the group.

Obviously, Gloria's behavior is that of a depressed person. But why is it happening—is she acting this way *because* she is depressed, or is feeling depressed perhaps *caused* by her social withdrawal? No one can say for sure, but Gloria's unpleasant social behavior may possibly be contributing to her depression. Certainly she is creating a situation that will help her stay depressed. The others in the circle are bothered by her unfriendliness, and they gradually say less and less to her. Next time she may not be included at all. Then she will feel even more lonely and depressed, and she will be even less pleasant to be around. This sets up a vicious circle which may get very hard for her to break.

It is very striking to observe a really depressed person like Gloria; the depression often shows clearly without the person ever saying that he or she feels depressed. Try observing someone you know who is depressed sometime. Like Gloria, that person (let's assume it's a female friend) is likely to smile very little, to look at the floor or her lap instead of at you, to sit slouched over rather than looking interested and alert. She may also speak very slowly or very softly so that it is hard to listen to her for very long. It is also likely that she will not use illustrative hand gestures while speaking; instead, she may use nervous gestures like playing with a paper clip or rubbing her hand on her leg. This may be distracting or irritating to you. Your friend may also fail to show much interest in what you say and, thus, make you feel like she would rather have you leave her alone. All these things will combine to create in you a vivid feeling that your friend is unhappy, even though you may not know why she is unhappy. You will probably feel uncomfortable while you are with her, and you may have a vague feeling of guilt because it seems like you are expected to do something for her. If this has happened several times, you may find yourself avoiding her in the future. Now, the real question is: Do *you* affect other people in this way when *you* are depressed? It is possible that you do. However, it will be difficult for you to judge this for yourself. Look over the following list and check off, as honestly as you can, all the behaviors that seem to be true of you. Discuss this information with a close, trusted friend if you possibly can; the two of you should make a decision together about whether this is a problem area for you.

_____ Not smiling; unpleasant facial expression

_____ Failing to make eye contact

_____ Not joining in conversations

_____ Whining

_____ Complaining or brooding out loud on your problems

_____ Slumping over while sitting or standing

_____ Poor grooming

_____ Nervous gestures

_____ Not asking questions or otherwise showing interest in what others are saying

_____ Speaking too softly; making it hard for others to hear you

_____ Slow, halting speech

_____ Telling your troubles to everyone

_____ Crying often in public

_____ Not responding to questions

_____ Criticizing others

_____ Ignoring others

_____ Other problem: _____

These problems illustrate the kinds of things that influence the impact we have on others. There may be other ways that are important in your case. If you feel you are having a negative impact on others, the important thing is to pinpoint a few areas which you can change and which are most likely to lead to success. You can do that using our list or by coming up with items on your own.

How do you go about changing these things? Remember the basic way we have set up changes throughout this book. First, set up specific goals for yourself that proceed in small gradual steps. Second, keep track of your behavior in order to make sure you are actually improving. Third, reward yourself for progress; reward small gains rather than insisting on immediate perfection.

To make these steps concrete, let's use the first item, *Not smiling*, as an illustration. Here is a sample set of small, gradual steps toward improvement; for illustration purposes, let's use Gloria's list:

1. Smile at myself in the mirror at least 3 times a day.

2. Smile at my co-workers at least twice a day.

3. Smile at my co-workers at least 5 times a day.

4. Smile at my co-workers at least once each time I speak to one of them.

5. Smile at friends outside of work at least once a day.

6. Smile at friends outside of work at least once each time I speak to them.

Gloria set it up this way because she felt most awkward smiling with friends, and she was most tempted to cry and whine with her friends. It was easier to start with co-workers. She gave herself a week for each step. By the end of the week she expected herself to meet or exceed her goal. If she did, she rewarded herself with either new clothes or a good lunch at a restaurant on Saturday; then she started the next step on Sunday. She progressed well at most steps; however Step 4 took her 2 weeks to accomplish and Step 6 also took her 2 weeks. Thus, the whole process of change took 8 weeks—or about 2 months. That may seem like slow progress, but because she kept at it steadily and in discrete steps she could see her improvement every week in the records she was keeping.

You should set up similar steps for yourself for any of the items that seem to be important for you. Try to keep in mind the overall goal: You want to stop driving people away with your negative behavior. You don't have to be fake, or give up honest emotions, or act like a cheerful circus clown. You simply want to be a reasonably pleasant person rather than someone to avoid. Use a good friend to help you keep track of how you are doing, if you possibly can.

MOVING TO A NEW SOCIAL ENVIRONMENT

James moved to San Francisco in January; by March he was ready to jump off the Golden Gate Bridge. His job was OK; his apartment was OK; his family loved him and missed him; his cat was always waiting for him when he came home; and he had read a lot of good books. He knew San Francisco had a symphony, an opera, beautiful parks, museums, restaurants, nightclubs, theaters—but he didn't know where they were, or how to get around in the city, or how to do things by himself, or where to meet people he might enjoy. So he stayed home with his cat, read books, and got depressed living in one of the most interesting cities in the world.

This kind of situation can occur when people move, when they change jobs or schools, when a company is reorganized, or for numerous other reasons. The missing skill for James, or others in similar situations, is a simple one—he doesn't know how to gather and act on information about social activities. This problem serves as a bridge between this chapter, which has emphasized learning new skills, and the next one, which will emphasize skills that are available but are not being used. Learning to collect information in a new environment doesn't fit exactly into either category, but we can offer a few brief hints here about getting to know a new environment; the next chapter should also be useful if this is one of your problems.

In your efforts to begin to feel at home in any new territory, you should ask the following questions: Where are the people? Where are the activities? What parts of town should be avoided? How formal or informal are people here? What is available to someone on a tight budget? What child care is available for single parents? These, and a host of similar questions, weigh on a new arrival and interfere with socializing.

Luckily, these questions are not all that hard to answer, as long as you display some initiative.

The following are some things you can do; many of these ideas are also found in *First Person Singular* by Stephen M. Johnson.[3] You also may want to read Johnson's book for further ideas.

1. Subscribe to the local paper and read the activities and entertainment section faithfully.

2. Ask the local Chamber of Commerce for information. They usually will have a good bit of information about groups and activities in the area.

3. Go out a lot and make *mistakes.* There's no teacher like experience; you may waste a few evenings or weekends, but you'll learn a lot and maybe you'll find someone else who is looking for answers.

4. Call someone—anyone you know at work, a neighbor, a classmate. Don't ask for friendship, just explain your situation and ask for information. You may get both information *and* friendship.

5. Spend some weekends exploring. Get a map of town and a good pair of shoes, and plan a number of exploring trips. Walk all over a section of town; scout out the shops, restaurants, theaters, and other areas where people might congregate. Make a list of what you find; now when you're looking for a good restaurant you will have lots of places to try that looked interesting to you.

6. Join a group that does interesting things in the area—a hiking club, or a theater group, or a sports club, etc. It is probably better at this stage to avoid groups that meet in the same place every week to do the same thing. That can come later; right now, you want to get a variety of experiences. If you know

---

[3] Johnson, S. M. *First Person Singular: Living the Good Life Alone.* Philadelphia: Lippincott, 1977.

you would really enjoy a group that meets regularly for one purpose, go ahead and join it. But don't stop there.

If you've tried all these suggestions and you're still having trouble, you need to wonder why. It may be that just learning about social environments is not enough for you. You may need a more systematic approach to increasing your social activities. The next chapter is designed to help do that.

SUMMARY

This chapter has covered three different kinds of problems with people; lack of assertiveness, having negative impact because of personal style, and failure to learn about social environments. For each problem area, a strategy was suggested for improvement. If you used this chapter, you should now have a clearer idea of what your own specific problems with people are and what you can do about them. You should have a plan of action and you should be keeping records of your behavior. Hopefully, you will be seeing changes in the behavior as you implement your plan. And, as always, you can use your daily records of your mood to see whether changing your social behavior is helping you become less depressed.

REVIEW

_____ I understand what assertion is and why it is important.

_____ I have taken the Assertion Questionnaire in Table 8–1 and evaluated my scores.

_____ If either of my scores on assertion was low, I am working on becoming more assertive and/or comfortable about assertion. To do this I have

_____ Made a Personal Problem List

_____ Been assessing everyday my comfort and assertive skill in each of the situations on my list.

_____ Been practicing, in imagery, behaving assertively in situations on my list

_____ Begun trying out my assertiveness in real life situations

_____ Evaluated my progress at least once.

_____ I have gone over the checklist of negative behaviors. If I decided that one or more of these are typical of me, I have

_____ Set up a change plan, using small steps, self-monitoring, and rewards for small gains.

_____ Worked on my plan for at least a couple of weeks.

_____ Evaluated my progress at least once.

_____ I have decided whether the section on learning about new social environments is applicable to my situtaion. If it is, I have

_____ Tried out at least one of the techniques suggested.

_____ Evaluated my progress at least once.

_____ Decided whether to go on to the next chapter to use a more systematic approach.

chapter 9

Using
Your Social
Skills

Janet is a lonely, depressed person. She wasn't always lonely.
In fact, until last year no one would have suspected that she
could be so lonely. Janet had always been friendly and easy to
know; she had a warm smile and a relaxed, comfortable personal style. She had been able to assert herself, and she was able
to make new friends when she tried. So why is Janet lonely?

There are a number of reasons. A year ago, she had her first
child and she voluntarily gave up a number of activities she
had shared with friends. She told herself this was only temporary, but somehow she didn't keep track of the time and 6
months later she realized that "temporary" was becoming "permanent." She and her husband no longer enjoyed the same
people or activities, they had stopped inviting couples over.
They had turned down so many invitations right after the
baby was born that they were no longer being invited out by

their friends. Janet still hasn't planned a new daily schedule for herself, so there is no regular time of day when she can count on making appointments to go out with friends.

In short, Janet is in a rut. She has set up a life schedule which leaves no room for friends, and she isn't doing anything to change that situation. She gets lonelier and more depressed every day. The more depressed she gets, the more helpless and tired she feels. She enjoys her family less, has less interest in life, and has less to talk about when she does see friends. Janet still has the potential to make friends and enjoy social inter-action, but she isn't using her abilities at all.

Janet illustrates a common problem. She knows how to be socially skillful, but she isn't using what she knows. She doesn't need to learn new skills; she mainly needs to arrange her life differently so that she can use the skills she has. This is a fairly common pattern among depressed people.

Another similar problem can come up with socially anx-ious people. They have the skills, but being in social situations in general, or in certain social situations in particular, makes them feel fearful or uncomfortable. For these people, like for Janet in the previous illustration, knowing *what* to do isn't enough. They need help in overcoming whatever prevents them from using what they know. Providing such help is the purpose of this chapter.

EVALUATING YOURSELF

By taking the following test you can evaluate your level of social participation. Table 9–1 lists activities which are usually shared with other people. You should go over this list twice. The first time you should rate each activity on how often it has occurred in the past month; the second time you should rate how com-fortable you were during the activity (or, if it did not occur, how comfortable you *would be* if it were to occur). There are no right or wrong answers to these questions; their purpose is to provide you with information about yourself. Please work quickly and rate *every* activity.

After you have rated each item on frequency and comfort, you can go on to the next section.

To score your activities, first add the ratings on comfort for each of the items. This is your *comfort score* (it can also be thought of as your social anxiety score). Compare your score to those in Table 9–2, which shows high and low scores based on normative data for nondepressed adults. If your score is lower than low score shown, then you should read Chapter 6, *Relaxation,* which presents a detailed plan for learning how to relax and how to use relaxation to overcome anxiety in your everyday life. You should also go on with the scoring in this chapter.

Next, add the frequency ratings for each of the items; this is your *frequency score.* Compare your score to those in Table 9–2. If your score on social participation was lower than the low score shown, you probably will want to plan ways to become more active with other people. The rest of this chapter is designed to help you with that goal.

If your comfort score was low and your frequency score was high, you will just need to work with Chapter 6. If comfort was high but frequency was low, you will just need to work with this chapter. If both were low, decide which to work on first, but plan to work on both. If both were high, pat yourself on the back and move on to another problem area.

OVERCOMING SOCIAL PARTICIPATION PROBLEMS

We have already encouraged you to go to Chapter 6 if you scored in the "anxious" range on your *comfort score.* This chapter assumes that your problems, like Janet's in the initial

Table 9-1

Social Activities Questionnaire

Rating how often social activities occur

Indicate how often you did each of the following activities by marking Column A, using the following scale:

1. . . . This has *not* happened in the past 30 days.
2. . . . This has happened *a few times* (1 to 6 times) in the past 30 days.
3. . . . This has happened *often* (7 times or more) in the past 30 days.

Rating how you feel about each social activity

Indicate how you feel about each of the following activities by marking Column B, using the following scale:

1. . . . I felt *very uncomfortable or upset* when this happened.
2. . . . I felt *somewhat uncomfortable or upset* when this happened.
3. . . . I felt *neutral* when this happened (neither comfortable nor uncomfortable; neither good nor upset).
4. . . . I felt *fairly comfortable or good* when this happened.
5. . . . I felt *very comfortable or good* when this happened.

Important: If an event has *not* happened to you during the past month, then rate according to how you think you would feel if it happened. If an event happened more than once in the past month, rate roughly how you felt about it *on the average.*

	A	B
1. Talking with a friend		
2. Going on a recreational outing (boating, camping, hiking, etc.)		
3. Being in a class, discussion group, or encounter group		
4. Going on my first date with someone		
5. Receiving a telephone call from a friend		
6. Initiating a conversation with a stranger		
7. Talking with my parent(s)		

                                                                    A   *B*

8. Being asked for my help or advice
9. Going to an office party
10. Talking with my child(ren) or grandchild(ren)
11. Visiting friends
12. Doing volunteer work or working on a community service project
13. Accepting a date or social invitation
14. Dancing
15. Being the first to say "hello" when I see someone I know
16. Having lunch or a coffee break with friends
17. Going to a bar or tavern
18. Introducing myself to someone
19. Talking with a stranger of the same sex
20. Introducing people I think would like each other
21. Going to a sports event (football, track meet, etc.)
22. Singing or playing a musical instrument in a group
23. Talking with my husband or wife
24. Going on a date
25. Being introduced to someone
26. Going to a church function
27. Playing cards or board games (checkers, Monopoly, etc.)
28. Going to a party
29. Inviting a friend or acquaintance to join me for some social activity
30. Walking up and joining a group of people
31. Going to a service, civic, special interest, or social club meeting
32. Going someplace where I know I must be sociable
33. Talking with someone on the job or in class
34. Talking with a stranger of the opposite sex
35. Joining a friend or friends for a social activity

Social Activities Questionnaire (*cont.*)

		A	B
36.	Giving a party or get-together		
37.	Calling a friend on the telephone		
38.	Having sexual relations		
39.	Going to a formal social affair		
40.	Having friends come to visit		
41.	Being at a party where I hardly know anyone		
42.	Going to the movies with someone		
43.	Playing competitive team sports (softball, basketball, etc.)		
44.	Going to lectures or hearing speakers		
45.	Engaging in recreational sports with someone (tennis, bowling, skiing, etc.)		
46.	Attending a concert, play, opera, or ballet		

Table 9–2

Social Activity Scores: Normal Range	
Comfort	150–198
Frequency	75– 95

case illustration, are a result of faulty life planning, not anxiety.

There are two main planning problems that seem to interfere with social activity. We will use the labels "Inadequate stimulation" and "Inadequate reward" to refer to them.

Inadequate Stimulation

This label applies to situations where you fall into a routine that doesn't provide you with *easy opportunities* to do things with other people. This can happen in lots of ways; the following are just some of the possibilities:

- You are tired from work in the evening and turn on the TV because it is the easiest thing to do.

- You aren't being invited out by friends and don't get around to inviting them yourself.

- You aren't working outside your home, or your job doesn't put you in contact with other people.

- You work odd or irregular hours so you can't easily plan activities with others.

- Your work requires you to travel a lot, so you have trouble building up a group of friends in one place.

- You have taken on a role, such as nurse for a relative or chauffeur for your children, which has taken up *all* of your spare time.

- You don't pay attention to the entertainment section of your newspaper, so you never know what activities there are in your area.

- You got used to being around one particular person, and now that person has moved away.

The list could go on and on, but you probably have gotten the idea by now. What they all have in common is that effort is going into activities that interfere with social interactions, or no active effort is being made to plan or create pleasant social interactions. It is hard to plan ahead when you have other demands on your time or when you are not used to planning, but that effort may be just what you need to create a more active and positive life.

The first thing you should do to begin working on this problem is to go back to the items you filled out at the start of this chapter. Go through the items and find all the ones you marked as potentially enjoyable (that is, all the items to which you gave a 4 or 5 for comfort), but which you rarely do (that is, you gave them a 1 or 2 for frequency). Write each of these activities down on the self-monitoring data sheet provided in Figure 9–1. Add any you wish which are not on the questionnaire and which you are not currently doing very often. Make the list as long as you want; you don't have to fill in all 20 spaces. You may want to copy the form and keep it in a conspicuous place (like your refrigerator door).[1] These are activities which could *get you out of your rut*. You need to make some specific plans to start including more of these in your life. A sample form is filled out in Figure 9–2.

It might help you to make another list to show the bad habits you have developed which interfere with interesting activities with other people. You will have to generate this list yourself, since we do not have a test that lists all the individual possibilities. To get you started, think about how much time you spent watching TV, doing things for others which they could easily do for themselves (e.g., picking up after your kids), complaining, or sitting and feeling blue. On the next self-monitoring data sheet (Figure 9–3), list any of these things which apply to you, and then go on to think of more things that are especially time-consuming, unnecessary, and interfering for you. You can list as many as you want; you don't need to fill all 20 spaces. These are the activities that could *keep you in your rut*. You need to make some specific plans to start spending less of your time doing these things. Again, you may want to copy this form and post it by your list of activities to increase.[2] Figure 9–4 shows an example of this sheet filled out. To help you turn these lists into practical plans, we urge you to follow this sequence:

1. Do all of the things already suggested in this chapter (fill out the Social Activity Questionnaire (Table 9–1), use them to make a personalized list of social activities to increase, and create your own list of interfering activities).

[1] The Social Activities to Increase Form is included in Appendix B so that you can make additional copies.

[2] This form is included in Appendix B so that you can make additional copies.

Figure 9–1
Social Activities to Increase

	Month:								
Item	Date:								
1.									
2.									
3.									
4.									
5.									
6.									
7.									
8.									
9.									
10.									
11.									
12.									
13.									
14.									
15.									
16.									
17.									
18.									
19.									
20.									
Daily Totals:									

Goal for Increasing: _____ per _____ .

Average Increase Achieved: _____ per _____ .

Figure 9-2

Item Date:	9	10	11	12	13	14	15
Month: January							

Month: <u>January</u>

Item Date:	9	10	11	12	13	14	15
1. Talking with a friend							
2. Going to an office party							
3. Accepting a social invitation							
4. Inviting a friend to join me for an activity							
5. Going to a service club meeting							
6. Talking with someone on the job							
7. Joining a friend for a social activity							
8. Giving a party							
9. Calling a friend on the telephone							
10. Having friends come to visit							
11. Going to the movies with someone							
12. Engaging in recreational sports with someone							
13. Attending a concert or ballet							
14. Introducing myself to neighbors							
15. Going on picnic							
16.							
17.							
18.							
19.							
20.							
Daily Totals:							

Goal for Increasing: __4__ per _week_ .

Average Increase Achieved: _____ per _____ .

Figure 9–3
Interferences: Activities to Decrease

	Item	Date:							
Month:									
1.									
2.									
3.									
4.									
5.									
6.									
7.									
8.									
9.									
10.									
11.									
12.									
13.									
14.									
15.									
16.									
17.									
18.									
19.									
20.									
Daily Totals:									

Goal for Decreasing: _____ per _____ .

Average Decrease Achieved: _____ per _____ .

Figure 9–4

Item	Date:	9	10	11	12	13	14	15
1. Ironing sheets								
2. Going to visit Aunt Jane at rest home								
3. Driving Susie places she could easily walk to								
4. Picking up Jimmy's room								
5. Waiting at home in case Susie needs a ride								
6. Complaining about Jimmy and Susie								
7. Watching daytime TV								
8. Reading movie magazines								
9. Baking cookies								
10. Afternoon "slump"								
11.								
12.								
13.								
14.								
15.								
16.								
17.								
18.								
19.								
20.								
Daily Totals:								

Month: ___January___

Goal for Decreasing: ___1___ per day .

Average Decrease Achieved: _____ per _____ .

208

2. You now want to begin increasing your pleasant social activities. Keep track each day on your self-monitoring forms when each item occurs. On the list of activities to increase (Figure 9–1), put a check mark each day for each item that occurred and was at least slightly enjoyable. At the bottom of the sheet add up and record your daily total. On the list of activities to decrease (Figure 9–3), put a check mark each day for each item that occurred. At the bottom, add up and record your daily total. Your goal is to begin gradually increasing your enjoyable social interactions and decreasing your interfering activities. As you do this, notice your daily mood in relation to your daily activities. You can expect to see your mood getting better when your interferences go down and your social activities go up.

The optimal level for each of these things varies a lot from person to person. You need to experiment and find the best mix for yourself. You probably don't want to spend *all* your time on pleasant socializing; many of those interfering activities may be important responsibilities you take seriously. Keep in mind that you are experimenting; you want to find a balance of pleasure and responsibility which works for you—that is, a level at which you feel happy instead of depressed.

To get started on your experiment, set a goal for increasing social activities; for example, you might try to increase by one per day or by three per week. Set your own goal, but then stick to it. Write your goal at the bottom of the self-monitoring sheet (Figure 9–1).

Next set a goal for decreasing interfering activities and write it at the bottom of Figure 9–3. Again, set your own goal, but really try to stick to whatever you set up.

3. Learn how to gather information about social activities in your area. Many of the activities on your list may require knowledge about your community. For instance "going on a recreational outing" may be easier if you know where to rent a canoe or what groups plan hikes together. Similarly, it will be easier to find an opportunity for "singing in a group" if you know about choirs, glee clubs, and musical comedy theater

groups in your area. All of this information is fairly readily obtained by carefully reading your local newspaper. Most papers have one or two particular days when they provide a detailed list of all the group activities in the area, along with information on how to contact the group. If you don't know what day your paper does this, call and ask. They will be glad to provide you with that information. Other suggestions for gathering information can be found at the end of Chapter 8.

4. In addition to all the preceding steps, be sure to read the next section, *Inadequate Reward*. You may want to incorporate its suggestions in your plan.

Inadequate Reward

Throughout this book we have emphasized the importance of rewarding yourself, especially when you are trying to change your behavior. The same message applies, just as powerfully, in the area of social participation. Certainly the joy of doing things with friends will eventually be all the reward you need, but as you begin trying to change, you will need some additional, more tangible, rewards to help you keep up your resolve. Below are just some of the reasons why you should reward yourself as you get started:

- You may have a few failures as you get started; people may turn down your invitations, or a party might be dull, or you might find a restaurant closed.

- It takes energy to get started; if you're used to doing things the easy way (for example, watching TV by yourself), you'll need a boost to help you get going.

- You may need to do some difficult things in order to arrange time for social activities (for example, telling your mother you won't be spending every afternoon with her anymore, or refusing to take on extra work on your job). You will need to reward yourself or else the immediate difficulty of these steps may be more powerful than the long-range rewards you hope to gain.

These are just examples of reasons why self-reward is important; in your own case, there may be a number of additional reasons. The important thing is to recognize that you are making an *effort* when you try to change, and efforts have to be rewarded if they are to be successful.

If you have not been rewarding yourself for social participation, or if you expect that you will need help in setting up a self-reward program, then you should go back to Chapter 4, *Introduction to Self-Change Methods*, and use the suggestions there to set up a self-reward plan to use as you begin to increase your social participation.

But what if you have tried giving yourself rewards, and you have increased your social activities, but you find that social interaction is just not turning out to be very rewarding? The things we have suggested in this chapter are based on the assumption that social activity will be reinforcing in itself once you get started. You may need external rewards to get going, as was just described, but usually social interaction doesn't need extra rewards once you find an optimal level of activity.

However, for some people this is not the case. You may find that you feel it is unpleasant to be with others, or you may have recurring fears of rejection, or you may find that you are tense during and after a social interaction. This brings us full circle, back to the start of this chapter; you may need to re-examine your definition of the problem. If you are anxious with others, Chapter 6 can help you learn to relax. Chapter 8 can help if you are uncomfortable because you lack social skills. If you are comfortable with others and your social behavior is pleasant and skillful, then social interactions will be intrinsically rewarding. If social behavior does not provide adequate reward for you, back up and decide whether Chapter 6 or 8 might help. If you don't feel that you need those chapters, but you really don't *enjoy* social interactions, you might want to discuss your problem with a counselor.

MONITORING YOUR PROGRESS

In Chapter 4, a general strategy was described for keeping track of how well you are doing when you try to change a behavior. It is likely to help you as you work on this chapter if you keep track of your success. The easiest way to do that has already been suggested, that is, keep track *every day* of how many of the social activities on your personal list you are actually doing. Keep each day's records and compare them at the end of the week. If your plan is working, the number should be gradually, but steadily, increasing according to the goal you have set. Of course the number will go up and down a little, but on the whole you should look for slow, steady progress. If that is not occurring, you need to re-evaluate your plan and try again. If you find that you need to re-evaluate your plan, the following checklist may help:

- Have you decreased the amount of time spent on interfering activities?
- Have you been rewarding yourself for small steps?
- Have you been gathering information about available social activities to help you carry out your plans?
- Have you set your goals in reasonable, small, steady steps?
- Have you given the plan enough time (at least 3 weeks)?

Use the information from the checklist to help you modify your plan to make it more effective.

A SAMPLE SUCCESS STORY

To give you an idea of how this can work, consider how Janet, the woman whose problems began this chapter, could use this chapter to help overcome her depression:

> Janet decided to do something about her rut. She worked out the following list of social activities:
>
> Janet's list of *Social Activities to Increase:*
>
> 1. Talking with a friend
> 2. Going on a recreational outing
> 3. Visiting friends
> 4. Dancing
> 5. Having lunch with friends
> 6. Going to a party
> 7. Giving a party or get-together
> 8. Having sexual relations with my husband
> 9. Going to the movies
> 10. Engaging in recreational sports with someone
>
> She also worked out the following list of interfering activities:
>
> Janet's list of *Interferences: Activities to Decrease*
>
> 1. Doing the wash every day; twice a week would be plenty
> 2. Baking "goodies" too often—takes time and we don't need the calories
> 3. Being "on call" constantly for the baby; he could stay at a day care center three mornings a week and with Grandma when I need time for something special
> 4. Sitting around feeling sorry for myself! I wasted three evenings that way last week

Janet then set up a plan to help herself change. She wanted to increase her social activities by three each week. She found out about a hiking group in her area and joined it. She and her husband scheduled a night a week for activities outside the home, and decided to alternate between going to the movies, dancing, and going bowling. Janet made an effort to call friends and ask them over during the day, especially on the mornings while her son was at the day care center. Janet and her husband gave a buffet dinner for a lot of friends with whom they had lost touch, and as a result they started to get more invitations. As Janet got more active and happy, she and her husband became happier with each other. They had more to talk about, and their sex life improved also.

Obviously not all of these things happened right away. Janet kept track, and found that in the first 2 weeks she increased by only 1 or 2 of the things on her list each week. She kept at it, however, and by the end of 4 weeks she was keeping up with her weekly goal. After that, she felt much happier and more energetic and found that she did more and more. By the end of 2 months she had stabilized at about 15 of the things on the list each week. That was an average of about 2 each day, but actually her pattern was to do about 1 a day during weekdays, and the rest on weekends. She also had decreased her interfering activities. She arranged day care for the baby, which immediately brought about a decrease of 3 per week. In addition she set a goal of decreasing the others by 1 per week until they were down to a weekly total of 4. That took about a month.

Janet was very pleased with her pattern after 2 months and no longer felt depressed. She stopped using her lists and plan at that point, but carefully put them away so that she could bring them out and use them again if she fell back into her old rut.

Janet is just one person, of course, but she illustrates what *you* can accomplish. If you try to use this chapter's suggestions, you may well create an actual success story much like Janet's example. If you find that these suggestions don't work, however, remember that you should not despair. Not everyone improves at the same rate or using the same methods. Your depression will improve when you find the right approach for *you*.

SUMMARY

This chapter has tried to set out a systematic approach for you to use to increase your social activities. It gives a step-by-step method to assess your difficulties, to set up a self-monitoring program, and to work on gradual increases in pleasant interactions with others. It also has some suggestions about how to use other sections of this book if you are anxious in social situations or if you need help setting up a self-reward system while you work on increasing social activities.

REVIEW

_____ I have filled out the Social Activities Questionnaire (Table 9–1) and figured out my scores.

_____ I have decided whether to work on this chapter, the relaxation chapter, or both.

_____ If I am working on this chapter, I have done the following things:

    _____ I have made a list of social activities to increase (Figure 9–1).

    _____ I have made a list of interfering activities to decrease (Figure 9–3).

    _____ I am keeping track of the activities on both lists every day.

    _____ I have set a goal for increasing social activities and a goal for decreasing interfering activities.

    _____ I am systematically working toward reaching the goals I have set.

_____ I am using self-rewards to help myself get going with the effort to change.

_____ I know what to do if I do not find myself enjoying social activities. I will *either*:

_____ Use Chapter 6 to decrease my social anxiety.

_____ Use Chapter 8 to increase my social skill.

_____ See a counselor.

_____ Other: _____

_____ I have evaluated my progress at least once.

chapter 10

Controlling Thoughts

Theresa, a 42-year-old woman, single-handedly raised her two children, David, now 16, and Lydia, 20 years old. Their father left the family when they were small, and Theresa had to struggle to provide for herself and the children. She managed to get a job as a secretary though she had not worked before, and by now has her house almost paid for. For the last year and a half she has had frequent crying spells, her ability to attend to her job and her home has suffered somewhat, and she feels overwhelmed by her duties.

According to Theresa, her activities at home and work have not changed much in the last couple of years. But since Lydia graduated from high school, Theresa has begun to think more and more that her life is nearly over. She repeatedly tells herself that the only thing she is good for is raising children, cooking and cleaning after them, and providing them with a home. Once they leave, she figures her job will be done and she could die without being missed. At times she even questions her competence as a mother. She blames herself for her husband's dissatisfaction and wonders whether she should have remarried to provide the children with a father. She worries about her daughter's plans to marry her boyfriend. She thinks they won't be happy together and wonders whether Lydia just wants to leave home. David has become less communicative lately, and Theresa berates herself for not having been more available to him—maybe if she hadn't had to work he would have learned to feel closer to her. She is continually wondering whether she'll be able to help David with college or whether he, like Lydia, will choose not to go on.

Theresa's head is constantly filled with fears of tragedies, with self-blame about choices made in the past, and with other negative thoughts. This kind of thinking is extremely destructive, energy-draining, and a source of much suffering. Yet she does not consider her thoughts as contributors to her depression. As far as she is concerned, they are merely a natural reflection of her difficult situation.

This chapter focuses on thoughts, their effect on depression, and ways in which you can learn to use them to your advantage. We will help you to

1. Become aware of specific thoughts, so that you can identify troublesome thoughts and beneficial thoughts.

2. Learn techniques to channel your thoughts into directions you decide are most appropriate at the moment.

Thoughts are especially good to work with for two reasons:

1. They are always with you. You can work with them anytime, anywhere.

2. They are pretty much under your control and no one else's. No one can directly change the way *you* think.

However, these characteristics of thoughts can also be disadvantageous:

1. *Because* they are always with you, you have learned to take thoughts for granted. It will be hard for you to pay attention to them and take seriously the need to change them. Unless you seriously attend to them, of course, you probably won't change them.

2. *Because* your thoughts are only known to *you*, there is no way anyone else can directly observe whether they are changing. This means that you will have to be very conscientious about doing the exercises designed to change the way you think. Only you will be able to tell whether or not you are applying what you learn here.

There will be one thought you need to learn before we get started. Many people who experience depression think of themselves as having an "illness" which must be "cured." This is one way of thinking about depression. An alternate way to think about it (the way on which this book is based) is to see depression as an experience produced by the way you have *learned* to think, act, and feel. Therefore, to deal with depression, you need to think of yourself as actively learning new ways to think, act, and feel. As you learn new patterns of thought and behavior, you will begin to have different nondepressed experiences.

SELF-ASSESSMENT OF
THNKING PATTERNS

The list of thoughts below were obtained by asking depressed and nondepressed people to rate the frequency with which they had a large number of thoughts. We picked the thoughts that were rated significantly differently by depressed and nondepressed people and present them to you here.

Indicate whether you have experienced each of the following thoughts in the past month by placing a check mark next to the appropriate thought.

Set A

_____ Life is interesting.

_____ I really feel great.

_____ This is fun.

_____ I have great hopes for the future.

_____ I have good self-control.

_____ That's interesting.

_____ A nice, relaxing evening can sure be enjoyable.

_____ I have enough time to accomplish the things I most want to do.

_____ I like people.

_____ I'm pretty lucky.

_____ That's funny (humorous).

_____ Don't want to miss that event.

_____ *Total sum for Set A* (Highest possible, 12)

Set B

_____ I'll always be sexually frustrated.

_____ I'm confused.

_____ There is no love in the world.

_____ I am wasting my life.

_____ I'm scared.

_____ Nobody loves me.

_____ I'll end up living all alone.

_____ People don't consider friendship important anymore.

_____ I don't have any patience.

_____ What's the use.

_____ That was a dumb thing for me to do.

_____ I'll probably have to be placed in a mental institution someday.

_____ Anybody who thinks I'm nice doesn't know the real me.

_____ Existence has no meaning, *or* life has no meaning.

_____ I am ugly.

_____ I can't express my feelings.

_____ I'll never find what I really want.

_____ I am not capable of loving.

_____ I am worthless.

_____ It's all my fault.

_____ Why do so many bad things happen to me?

_____ I can't think of anything that would be fun.

_____ I don't have what it takes.

_____ Bringing kids into the world is cruel because life isn't worth living.

_____ I'll never get over this depression.

_____ Things are so messed up that doing anything about them is futile.

_____ I don't have enough will power.

_____ Why even bother getting up?

_____ I wish I were dead.

_____ I wonder if they are talking about me.

_____ Things are just going to get worse and worse.

_____ I have a bad temper.

_____ No matter how hard one tries, people aren't satisfied.

_____ Life is unfair.

_____ I'll never make good friends.

_____ I don't dare imagine what my life will be like in 10 years.

_____ There is something wrong with me.

_____ I am selfish.

_____ My memory is lousy.

_____ I am not as good as so-and-so.

_____ I get my feelings hurt easily.

_____ *Total sum for Set B* (Highest possible, 41)

Now summarize your results as follows:

Positive thoughts (Set A Total): _____

Negative thoughts (Set B Total): _____

Ratio of positive to negative thoughts (Set A Total ÷ Set B Total): _____

If your ratio is less than 2, you can profit from putting into practice the techniques explained in this chapter.

Mr. Jackson checked 2 thoughts from Set A and 16 from Set B. His ratio was $2 \div 16 = 0.125$. He therefore decided to read and put into practice this chapter.

Mr. Hall checked 10 thoughts from Set A and 3 from Set B. His ratio was $10 \div 3 = 3.33$. He decided to work on another chapter but read this one out of curiosity.

IDENTIFYING THOUGHTS

To begin working with thoughts, you need to learn to identify them. A fairly easy way to do this is to begin to keep track of "positive" and "negative" thoughts. Positive thoughts are those that have a positive effect on your mood and reflect the good points of whatever they refer to. For example, they may reflect your good characteristics ("I am intelligent," "I am dependable," "I know how to enjoy myself)." Or they may reflect the good parts of your life ("My family is great," "My work is satisfying," "Our health is good)." Negative thoughts are those that have a negative effect on your mood, usually because they focus on bad points ("I am worthless," "I can't do anything right," "My wife is a nag," "My husband is lazy)."

Directions

1. Using a 3″ × 5″ card, label one side of the card with a plus sign ("+" for positive thoughts) and the other side with a minus sign ("−" for negative thoughts). Use one card per day and date it.

2. Jot down positive and negative thoughts on the appropriate side of the card as soon after they occur as possible. (If you have trouble remembering to do this, make it a habit to take a few minutes before breakfast, lunch, dinner, and bedtime to jot down the important positive and negative thoughts of the last few hours).

Figure 10–1 shows an example of these cards.

You won't be able to write down *every* thought you have, of course. If you can note down 10 positive thoughts and 10 negative ones each day, you'll be doing well. By the end of a week you will have a good sample of positive and negative thoughts. You may find that some thoughts occur to you re-

Figure 10-1

+   Date _____

I really feel great
That's interesting
I have great hopes for the future
I like people
A nice, relaxing evening can sure be enjoyable

−   Date _____

I am worthless
Can't think of anything that could be fun
I am not capable of loving
I'll never get over this depression
Nobody loves me
There is something wrong with me

---

peatedly, that some are more disturbing than others, and, in general, that some seem to be particularly powerful in influencing your mood.

Make a personalized list of the most important thoughts you have found during your week's self-observation on Figure 10-2, *Inventory of Thoughts*. Place a star next to those which are particularly helpful to you in regard to your mood. Add more thoughts to your list if you remember important ones not already included. You may want to look at Set A and Set B earlier in this chapter for ideas.

Figure 10–2
Inventory of Thoughts

Negative	Positive

COUNTING THOUGHTS

Now that you have identified the kinds of thoughts that are most likely to occur to you, it will be easier to count them.

For 1 week, tally each positive thought and each negative thought as it occurs during the day. A 3″ × 5″ card labeled, as before, with a "+" on one side and a "−" on the other works very well. Total your tally marks at the end of each day. Record your totals on Figure 10–3.

Figure 10–3

	Number of Negative Thoughts	Number of Positive Thoughts
Day 1	⎯⎯⎯⎯	⎯⎯⎯⎯
Day 2	⎯⎯⎯⎯	⎯⎯⎯⎯
Day 3	⎯⎯⎯⎯	⎯⎯⎯⎯
Day 4	⎯⎯⎯⎯	⎯⎯⎯⎯
Day 5	⎯⎯⎯⎯	⎯⎯⎯⎯
Day 6	⎯⎯⎯⎯	⎯⎯⎯⎯
Day 7	⎯⎯⎯⎯	⎯⎯⎯⎯
Total for the week	⎯⎯⎯⎯	⎯⎯⎯⎯
Average for the week	⎯⎯⎯⎯	⎯⎯⎯⎯

These are your "Base-line" averages.

If your average of negative thoughts is greater than your average of positive thoughts, go on with the chapter. If your average of positive thoughts is greater than your average of negative thoughts, you may already be changing your thinking patterns. In this case you may want to skip this chapter. Before you do, however, please skim through it and read the summary at the end.

MANAGING THOUGHTS:
DECREASING NEGATIVE THINKING

When you are depressed, you tend to engage in a higher number of negative thoughts than when you are not depressed. These thoughts, which may have been originally caused by feelings of depression, in turn produce more depressed feelings, thus starting a destructive downward spiral. By breaking up this process, you can reduce feelings of depression and get yourself back into a more pleasant state of mind.

The following three techniques have been found helpful in controlling negative thoughts. Choose one of the techniques and try it for 1 week, keeping a tally of the number of negative thoughts you have each day. If at the end of the week your average is less than your base-line average, the technique is working. If not, you should switch to another technique and test *it* for 1 week. Do not give up on a technique without giving it a reasonable time to work for you.

Thought Interruption

Immediately upon noticing that you are producing a negative thought, interrupt it and go back to whatever non-negative thoughts you were having. To interrupt the thought, instruct yourself as follows: "I am going to stop thinking about that now." Then, without getting upset, let your attention flow back into non-negative ideas. This is probably the easiest interruption method, and the one we recommend most highly. There are two other methods that have been found useful by some and which we should mention:

One involves a stronger interruption. You should begin practicing this method someplace where you are not likely to be heard (for example, when you are home alone or when you are driving by yourself). When you are ready to begin, start thinking a negative thought and, as soon as you notice the thought clearly in your mind, yell the word "STOP!" as loudly as you can. You'll notice that the negative thought will be pushed aside for a few seconds by the very force of the act of yelling. You should then go on thinking non-negative thoughts. Repeat the actual yelling technique for about 3 days, then begin reducing the volume of the yell, while at the same time maintaining the force behind it. Continue this process until you can "yell" the word "STOP!" mentally, feeling the full force of the yell without making a sound. Now you are ready to use the technique in public.

The other technique originates from the notion that an act which is punished consistently will show a reduction in its frequency. In this case the act is the negative thought. The punishment is a "slap on the wrist" with a rubber band. Specifically, you begin by wearing a heavy-gauge rubber band around your wrist. As soon as you notice a negative thought, you snap the band against your wrist. If you do this consistently, you will soon begin to catch negative thoughts almost at their inception, and the frequency of such thoughts will drop.

For all three of these techniques, remember to record your positive and negative thoughts and inspect the record regularly to ascertain whether the negative thoughts are diminishing. Choose one of the three interruption methods now, and use it for the next week. Remember to record your positive and negative thoughts.

Worrying Time

One of the many sources of depression is an inability to keep some negative thoughts away. These may be particularly bothersome ideas that intrude into your train of thought again and again, draining your energy and distracting you from the task at hand. This is sometimes called "obsessive thinking."

If you feel that you need to spend some time mulling these thoughts over, this technique is exactly what you need. Decide how long you think you should spend on these intrusive but necessary thoughts and then schedule them into your day. Do not allow these thoughts to interfere with your mood or your work or play at any other time. If you feel that it is hard for you to set aside a thought completely when it occurs for fear you may not remember to think about it during your "worrying time," then keep a pen or pencil and paper handy to jot down a word or two that will remind you of particularly important thoughts.

The point of this technique is not to avoid thinking about unpleasant subjects completely. Rather, it is to let you decide *when* is the best time to devote to what you consider necessary thinking, and to free you from having to carry your mental burdens everywhere. Half an hour of worrying time a day should prove sufficient for most people. The technique works best if you refrain from doing anything else except thinking during your "worrying time." For example, pick one particular chair in which to sit and think—no talking, eating, drinking, working, or playing. Knowing you have the daily "worry time" may make it easier to forego ruminating over worries at other times.

Fill in: My worrying time will start at _____ o'clock and last _____ minutes.

Note: If you use this technique, only tally negative thoughts that occur *outside* of your "worrying time" in your daily total.

The Blow-Up Technique

This is a technique designed to reduce the impact of a disturbing negative thought by exaggerating it beyond all proportion and thus making it so ridiculous that it ceases to be fearful.

Marsha had been worried about having to tell her supervisor

that she had made an important error on an order she had taken care of at the shipping department of a major store. But, in order to correct her error, she *had* to tell her. She fretted about it for a few days, losing some sleep over it, and becoming so quiet at work that one of her co-workers even asked if something was wrong.

Marsha realized then that she couldn't put it off any longer, and began to ask herself why she feared to tell her supervisor. She decided that she was afraid of having the supervisor think that she was "incompetent" and maybe tell her co-workers, who then would also consider Marsha "stupid" or "careless."

The way Marsha used the blow-up technique was to imagine that her supervisor became terribly upset at her error, began screaming at the top of her lungs, throwing stuff at Marsha, and stomping up and down on the resulting wreckage. Her co-workers heard the commotion and joined in on the ruckus. They finally placed a big sign on her chest which read "STUPID" and outfitted her with a "dunce" cap. The store's loudspeaker blared out Marsha's error throughout the day, and as Marsha rode on the bus (with her cap and sign still on) she could see newspaper headlines proclaiming her error being read by the bus riders. The people in the streets booed her, and little children stuck out their tongues at her.

Marsha found the process of letting her imagination run wild somewhat funny. The ridiculous flavor of her exaggerated images blended with her earlier fear of telling her supervisor and gave it a less threatening tone.

She went ahead and did it. And survived!

MANAGING THOUGHTS: INCREASING POSITIVE THINKING

Reducing the number of negative thoughts will not automatically increase the number of positive thoughts. You need to learn techniques designed to accomplish each of these objectives.

To increase the number of positive thoughts you generate, choose one of the following techniques and keep a daily count of positive thoughts for 1 week. If your average for that week is greater than your base-line average, the technique is working. If not, choose another technique and test its effectiveness for a week.

Priming

Priming is a technique designed to increase positive thoughts. Its name comes from the phrase "priming the pump" (which originally meant placing water in the barrel of a dry pump to begin the pumping action that would start the desired flow of water). In our case, the word refers to placing positive thoughts in your mind systematically so that you can break the pattern of thinking negative thoughts and thus you can start the flow of positive thoughts.

First, you need to put together a list of positive thoughts. Use the list in Set A, earlier in this chapter. Add any thoughts you came up with on your index cards. And now add still more. Think especially about thoughts that refer to *yourself*. If necessary, ask people you trust to tell you what they consider your good points.

Second, write down these thoughts on 3" × 5" cards, one thought per card. You will then have a deck of positive thoughts.

Third, begin to prime your "positive thought pump" by carrying the deck of cards with you, pulling a card out at random intervals throughout the day, and reading it, paying serious attention to it.

Add new positive thoughts about yourself to the deck as they occur to you. Also, begin placing "wild cards" in the deck. When you get to a card labeled "wild card," you are to generate a positive thought about yourself on the spot. This will help you to begin to come up with positive thoughts on your own.

Using Cues

Use frequent behaviors as reminders for yourself to have a positive thought. Since positive thoughts are infrequent occurrences in your daily routine, you can increase their frequency by pairing them to things you do frequently.

For example, remind yourself to think a positive thought each time you eat, brush your teeth, talk on the phone, read something, get in your car or on the bus, and so on.

Noticing What You Accomplish

Many depressed people don't give themselves credit for what they do. Instead, they belittle themselves when something doesn't work out right.

To see if this is true in your case, begin to keep track of all the things you accomplish during the day, even things you may consider trivial. Carry a couple of 3" × 5" cards with you and note down every task you complete throughout the day. A typical list may look like this:

Got up on time.

Cooked and ate a substantial breakfast.

Dressed neatly.

Got to work on time.

Conducted myself properly at a meeting with my boss.

Finished a project.

Planned out an effective schedule for the day.

Picked a nice place for lunch.

Had a good conversation with a co-worker.

Accomplished 3 out of 5 things I wanted to finish today.

Drove home skillfully—didn't let traffic get me angry.

Cooked a good dinner.

Saw a TV program I really wanted to see.

The object of this technique is to notice what you do during your day. Many people feel that they don't do anything when, in fact, their days are full of activities for which they don't give themselves credit.

Positive Self-Rewarding Thougths

Hearing someone telling us they appreciate what we have done usually feels good. This may be because our contribution is noticed, our efforts are considered worthwhile, and our value is acknowledged. These three elements can also be present within our thoughts.

The result of being praised or encouraged is usually an increase in the desire to continue to do well. You can often produce a similar effect by praising or encouraging yourself.

If you were to tell other people that they are lazy or incompetent, or that their work is unimportant or lousy, they would probably be less likely to feel good about themselves or their efforts. They might give up and stop trying. The same result can take place if you tell yourself those things.

Since one of the problems depressed persons have is that they don't do much, it makes sense to notice if you are encouraging this inactivity by punishing yourself with negative thoughts before, during, or after you do something. For example, when you *consider* getting together with friends, do you think to yourself "It will be boring" or "I really don't feel like it"? *During* an outing or a visit do you say to yourself "I don't fit in here" or "Everyone is looking at me"? *After* you have done something you were looking forward to, do you come down hard on yourself and focus on all the disappointing parts of the experience instead of enjoying the fact that you finally did it? Do you think, for example, "I really could have done a lot better," "I looked like a fool," or "No one really enjoyed it"?

By increasing your level of positive self-reward, you can increase your level of activities and your level of positive thoughts. The trick is to reward yourself silently after you do or think something positive by "patting yourself on the back." For example, let's say you are again considering getting together with friends, you could think to yourself: "That's a constructive idea. Having this type of idea means I am making progress. I am headed in the right direction." Or during an outing: "I haven't done this in so long. It took guts to try it. I am proud of myself." And, afterward: "I did it! I really did it! Not bad!"

We have found that many people are reluctant to praise themselves because they see that as being too proud, or egotistical, or self-centered. The fact is that *all of us need encouragement.* If it is good to compliment others for good work, then it certainly makes sense to do the same for oneself.

Time Projection

One of the most frightening things about depression is that while you are thinking, feeling, and acting depressed, you believe that the state you are in is never going to end. The time projection technique breaks through this tendency by having you mentally travel forward in time far enough so that, in your estimation, the stressful period has ended.

The stressful period may be as short as a visit to the dentist or as long as a period of mourning. In the first case, for example, the idea is to acknowledge the anxiety and discomfort you are experiencing in the dentist's chair, and then "jump forward" in time a couple of hours to when the only discomfort will possibly be a residual numbness from the anesthetic, and then again a week or so later, when you won't even be thinking about the fact that you were at the dentist's today.

In the case of mourning or separation, you would acknowledge the memories, the loss, and the pain you now feel, and then think about the fact that the pain—which may be almost unbearable at times now—*must* decrease as time goes on, and that in a few months the memories will be free from the intense, tear-eliciting pangs that are so common now.

Time projection can be used to help yourself survive a crisis, to produce hope of having your suffering alleviated, and to make salient the idea that psychological pain is *not* fatal.

At the same time, we would like to underscore a basic concept often overlooked by many depressed people. Feelings of sadness, pain, and depression are natural parts of life. They come at all levels, from very minor to most intense. *It is OK to feel depressed.* This in itself will cause no problems. Human beings can bear very intense levels of depressive feelings. It is when you become demoralized, lose hope, and forget that you can endure the pain and go on living that the trouble starts. Time projection acknowledges the pain and helps you see a more satisfying future.

EVALUATING YOUR EFFORTS

The goal of this chapter is to help you identify thoughts that make you depressed, learn to count them, and to control them.

To do this we have focused on negative thoughts—those thoughts that have a negative influence on your mood; and positive thoughts—those thoughts that have a positive influence on your mood. Your base-line averages can serve as a guide for your self-change project. Your goal is to increase positive thoughts and decrease negative thoughts until you have as many or more positive thoughts as negative thoughts each day. Remember the social learning concepts we mentioned in Chapter 2:

1. *Antecedents:* Note when and where you are most likely to have negative thoughts. Are you in certain places, with certain people, or at certain times of day? If so, devise alternative plans for yourself so you can avoid or deal differently with these situations.

2. *Consequences:* Do you reward yourself for thinking negative thoughts? For example, do you postpone an unpleasant chore because thinking about some unrelated problem has made you too depressed to do it?

3. *Mental factors:* Do you punish yourself mentally when you have positive thoughts? For example, do you label yourself conceited for thinking you do something well? Or do you belittle what you did and tell yourself you didn't really do it well enough?

Use the self-change elements also:

1. *Self-reward.* Reward yourself for putting these techniques into practice.

2. *Step-by-step change.* Notice small changes in your thinking. If you reduce your average negative thoughts by even one thought per week, you are being successful in your self-change program. Don't expect to have no negative thoughts. That's not a realistic goal.

3. *Modeling.* Imagine how some nondepressed person you like might think. Ask yourself how your model would deal with a negative thought. What kind of positive thoughts would this person come up with if he or she were in your shoes?

4. *Self-observation.* By keeping records you make it easier to pay attention to your self-change project. This also helps you with self-reinforcement, since it gives you a clear picture of how much you are changing.

THINKING AND DEPRESSION

The ways you have learned to think, act, and feel make it more or less likely you will feel depressed. To control your feelings of depression, you need to relearn how to think, act, and feel.

Thinking affects feelings and actions. You can learn to think in constructive ways. To do this you need to learn to identify thoughts, count them, and modify them. In general, you want to stop distorting reality in a negative direction by beginning to focus on positive perspectives.

SUMMARY

This chapter explains how thoughts affect depression and how one can learn to manage one's own thoughts to deal effectively with depression. It includes an exercise for self-assessment of thinking patterns, techniques for identifying, counting, and managing thoughts, and for evaluating your thoughts.

As you finish the chapter you should know how thoughts affect mood, how to decrease frequency of negative thoughts, and how to increase the frequency of positive thoughts.

REVIEW

_____ I understand how a person's thoughts affect his/her mood.

_____ I have completed the *Self-Assessment of Thinking Patterns section*. My score was _____. That meant

_____ I needed to change my thinking.

_____ My ratio of positive to negative thoughts is OK as is.

_____ I used 3″ × 5″ cards to identify my positive and negative thoughts.

_____ I filled out the Inventory of Thoughts (Figure 10–2).

_____ I counted my negative and positive thoughts daily for a week.

_____ I tried (for at least a week) the techniques called:

    _____ Thought Interruption.

    _____ Worrying Time.

    _____ The Blow-Up Technique.

    _____ Priming.

    _____ Using Cues.

    _____ Noticing What I Accomplish.

    _____ Positive Self-Rewarding Thoughts.

    _____ Time Projection.

chapter 11

Constructive Thinking

In the last chapter we discussed how thoughts are very closely connected with both feelings and actions. For some people, changing their thoughts or attitudes about problems and difficulties can be a helpful way to begin feeling less depressed. In this chapter, we focus on ways to change the way you think about problems and difficulties so you will be less upset by them, and, therefore, can approach and deal with them more constructively.

In order to help you evaluate whether this chapter will be useful for you, we have included a test. For each of the 13 statements listed below, rate how much you agree or disagree using the following scale:

1 = I disagree completely
2 = I disagree slightly

3 = I am neutral about this statement
4 = I agree slightly
5 = I agree completely

There are no right or wrong answers. It is important that you rate each item according to what you really believe.

_____ Considering the blatant and widespread sexism in our society, it is unlikely that any concerned woman can be truly happy.

_____ Some people could not be happy living in a small town or a large city because some of the things they need are not available there.

_____ There are some people in this world who truly can be described as rotten.

_____ If things are not the way one would like them to be, it is a catastrophe.

_____ Given the kind of home life some people have had, it is almost impossible for them ever to be happy.

_____ What others think of you is most important.

_____ Persons living in slum conditions are almost certain to feel depressed or miserable.

_____ Love and success are two basic human needs.

_____ Avoiding life's difficulties and self-responsibilities is easier than facing them.

_____ The main goal and purpose of life is achievement and success.

———— Failure at something one really wants to do is terrible.

———— People really can't help it when they feel angry, depressed, or guilty.

———— One should blame oneself severely for all mistakes and wrongdoings.

To score the test, add up all of your ratings. If you find that your score is above 39, then you are likely to find this chapter helpful. A high score indicates that you, like many depressed persons (and many other people, too), may tend to overreact to problems and difficulties that occur in your day-to-day life. If your score was within or below the 27 to 39 range (the average range) but you feel you do tend to overreact to problems, you still might find this chapter useful. You can, however, choose to skip this chapter and go on to a different chapter.

OVERREACTING TO PROBLEMS AND DIFFICULTIES

What do we mean when we say you may overreact to problems and difficulties? Perhaps the following examples will illustrate what we have in mind:

> Jack has started taking night classes at the community college in his city. It has been quite some time since he finished high school, so learning to study and take notes in class has not come all that easily. He has worked hard all term, partly because his courses will help him get the certification he needs for a job promotion, but mostly because it has always been

important to Jack to do well at whatever he does. His toughest class has been algebra, and he has been spending a lot of time preparing for the final exam. With the help of a tutor, he now feels quite confident that he can get an *A* on the exam. After the exam, he is sure he did well and tells his tutor, his closest friend, and his boss that he thinks he'll get an *A* in algebra. When he gets the exam back, Jack is shocked to see that his grade is not an *A* or even a *B* but a *C*. Jack is very upset and, at first, is sure there must be a mistake but soon finds out that the grade is correct. He feels like a total failure, very discouraged and down. He thinks he might as well give up on the idea of trying to earn more college credit because it seems so obvious to him that he's too "dumb" to do the work.

Melanie comes home late one afternoon. She has just returned from the beauty parlor and has had her hair cut in a new, different style. Melanie thinks she looks pretty good but is anxious to see what Jim, her husband, thinks. When Jim arrives home, he mixes himself his usual before-dinner drink and sits down with the newspaper. Melanie is disappointed that he didn't notice her hair but decides not to say anything. After a little while, Jim starts talking to Melanie about his day at work. Melanie pretends to be listening but is getting more and more upset that he hasn't said anything about her new haircut. Finally, she bursts into tears and runs into the bedroom, slamming the door behind her. She is both very angry and very hurt. When Jim comes to find out what's wrong, she yells, "Go away!" and continues sobbing.

Jan has just been out on her first date with Allan, a very handsome man who recently took a job at the office where she works. Jan had a good time on their date and thinks he did too. She hopes that Allan will ask her out again soon. The next day at work, she is chatting with John, a good friend of hers. Knowing that John and Allan talk with one another quite a bit, she asks John if Allan had said anything about her or their date. John hesitates and then says, "Well, I don't really know— I guess I don't think you ought to count on going out with him again." When Jan presses him for more information, he says that the only thing Allan had said about their date was "Jan's a nice person, but she's just not my type." Jan is upset to hear this and the more she thinks about it, the worse she feels. She now thinks of herself as an unattractive woman and feels unloved and unlovable. She decides that if she goes out at all in the future, it will have to be with men she really doesn't like very much. For the next several days, Jan feels very discouraged, lonely, and down.

All three of these people had unpleasant things happen to them. It seems quite natural to feel disappointed in such circumstances. Certainly it would be unrealistic to expect Jack to not feel disappointed when he got a C instead of an A on his exam. Similarly, we wouldn't expect Melanie not to be annoyed about her husband's failure to comment on her haircut or Jan not to feel a little hurt when she learned that Allan wasn't as attracted to her as she had hoped. But their reactions went far beyond being disappointed or annoyed or "a little" hurt. Jack concluded that he was dumb and felt like a total failure. Melanie felt very angry and hurt and couldn't help her husband understand what was wrong. Jan decided she was an unattractive, unlovable woman and felt very down for several days. Each of these people overreacted, making it more difficult to approach constructively the problem situation.

Listed below are some of the kinds of situations that lead many people to overreact and become quite upset:

1. Being rejected by someone or realizing that someone doesn't care about you to the same degree that you care about him or her.

2. Being disapproved of or criticized by someone.

3. Feeling unappreciated by someone who has received quite a bit of your attention, caring, or effort.

4. Doing more than your share of work and not getting credit for it.

5. Failing at something, making a mistake, or doing something less well than you think you should have.

6. Having someone *not* do or say something you think they should have done or said *or* having someone do or say something you think they should *not* have done or said.

7. Having things not turn out as you had expected or hoped.

8. Being unfairly accused of something you did not do.

Can you think of times when you have experienced one or more of these unpleasant events? On some of those occasions, did you overreact (that is, become excessively upset)?

THE A–B–C METHOD

A well-known psychologist, Dr. Albert Ellis, has developed an approach for helping people learn to think more constructively about these kinds of difficulties.[1] He calls his approach "Rational-Emotive Therapy" as a way of stressing the connection between what you think and how you feel. As part of this therapy, Dr. Ellis presents a fairly simple method to help people learn to identify the kinds of beliefs or attitudes they hold that may lead them to overreact to problems or difficulties.

Our suggested plan is based on Dr. Ellis' techniques and on the self-help method developed by Dr. Gerald Kranzler. The technique is called the A-B-C method. *A* stands for *Activating Event*, the event you feel upset about. For Jack, *A* =

[1] Ellis, A., and Harper, R. A. *A Guide to Rational Living*. No. Hollywood, Calif.: Wilshire Book Co., 1973.

receiving a low grade on his exam. For Melanie, A = her husband not commenting on her new haircut. For Jan, A = learning that Allan doesn't consider her "his type." For the moment we will skip B and discuss C, which stands for *Emotional Consequences*. For Jack, C = feeling very upset and discouraged. For Melanie, C = feeling very angry and hurt. For Jan, C = feeling very hurt and down.

Most people assume that A causes C. If we asked Jack why he was so upset, he would probably say, "because I got a low grade on my exam." Assuming that A causes C is often accurate if you are talking about physical pain. For example, if you stub your toe (A) and feel pain (C), it is accurate to say that A caused C. But it is *not* accurate to say that A causes C when we talk about psychological pain. When you feel angry or hurt or very down (C) it is not A (the Activating Event) that causes your emotional reaction; rather it is B, what you believe or say to yourself about A, that results in your emotional reaction (C). It's your *interpretation* (B) of events (A) that leads to emotional upset (C).

```
A = Activating Event
          ↓
B = Belief or Self-talk about A
          ↓
C = Emotional Consequence
```

For Jack, B = his belief that he *should* have gotten a higher grade on his exam and that, since he didn't, he was a *total* failure and very dumb. For Melanie, B = telling herself that it was *awful* that her husband didn't notice and comment on her new haircut. For Jan, B = telling herself that it was *terrible* that Allan didn't think she was "his type" and that, since *he* didn't find her attractive, *she* must be very unattractive and unlovable.

In order to change C, your emotional overreaction, you

need to learn how to change *B*, the kinds of beliefs you hold or what you tell yourself about problems and difficulties that are bound to occur in everybody's life. The procedure we describe below is based upon the method described by Dr. Kranzler's booklet, *You Can Change How You Feel.*[2]

Step 1

Using Section *C* on Figure 11–1, briefly describe an unpleasant emotion you have experienced today. (It may be helpful to say to yourself, "I felt _____" and use a word such as angry, depressed, guilty, sad, hurt, used, disgusted, anxious, or down in completing the sentence.) Also, rate how upset you were, using a scale from 0 (only mildly upset) to 5 (extremely upset).

Step 2

In Section *A* on the form, describe briefly the activating event, the situation or event that seemed to lead to your emotional reaction.

Step 3

As accurately as possible, list the kinds of things you seem to be saying to yourself at point *B*. Place a check mark (√) beside those statements that are *not* constructive or reasonable.

Step 3 may be difficult to do at first because the emotional consequences (*C*) seem to follow the activating event (*A*) so automatically. Even though it is difficult at first, most people can learn to become aware of their self-talk at *B*. Some of this self-talk is not constructive because it almost guarantees that

[2] Kranzler, G. *You Can Change How You Feel.* Eugene, Ore.: University of Oregon Press, 1974.

you are going to feel quite upset or bad. Dr. Kranzler lists three good indicators of nonconstructive self-talk:

1. *Highly evaluative words* like "should," "ought," or "must" (for example, he *ought* to say what I'd like him to say or I *should* be able to do this well.

2. *Catastrophizing* words like "it's awful" or "it's terrible" or "I just can't stand it."

3. *Overgeneralizations,* such as "I'll *never* be able to do this" or "*nobody* will *ever* like me" or "I'm really a bad or rotten person."

Of course, some of your self-talk at *B* may be quite reasonable. Examples of reasonable self-talk are statements that begin with: "I wish . . ." or "I would have preferred . . ." or statements like "I am disappointed that . . ." or "I don't like. . . ." Statements about your wishes, preferences, likes, and dislikes are perfectly reasonable. If that's *all* you are saying to yourself when an unpleasant situation occurs, you may feel annoyed or disappointed, but you *won't* feel prolonged or intense hurt, sadness, anger, etc.

For the next week, use these forms to keep track of your reactions and self-talk about *one* unpleasant event each day.[3] At the end of each day, first complete Section *C,* then Section *A,* and then Section *B* on the form. For the time being, ignore Section *D.*

Figures 11–2A, B, and C are the forms Jack, Melanie, and Jan filled out for the days on which the events we've described occurred.

After 1 week of self-monitoring, you should go on to Step 4, which follows. We suggest that you complete Sections *A, B,* and *C* for one situation per day for 1 week *before* going on with the rest of this chapter.

---

[3] This form is included in Appendix B so that you can make additional copies for your daily monitoring.

Figure 11–1
Daily Monitoring Form [a]

Daily Monitoring Form[a]

Date _____

A. Activating Event

   (Briefly describe the situation or event that seemed to lead to your
   emotional upset at C.)

B. Beliefs or Self-Talk

   (List each of the things that you said to yourself about A.)

   1.

   2.

   3.

   4.

   5.

   (Now go back and place a checkmark beside each statement that is non-
   constructive or "irrational.")

C. Emotional Consequences

   (Describe and rate how you felt when A happened.)

   I felt: _____

   _____

   Rating (0 = mildly upset; 5 = extremely upset): _____

D. Dispute of Self-Talk

   (For each checked statement in Section B describe what you would ask
   or say to dispute your non-constructive self-talk.)

---

[a]Note: You should first complete Section C. Then go back and complete Section A and
   Section B. After the first week of self-monitoring, also complete Section D.

Figure 11-2A
Jack's Daily Monitoring Form

A. Activating Event
Getting a C on my exam.

B. Beliefs or Self-Talk
✓1. *It's terrible that I didn't get an A.*
✓2. *I'm a total failure.*
✓3. *This shows how dumb I am.*
4.
5.

C. Emotional Consequences
I felt: *very upset*

Rating: *5*

Figure 11-2B
Melanie's Daily Monitoring Form

A. Activating Event
Jim didn't say anything about my hair.

B. Beliefs or Self-Talk
1. *I wish Jim had said something about my hair*
✓2. *Jim should have said something*
✓3. *It's terrible that he didn't*
4.
5.

C. Emotional Consequences
I felt: *very angry; hurt*

Rating: *4*

Figure 11-2C
Jan's Daily Monitoring Form

A. Activating Event
Allan said I wasn't his type.

B. Beliefs or Self-Talk
✓1. *It's awful that Allan doesn't like me.*
✓2. *I must be very unattractive.*
✓3. *Nobody will ever like me.*
4. *I wish Allan would have liked me.*
5.

C. Emotional Consequences
I felt: *upset & down; hurt*

Rating: *5*

DISPUTING YOUR NONCONSTRUCTIVE
SELF-TALK

After 1 week of self-monitoring, you'll probably become more aware of the kinds of things you say to yourself at B that lead to the emotional overreaction you experience at C. Perhaps just becoming aware of some of your self-talk has helped you react with less upset to unpleasant situations or events in your day-to-day life. An additional helpful step is to dispute actively the things you say to yourself at B. By disputing self-talk we mean coming up with arguments to use against your "should" and "ought" statements, against your beliefs that certain things are "awful" or "terrible," and against your overgeneralizations —the "always" and "never" statements. Some examples of disputing are given below:

For "shoulds" and
"oughts":

"*Why* should I or the other person behave in this particular way?"

"*Why must* an event occur just the way I wanted it to?"

For "terribles" and
"awfuls":

"I would have liked this person to do or say this, but is there any good reason why he (or she) must do or say what I'd like?"

"I would have liked for this to have happened in a different way, but is it really *awful* (or *horrible* or *terrible*) that it didn't?

"It would have been nice if that person had done or said this, but is it really *terrible* that he (or she) didn't?

For overgeneralizations: "Just because this didn't work out
                                    the way I wanted, is there any good
                                    evidence that it can't work out bet-
                                    ter another time?"

                                    "Just because that person said
                                    something about me that I didn't
                                    like, does that really mean that
                                    everyone is going to feel that way?"

From now on, when you complete the daily monitoring
form, be sure to complete Section *D*. For each of the nonconstructive things you said to yourself in Section *B* (the checked
statements), write in Section *D* how you would dispute or argue
against them. Examples for Jack, Melanie, and Jan are shown
in Figures 11–3A, B, and C.

As you complete Section *D*, follow our general guidelines,
but use your own words in disputing your self-talk. For practice, go back over your daily monitoring forms for the past
week and complete Section *D*. From now on, complete all four
sections for one situation each day: first, Section *C*, then *A*,
then *B*, and finally, *D*.

You may soon notice that you are substituting constructive self-talk at *B* and that your emotional consequences are
less upsetting and/or briefer. That, of course, is the goal for
people using this approach. But don't worry if your progress
seems slow at first. The self-talk most of us engage in at point
B has developed over a number of years and operates much like
an automatic habit. Like other habits that have bad consequences (smoking, for example), such habits are not easy to
change, and changing them requires much effort and patience.
Even when you realize afterward that you have overreacted to
an unpleasant event, there is still much to be gained from the
experience. Analyze what happened, using the procedure we've

Figure 11–3A
Jack

D. Dispute of Self-Talk

1. Sure I'm disappointed but is it really <u>terrible</u> that I didn't get an A grade?

2. Does getting a C grade really mean I'm a <u>total failure</u>?

3. Just because I'm not a real whiz at algebra, does that mean I'm <u>dumb</u>?

Figure 11–3B
Melanie

D. Dispute of Self-Talk

1. OK (reasonable)

2. Yes, it would be nice if Jim had said something, I would have liked that. But is there any good reason why he <u>must</u>?

3. I was disappointed but is it really <u>terrible</u> that he said nothing?

Figure 11–3C
Jan

D. Dispute of Self-Talk

1. I would have liked it if Allan had liked me better but is it really <u>awful</u> that he didn't?

2. Just because Allan didn't find me attractive, is that good evidence that I'm <u>unattractive</u>?

3. Just because Allan didn't like me does that really mean <u>nobody ever</u> will?

4. OK (reasonable)

presented. Try to identify your self-talk at B that caused your emotional upset at C. Then think of ways to dispute your nonconstructive self-talk. Next time when that event or a similar one happens, you will be better able to cope with it constructively.

Also, keep in mind that nobody is happy, content, and calm all or even most of the time. The goal of this method is *not* to help you be some kind of robot who responds calmly and with little emotion to negative, unpleasant events. Being human, you are going to continue to feel hurt, disappointed, angry, or sad when some kinds of events occur, just as you are likely to feel pleased and happy when pleasant events occur. We hope that by using this method, you will be able to keep feelings of disappointment, anger, hurt, and upset at a more manageable level so that you can deal with life's difficulties and problems more constructively.

SUMMARY

This chapter presents a strategy for changing how you think about unpleasant, difficult situations so that you will be less upset by them and, therefore, able to deal with them more constructively. The basic idea of this approach is that it's *not* the unpleasant events that cause us to feel excessively bad or upset; rather, it's how we interpret or what we say to ourselves about the events that leads to our emotional overreaction.

We presented the A-B-C Method as a way for you to learn to identify your nonconstructive self-talk and then suggested some guidelines for you to use in actively disputing and changing what you say to yourself when unpleasant situations occur.

REVIEW

_____ I understand how what I say to myself about difficult or unpleasant situations can lead to my emotional overreaction.

_____ I have learned to identify my nonconstructive self-talk about difficult or unpleasant events.

_____ I have begun actively disputing my nonconstructive self-talk by challenging:

_____ My highly evaluative ("should" and "ought") statements.

_____ My catastrophizing ("awful" and "terrible") statements.

_____ My overgeneralizations ("always" and "never" statements).

_____ I have been completing the self-monitoring form (Figure 11–1) each day.

_____ For the first week I chose one unpleasant event and identified the activating event (A), the emotional consequences I experienced (C), and then my beliefs or self-talk (B), about A which led to C.

_____ After the first week I began disputing my self-talk and recording how I did this (Section D).

chapter 12

Being Your Own Coach: Self-Instructional Techniques

Kevin was a fast learner. He could understand how to use the techniques we presented to him and could give examples of how they might be used in a real-life situation. Thus, it was hard to understand why he did not appear to be making much progress.

On questioning him carefully, we found that, although he understood what he wanted to do, he had a hard time thinking of it when the opportunity to try it presented itself. He was a good planner and a good hindsight critic, but when it came to implementing a course of action, he totally forgot all his plans.

What Kevin needed was someone at his side, reminding him of his well-laid plans. And that is exactly what he was able to get by learning how to be his own coach. What Kevin learned was how to give himself instructions at strategic times, that is, how to use what he had already learned in his day-to-day life. The kinds of techniques he learned are described in this chapter. They are useful when you know what you want to do but have a hard time doing it.

Many people who "know better" engage in behavior that either gets them into trouble or does not help them deal with difficult situations. Yet, they are able to point out what they could do to handle things in a more constructive way and may be able to give good advice to others.

The question we can ask ourselves, then, is how we can make the knowledge we have work for us when it counts. This chapter deals with one such technique, called self-instruction that is, talking to yourself. This technique is neither childish nor crazy. It can be an effective way of helping yourself do what you plan to do. Everyone talks to himself to some extent although one only notices it during fairly complex activities. For example, if you have to drive to a certain destination, you may find yourself carrying on a conversation in your head such as the following:

> "Need to take the freeway exit from Watt Avenue South. Ahh, here it is. Now to Folsom in the middle lane so that I can be on the extreme right lane after I turn left. Then right at the light. There should be some railroad tracks. Good. Must be on the correct street. Left at the stop sign. Then right at the light and down one block."

Of course, the conversation may be less grammatically correct. It probably sounds like:

> "Watt South? Middle Lane. Folsom? Left. Stop light? Good. Right turn. Tracks? Yep. Stop sign. Left. Light. Right. Good. Phew! Made it! On time? Hope so, etc. . . ."

This internal dialogue sounds very similar to one you might engage in if a friend were with you, giving you directions. In effect, you are silently talking with yourself. In this case, you are doing so in order not to get lost, in order to get where you want to go. When used appropriately, self-talk helps us guide our behavior, gives us a sense of direction, keeps us on track. It does this by making our goals concrete, by focusing our attention on the situation at hand, and by activating our memory so that we remember what our chosen plan of action is.

Another reason for the success of self-instruction is its distancing effect. You may have noted that it is much easier to give advice to someone else in a tough situation than it is to think of it yourself when in similar straits. This is partly because one can be more objective and see a bigger picture when at a distance—psychologically as well as physically. You can create a beneficial distance by instructing yourself as you would a friend. Imagine yourself trying to coach someone in your situation and you almost immediately get some perspective. By planning ahead, you can be prepared to coach yourself. By having a game plan, you'll be less likely to freeze when the moment comes.

If you have tried self-change programs before and haven't kept them up, or if you know what would get you out of your depression but you just haven't gotten around to do it, this may be a useful skill for you to use systematically.

Self-talk helps you cope with situations in your daily life by:

1. *Anticipating* what you want to accomplish in a given situation ("I want to chat with Lawrence after the sermon"), what the situation is going to be like ("There will be a lot of people milling around"), how you plan to handle it ("I will have to catch him early"), and exactly what you will do ("I will ask him about his job").

2. Keeping you *on track* and calm during the actual situation ("There are more people here than I expected, but

I still want to talk with him. I've got to keep cool, and do what I planned anyway").

3. Helping you *handle good or bad situations* ("I am glad I talked to him. He is really nice," or "He was kind of nasty. Wonder what's bugging him?").

4. *Motivating* you to continue doing something you know will benefit you. ("I don't feel like putting in the energy to get out of this depressive pattern I'm in, but I know that once I get going I'll feel better. Why punish myself by continuing to feel down?")

EXAMPLES OF SELF-INSTRUCTION

Bad Memory Bill. One of the things that upset Bill the most was his bad memory. As he began to change his depressive behavior, he decided to work on his memory, too. A book we have found helpful in this area is *The Memory Book* by Harry Lorrayne and Jerry Lucas.[1] Bill liked many of the ideas in the book but found that he neglected to put them into practice. So he wrote out a set of directions for himself which he practiced and finally used to instruct himself: "OK. This is something I want to remember. Must make a ridiculous mental image of it and combine it with another such image so that one will bring up the other. Since I want to get typewriter ribbon before coming home, I'll imagine that I won't be able to get into the bus this afternoon because it is wrapped up with typewriter ribbon from a giant typewriter. The idea of not being able to get on the bus will trigger the image and remind me of the ribbon."

Bill found that telling himself what to do helped him to do it. And when he found himself feeling discouraged about his bad

[1] Lorrayne, H., and Lucas, J. *The Memory Book.* Briarcliff Manor, N.Y.: Stein & Day, 1974.

memory, he began to reassure himself as if he were talking to a friend: "As one gets older, some memory loss is normal. As long as you find a way around that, such as the memory skills you are learning, it won't become a nuisance. The more upset you get, the more grief you pile up on yourself. And getting upset about it doesn't help your memory a bit."

Bill found, in fact, that the more upset he became, the harder it was to remember things. By concentrating on his memory training and not allowing every minor instance of forgetting something to rattle him, he was able to feel better about himself and throw off one more obstacle to getting rid of his feelings of depression.

High-Expectations Hank. Like many other depressed people, Hank felt that he had never accomplished much. Yet, by any objective measure, Hank was clearly a competent person. The trouble was that Hank expected to be one of the best in a number of areas, and since he placed his goals at the highest possible levels, he couldn't always reach them. On top of that, he took for granted his accomplishments but was regularly miserable when he failed to do as well as he expected he should do.

Talking to Hank about lowering his expectations was futile. He had an answer for every argument we could bring up. So it was decided to have him work on himself. And, as usual, he did a good job:

"I know that having high goals helps me do my best and that I don't know if a goal is really *unrealistic* until I try, but the fact that I am periodically disappointed enough to feel seriously depressed may indicate that I am setting self-expectations too high. Maybe instead of always comparing myself to the best in my field, I could compare myself to the average sometimes. I'd come out looking good then. Or, I could just notice the things I have done and not compare them to my goals or anyone else's. Setting high goals wouldn't be so bad if I also paid attention to medium ones."

In this case, consciously talking to himself helped Hank work through a very important issue. He continued to use self-instruction by periodically asking himself whether he had any "medium" goals at present, and by reminding himself that getting depressed over a disappointment was a waste of time and energy.

"Realistic" Rachel. After reading each of the chapters which give instructions on how to break the depressive cycle, Rachel felt that they were unrealistic. "If things are lousy, why should I do something pleasant, or be sociable, or think positive thoughts? That wouldn't be honest or realistic, that would be just putting on an act, faking it. I'd just feel more depressed about lying to myself."

Rachel knew these techniques could help her control her depression. But she needed to convince herself to use them. She finally latched on to the distinction between constructive and destructive alternatives and began to instruct herself to look for constructive ones.

A "constructive" alternative is one that helps you "put yourself together." Rachel found this distinction helpful and "realistic" when she remembered that a song she liked could make her feel really happy at times and really sad at other times. Since it was the same song, the happiness or sadness must be coming from her, not directly from the song.

Rachel's self-instructions began like this: "I know I am feeling depressed, and I know that when people feel depressed their "reality" is distorted in negative directions. Since that's the case, I need to balance things out by emphasizing constructive perspectives in my view of reality. What's the best way I could interpret what is happening right now?"

When her earlier doubts got in the way of her self-change efforts, she instructed herself to set them aside and consciously directed herself to continue with her plans and give them a proper test.

Once she overcame her depression, it was the negative, destructive perspectives she had once defended that seemed unrealistic to her.

Self-talk can be used in combination with any of the other self-change strategies described in this book. It can help you put the other technique into practice.

USING SELF-INSTRUCTION

Receiving instructions from someone else is most helpful when the instructor knows what he or she is talking about. Getting instructions on how to fix your auto from a brain surgeon who has never looked under the hood of a car would be a futile exercise. Similarly, giving yourself instructions works best when *you* know what *you* are talking about.

1. *Understand what you want to accomplish.* Be specific. "I don't want to be depressed" is much too general.

Good: "I want to stop thinking depressed."

Better: "I want to think in a less pessimistic manner."

Better still: "I want to remind myself 10 times each day that I *can* change the way I feel."

2. *Understand how you plan to accomplish it.* Be specific. "I'll make an effort to remind myself" is too general.

Good: "I'll reward myself for thinking that I *can* change how I feel."

Better: "Each time I think to myself that I *can* change how I feel I'll reward myself."

Better still: "Immediately after I think that I *can* change how I feel, I'll place a dime from my change purse into my left pocket. All the dimes I earn are mine to spend as I please."

Excellent: "Immediately after I think that I *can* change how I feel, I'll place a dime from my change purse into my left pocket. I'll place 10 dimes in my purse each morning, which means I can make a dollar each day by thinking it 10 times, not less than 15 minutes apart. With the money I get each week I can buy myself one of the following items: a table game, a record album, a book, an art print, a photography book, or a glider ride (which may take more than 1 week)."

3. *Write down your instructions.* It is easier to use self-instructions after you have written them down. Writing forces you to come up with *exact* words. This way you won't just *think* you know them. You'll see exactly what you know and what you are uncertain about.

4. *Practice using the instructions.* There are three good ways to practice:

Do It: Go through the process you have targeted and instruct yourself as planned. For example, if you have a hard time increasing positive thoughts, and you have decided to tell yourself a positive thought before you eat anything during the day, tell yourself: "OK, before I take the first bite, I need to think one positive thought." Then think the positive thought, and take that first bite.

Imagine Doing It: Imagine instructing yourself during an important situation. For example, if you want to practice disputing your irrational ideas, think about a typical situation in which you are prone to let others' remarks trigger depressive reactions in you. Then, imagine the whole scene, just as if you were seeing it on film. Listen to the spoken remarks that usually depress you. Then imagine instructing yourself: "OK, this is something that always gets to me. What am I telling myself to make myself depressed? How can I dispute that belief?" Actually pick out the irrational belief and dispute it on the spot. Replay the scene until you feel you have handled it comfortably.

Imagine Someone Else Doing It: Pick someone who, in your opinion, satisfactorily handles situations you find difficult. Then use this person as a model. Again, imagine a whole scene, but this time it's not you but your chosen model who is starring. The model could be a friend, acquaintance, public figure, movie star, or a character from a book you've read. As the scene progresses, try to read your model's mind. What kind of self-instructions are going through his or her mind? For example, is he or she thinking: "I'll never get out of this mess, I just can't handle it. I'm just no good. Might as well give up." *Or* "How can I get out of this mess? Let's see. Relax. Think clearly. If I do this, what will happen . . . ?" In other words, is the self-talk your model engages in destructive or constructive? Is it filled with hopelessness or optimism? Does it contain negatives or positives?

You can practice by placing your chosen model (or different models) in many situations in which *you* want to feel comfortable.

5. *Modify your self-instructions.* You may realize as you practice that there are better self-instructions than the ones you came up with at first. Go ahead and change them until you feel comfortable with them.

6. *Build self-instructions into a routine.* As soon as you begin to feel depressed, begin using self-instructions. You might tell yourself: "Is this something I want to think about right now? Do I want to save it for my worrying time or deal with it right now? What haven't I been considering lately? Have I been keeping up my pleasant activities? My social activities? My positive thoughts?" Once you have decided how you want to handle this particular feeling, coach yourself as you go about implementing your plan.

7. *Reward yourself for using self-instructions.*

SUMMARY

1. Self-instructions help you to

- Remind yourself to do what you had planned.
- Keep your task in focus.
- Motivate yourself in tough situations.
- Maintain some beneficial psychological distance.

2. To learn to use self-instructions:

- Understand *what* you want to do.
- Understand *how* you want to do it.
- Write down your instructions word by word.
- Practice by doing it, by imagining yourself doing it, or by imagining a "model" doing it.
- Modify your instructions as needed.
- Build them into your daily routine.
- Reward yourself for using them.

REVIEW

_____ I have read and understood what "self-instructions" are.

_____ I have read and understood the examples of people who used self-instructions.

_____ I have decided not to try this technique at this time.

(If you check this, skip the rest of the items and go to another chapter.)

———— I have decided to try this technique.

———— I have written down *what* I want to accomplish.

———— I have written down *how* (specifically) I want to accomplish it.

———— I have written down my self-instructions.

———— I have practiced using self-instructions by

    ———— Doing it.

    ———— Imagining doing it.

    ———— Imagining someone else doing it.

———— I have modified my self-instructions at least once.

———— I have noticed myself using self-instructions spontaneously.

———— I reward myself when I use self-instructions.

———— I have used self-instructions to help myself practice techniques from Chapters ————, ————, ————.

———— I have kept track of my mood to see how using self-instructions influences it.

part III

Looking Toward the Future

chapter 13

Maintaining
Your Gains

Let's get a reading on what you have done so far. By now you
have made progress on several important goals. To help you
assess your progress toward each goal, we will list them. You
might place a check mark (√) in front of statements to which
your answer would be "yes."

_____ Most importantly, *you* have been able to significantly reduce your depression level. To help you
determine the validity of this statement, you
should now fill out the Beck Depression Inventory
again (using the copy in Appendix B) and compute your new score. At least 1 month should
have elapsed since you first took this inventory.

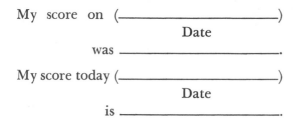

My score on (————————————)
                    Date

      was ————————————.

My score today (————————————)
                    Date

       is ————————————.

———— You have become more knowledgeable about the key manifestations of depression.

———— You have become more sensitive in being able to recognize depression in yourself.

———— You have acquired a better understanding of what causes people in general to feel depressed.

———— You have acquired knowledge about the kinds of situations, behaviors, and thoughts that contribute to your feeling depressed.

———— You have learned how to design and how to implement a self-change plan.

———— You have been able to put this skill to work for you (Chapters 6, 7, 8, 9, 10, 11, 12). By changing your behavior, and your life situations, you have been able to counteract your depression.

The purpose of the remainder of this chapter is

1. To assist you in integrating what you have learned;

2. To encourage you to monitor your depression level periodically so that you can recognize recurrences quickly;

3. To alert you to certain stressful life events that often cause depression.

INTEGRATION

In this section we will briefly review Chapters 6–12 in order to personalize their content for you. The goal is to heighten your awareness of the kinds of behaviors and situations that lead to your feeling depressed. You can do this by assigning a priority rating to each of the statements in Table 13–1. Give a priority rating of 2 if the statement has a high degree of relevance to your becoming depressed, a rating of 1 if it is somewhat important, and a rating of 0 if it is not relevant to you. While making your priority ratings you should also briefly describe the technique(s) you have found most useful for the particular problem.

> *Example:* You know that you feel tense and anxious in many situations. This interferes with your performance in those situations and makes you feel discouraged and dissatisfied with yourself. You would then give a priority rating of 2 to Statement 3 below. You have found that by practicing relaxation for 10 minutes before breakfast every day *and* before specific problem situations, you can avoid feeling tense and also reduce the frequency of your headaches. In the space provided you would indicate your technique for coping with this problem: (1) Practice relaxation 10 minutes before breakfast; (2) Relax for 3 minutes before (a) social gatherings, (b) business meetings, (c) giving a talk to a group.

Assigning priorities to your problems and describing your methods of coping with them will alert you to interventions which you may want to repeat if you feel yourself becoming depressed again. Remember, an ounce of prevention is better, easier, and much less painful than a pound of treatment.

Table 13–1

Statement	Priority Rating	Useful Technique(s)
Chapter 6, *Learning to Relax* *I may become depressed when:*		
1. I feel tense and upset a lot of the time.		
2. Feeling tense and anxious causes me to sleep poorly, to have headaches, and to feel tired.		

3. I feel tense in specific situations, which
  a. Interferes with my performance in, and with my enjoyment of these situations.
  b. Makes it difficult for me to participate in situations and to be as active as I would like to be.		

Chapter 7, *Pleasant Activities* *I may become depressed when:*		
4. I allow my rate of pleasant activities to drop below a certain level. Estimate the daily number of pleasant activities needed to allow you to feel good. List those pleasant activities (aim for 10) that are especially important (good) for you.		

Table 13-1 *(cont.)*

Statement	Priority Rating	Useful Technique(s)
5. I am unable to control my time so as to allow me to achieve a balance between what I must do and what I really want to do.		

Chapter 8, *Learning How to Be Socially Skillful,* and Chapter 9, *Using Your Social Skills*
    I may become depressed when:

6. My rate of social interactions and comfort drops below a certain level.

    What relationships and interactions do you see as most important to your well being? What problems do you see as still existing, or as potentially arising in the future, in these relationships?

    Is there anything you can do to anticipate, avoid, or cope with these problems?

7. I encounter social situations in which I feel rejected, disliked, and inferior.

8. I encounter situations in which I find it difficult to be appropriately assertive.

9. My interpersonal behavior becomes aversive to others, and, therefore, I am not being rewarded for my interactions.

Table 13–1 (*cont.*)

Statement	Priority Rating	Useful Technique(s)
Chapter 10, *Controlling Thoughts* *I may become depressed when:*		
10. I fail to generate enough positive thoughts about myself.		
11. I generate a larger than average number of negative thoughts about myself.		
Chapter 11, *Constructive Thinking* *I may become depressed when:*		
12. I overreact emotionally to situations because of what I tell myself about problems and difficulties.		
Chapter 12, *Self-Instructional Techniques*		
13. I fail to anticipate what I want to do and lose the chance to do it.		
14. I plan what I want to do but don't follow through when the time comes.		

In case you feel yourself becoming depressed again, focus on those problems you have judged to be of greatest importance to you. Put back into practice the techniques you have found most useful. Do you still have your self-change plans? Could you use them again? On the basis of your experience with them, are there changes you would want to make? If so, note these changes now.

REGULAR AND PERIODIC
REASSESSMENT

There is complete agreement among the experts (a rare event!) that preventive measures are superior to treatment and that mild forms of any disorder are more easily helped than more severe and advanced forms. The key ideas are *prevention* and *early recognition*. Since you know what it is like, we don't need to convince you that it is painful to be depressed. It is something that you want to avoid if you can. Furthermore, depression often has a destructive impact on our immediate family as well as a negative effect on our own lives. You also probably know from your own experiences that it is much easier to work yourself out of a mild depression than a more severe one. Nevertheless, it is hard for people to think preventively. Typically, we pay attention to our state of well-being only after something is drastically wrong. *It will take an active and conscious effort on your part to be alert to recurrences of depression.* You have an advantage over most people because you have learned how to recognize your own depression.

After you have stopped using this book regularly (we hope that's because you are not depressed any longer), we urge you to evaluate your depression level from time to time by filling out the Beck Depression Inventory (Appendix B). You should do this *regularly*. To do anything regularly, we need something to remind us. So, if you are going to evaluate yourself on a monthly basis (we think that's a fine idea), you might want to do it on payday (assuming that you get paid on a monthly basis). You could use any other "cue" which makes its appearance at regular monthly intervals. For example, you could use the arrival of your utility bill as a reminder. If you find that you are becoming more depressed, you should go back to using *systematically* the particular techniques you have found useful;

275

or, if your situation has changed, you should go back to Chapter 5 to decide whether some other technique might be more useful to you.

MAJOR LIFE EVENTS AND LIFE CHANGES
THAT OFTEN CAUSE DEPRESSION

A great deal has been learned in the past few years about the impact of stress on health in general and on mental health in particular. Stressful life events do happen, and, especially when too many of them happen to us, they make it considerably more likely that we will develop physical as well as mental problems, including depression. Depression is an especially common re- action to the death of loved ones and other social separations (for example, children leaving home to get married or to go to college, accepting a position in a different part of the coun- try, having close friends or relatives move away, getting sepa- rated or divorced from one's spouse).

It is easy to understand why stressful life events that hap- pen to us affect us as much as they do. They often seriously disrupt and sometimes permanently change the pattern of our interactions and our life-style. Somewhat more subtle is the fact that stressful life events that happen to others are also likely to affect us. We, and the people with whom we interact, are all part of a social system, and anything that affects one member of the system is likely to have an impact on the others as well. Thus, if your husband's mother dies, he is likely to feel de- pressed, be more withdrawn, and be less interested in you; this, in turn, will have an effect on *you.* Stressful life events of all kinds are likely to cause depression and require minor or major readjustments on our part. Table 13–2 lists events that may cause depression.

Table 13–2

List of Life Events that May Cause Depression

A. Social Separations
1. Death of spouse, close family member, or close friend
2. Divorce
3. Marital separation
4. Son or daughter leaving home
5. Change in residence
B. Health-Related Events
1. Major change in health of self or close family member
2. Personal injury or illness
C. New Responsibilities and Adjustments
1. Marriage
2. Addition of new family member
D. Work-Related Events
1. Change to different jobs
2. Promotion and/or major change in work responsibilities
3. Being fired
4. Trouble with boss
5. Retirement from work
6. Spouse starts or stops work
7. Change to new school
8. End of formal schooling
E. Financial and Material Events
1. Burdensome debts
2. Financial setbacks
3. Loss of personal property through fire, theft, etc.
4. Legal problems

PREPARE AND PLAN FOR
STRESSFUL LIFE EVENTS

Many stressful life events are predictable. You usually know ahead of time that your child will go to college, will get married, or move out of your home; that your close friend or someone in your family is going to move; that your spouse is going to retire (or you are); that a cold and dreary winter is approaching; that you and your spouse will separate; that you are going to lose your job; or that you are getting older and will find it more difficult to do some of the things that you have enjoyed doing.

You can prepare for stressful life events in three ways:

1. *Carefully anticipate the specific ways in which the stressful life event will affect your behavior and your interactions.* Separations (permanent or temporary) from people with whom you have been intensely (positively and/or negatively) involved are likely to leave a big *void* in your life. Many of the ongoing interactions to which you have been accustomed and which have been a major part of your life will no longer occur.

2. *Prepare for stressful events by developing a self-change plan.* Make use of the skills you have acquired in Chapter 4 and in the other chapters to deal with the problem(s) the event will create for you.

3. *Self-observe your depression level more closely* and if you find yourself becoming more depressed, put back into practice some of the techniques that you have found useful.

Unfortunately, some stressful life events are unpredictable. We cannot prepare for them, but we *can* plan to cope with them after they have happened. A physically disabling disease or accident may make it impossible for us to engage in many of the activities we are used to doing and which have been important sources of pleasure for us. A stroke may leave a person with impairments in his ability to communicate, an obviously very important skill in social interactions. Many chronic health conditions seriously lower our ability to get around, our coordination, and our energy level. All of these are stressful life events that seriously interfere with and limit our ability to engage in interactions with positive outcomes. These events are, therefore, likely to lead to depression. By pinpointing specific problems, a self-change plan can be developed to avoid, or at least to minimize, the resulting feeling of depression.

Stress (and hence depression) may also be associated with positive events that require change and new adjustments. Some life events are not *obviously* stressful but nevertheless place demands on a person and involve major readjustments because they change the pattern of the person's interactions. These include the following:

1. *Graduating from school:* Deadlines, time schedules, exams, grades, fear of failure, pride of being in a particular program or class, and other factors that have acted to motivate the person and to organize his time are lost.

2. *Promotions*: Getting "kicked upstairs" is likely to interrupt existing relationships; buddies become subordinates, and the quality of the relationships is likely to be affected. Customary work with which the person felt comfortable and pleased is replaced by new assignments with uncertain outcomes.

3. *Getting married*: Brings a host of new responsibilities and adjustments in day-to-day living.

4. *Addition of child, or anyone else, to the household:* Places additional demands on one's time and may drastically affect one's marital relationship.

5. *Change in residence:* Disrupts a person's ongoing relationships and many other interactions; requires a person to develop a new set of friendships and relationships.

6. *Changes in life-style of spouse* (for example, one's spouse goes back to school, takes a job after being a housewife, or retires): Introduces major changes in spouse's activities, the amount of time a couple spends together, etc.

The key idea is to be alert to the potential impact *on you* of the life event. The questions to ask are:

1. *Specifically* how will the event effect my life? Will it result in my having a lot of time on my hands? Will it separate me from people with whom I have been close and with whom I have enjoyed interacting? Will it make it more difficult for me to do many of the activities I like to do? Will it change the behavior of others toward me?

2. Is the event likely to cause me to feel depressed?

3. What can *I* do to prepare for, and to cope with, the changes in the pattern of my interactions that will be brought about by the event? The priority ratings you assigned to the behaviors and situations that lead to your feeling depressed in Table 13–1 and the techniques you have found most useful for controlling your depression may be useful guides for the design of a self-change program to deal with the problems the event will create for you.

REVIEW

_____ I have re-evaluated my depression level by taking the Beck Depression Inventory again.

_____ I have a pretty clear idea of what types of conditions are associated with my feeling depressed, and I have listed the techniques I found useful for controlling my depression.

_____ I will assess my depression level with the Beck Depression Inventory at regular intervals (preferably once a month).

_____ I understand the importance of being especially alert to the occurrence of stressful life events and life changes that might happen to me and/or people who are part of my "social network."

_____ I understand the importance of actively coping with life events by specifying (pinpointing) how they will affect my life pattern and by developing a self-change plan to cope with the problems the event will create for me.

chapter 14

Changing Your Personality

We believe that people can change. Some argue that our personalities are rather permanently formed after the early years of life and that change thereafter is very difficult, if not impossible. We don't agree. As long as you are alive, you will be growing and changing. Humans are the most adaptable and flexible form of life on earth. If you try to plant your feet too firmly in one spot, you may slow down change, but you will also be giving up one of your most precious human abilities.

You may have already changed a great deal as you have worked on this book. However, you should not feel that your changes are over! As long as you live, you will need to keep changing and adapting, as the world around you changes, as your own body changes, and as your friends and loved ones change. We are different at age 30 than we were at 20 or will be at 60.

The issue of this chapter is not what specific changes you want to make, but a larger question: Who are you and who might you become? Change and growth as lifelong processes are important to understand; change is a part of your rich human capacity. This chapter should help you plan in what direction your changes are heading. Since people often have objections and fears when thinking about making changes, this chapter will begin by spelling out some of the most common fears and arguments (convincing ones, we hope) that each fear should be abandoned. The chapter will then address the questions of how you create yourself by the choices you make and how to plan changes that will shape and define much of your life.

COMMON FEARS ABOUT CHANGING

Fear of Losing the Status Quo

Some people feel a safety in stability even if they are unhappy with their current situation. It may not be good, but at least it is familiar. Noticing change in ourselves or in people close to us can be threatening because it means there may be new dangers ahead. Also, being aware of change means becoming aware of the fact that we, and others, are inevitably getting older. This is an easy fear to understand because, to some extent, we all share it. However, it is not a good reason to avoid thinking about change. The fear is based on the recognition that change comes to us all and change brings unfamiliar experiences. But this will happen, like it or not. How much better to accept it and plan for it than to pretend you can prevent it! You can learn to anticipate change not as a danger but as an opportunity to plan new and positive life experiences.

Fear of Inconsistency

Sometimes people are afraid to change because they do not want to appear fickle or inconsistent. They fear that behaving in a new way will "cheapen" their self-image or that others will consider them "two-faced." Such a view implies that most people behave in a very consistent manner and, thus, that consistency is "normal." However, psychologists now know that, in fact, most of us are not extremely consistent. Flexibility seems to be the rule rather than rigid consistency. People's behavior tends to change to fit the situation; for example, you may be very friendly at a neighborhood gathering but very stiff and formal at a fancy restaurant. Similarly, you may be very meticulous and careful in your work but carefree and happy-go-lucky on weekends.

Ralph Waldo Emerson, an early American writer and philosopher, wrote about human adaptability before psychologists began to understand it. He said, "a foolish consistency is the hobgoblin of little minds." Those who fear adaptive change are limiting themselves, and they will lead small lives. And, we might add, unhappy lives as well.

Fear That Change Is an Admission of Failure

Sometimes people are afraid to change because they think others would interpret change as an admission of personal failure. This is a destructive attitude, and it also implies a very negative view of human adaptability. Our own feeling is different. We believe that all people do the best they can at any given time; you are doing the best you can now, given such things as what you know, where you live, and what others help you to do. But that doesn't mean that you will always want to do just what you are doing now. You may want to be different; you may be able to solve some life problems better at a later time. Or you may just feel that it's time for a change. Changing simply means that you are adapting, either because you know something you didn't before or because your world changed. Dinosaurs remained the same when their world changed, and then they became extinct. Change would have been a success for the dinosaurs; *lack* of change is often the *real* failure. You are a human, blessed with great adaptability. For you, too, change can be a great success rather than a sign of failure.

Fear of Losing Spontaneity

Sometimes people resist change because they feel that life should just flow naturally, without any conscious effort or careful planning. However, in reality that goal is seldom, if ever, achieved. All of us *create ourselves each day* by choosing to behave in certain ways. Our choices are not completely "free." They are certainly influenced by the environment we inhabit, the consequences of our choices, and the behavior of our peers. However, as humans we can *process* a great deal of information, including all these factors and more, in making choices. Often you do this so spontaneously or automatically that you are hardly aware of the activity of choosing; for instance, you probably get up and begin your daily work without thinking about the fact that you are making a *choice* about how to spend the day. At other times, decisions may seem painfully conscious. Whether your choices are simple or complex, you make them all the time, and you can always make new ones. Humans become spontaneous and natural by choosing well and wisely, not by refusing to make any choices at all (which is, after all, a choice in itself).

Fear of Experimenting

Change is risky; we never know ahead of time just what a change will bring. Sometimes, we just might make things worse; that is a real risk. Other changes may work out very well, but you will never know ahead of time which changes will work and which will not. The important thing is to stay flexible and to be tuned in to what is happening. That way, if things don't work out we can back off and try something else. By taking a risk now and then, we are able to improve our lives in the long run. George Kelly, a noted psychologist, was fond of using science as an example. The client, just like the scientist, must continually experiment, trying out possibilities and learning from what works and what doesn't work. Refusing to experiment is, in the long run, much more risky.

CREATING YOURSELF

Who You Might Be

Being eager for change is only one step along the road, although it is a very crucial one. The next step is knowing what kinds of changes you want and how to go about creating them.

One of the first important things for you to realize is that there is no *one* way to create a good life. Unhappy people sometimes think there is a "secret to life" that would unlock happiness if it were only known. But there is no secret; life is very complex and we all have to find our own way—primarily by helping to create it. We will highlight that complexity by describing a few people. These brief sketches have just one purpose: to demonstrate that a successful life can be fashioned in a number of ways.

"Susie"—This sketch describes a woman in her mid-30s who has a successful business career:

> Susie is an extremely competent person. She knows what she wants and she usually knows how to accomplish what she plans. People like and respect Susie because they can count on her; if she makes a promise, she keeps it.
>
> Susie is not always easy to get to know, partly because she is a busy person. In addition, because she is bright and active people are sometimes reluctant to bring up personal things with her. Consequently, Susie has a few very close friends who really understand her, but a large number of casual acquaintances with whom she has worked at one time or another.
>
> Susie is happy and successful because she uses her intelligence wisely both at work and in her personal relationships.

"Sharon"—This sketch describes a young woman who has just begun working after completing high school. She hopes to marry and has no particular career plans.

> Sharon is a gentle person. People like her because she is willing to give up time to help them and always has a kind word to say. She speaks softly and listens a lot. At parties, she usually talks to one person at a time instead of being part of a noisy group. When Sharon gets upset about something, she usually turns to her closest friends for support. She's not afraid to share her feelings with them because she trusts their feelings for her. They are glad to help her, because she can always be counted on to help others herself.
>
> Sharon is happy and well-liked because she is kind, interested in others, and willing to offer *and* receive help.

"Sam"—This sketch describes a man in his early 40s. He has a good job and makes a good salary; he does not expect or desire much advancement in his business.

> Sam is extremely self-confident and attractive. He uses these

attributes well and without arrogance. He enjoys his life, expects to make friends easily, and expects to be able to do most things he would like to do. People say he has an "easy, graceful" manner that is enjoyable. Sam is not a great conversationalist, nor does he have major life goals and plans. Instead he relies on his abilities and trusts that things will continue to work out for him.

Sam is happy and successful because he has self-confidence based on an honest assessment of his talents. He allows his natural talents free rein, but does not think that he is better than other people because of the skills he possesses.

"*Joe*"—This sketch describes a 20-year-old college student. He majors in elementary education and plans to be a teacher.

Joe is an extrovert. He is out-going, cheerful, and full of energy; as a result, he's usually the one to get things going among the people he knows. He likes fun; his projects are rarely "productive." Instead he focuses on physical activities, large parties, trips to the beach, etc. At a party, he is usually either dancing or talking in a group.

Joe has lots of friends, and he is constantly making new ones. His relationships are not superficial; he honestly enjoys others and he shares himself openly. However, his relationships usually do not proceed to depth or intimacy since there is little chance to sit and talk quietly with Joe.

Overall, Joe is happy because he has the active life full of friends that he wants.

"*Jeanine*"—This sketch describes a woman in her 40s who has been married to the same person for twenty years. She completed high school and two years of college; she does not work outside the home.

Jeanine is a happy woman whose life centers on her family. She is married and has two children; these relationships are enormously important to her. She likes others and has friends, but it is clear that home is her highest priority. Her family loves her, partly because of her love and devotion to them. But they also love her because of her enthusiasm and eagerness for life. Jeanine plans hikes and raft trips for the family; she maintains a garden and grows much of their food; she reads and shares new ideas with the whole family.

Jeanine is a happy person because she knows what she really wants in life, and she works hard at making that a success. She doesn't let her love of family become dull or boring; she stays active and she keeps growing, but she does that within a solid framework of family love.

CREATING YOUR OWN ROLE SKETCH

The examples above are diverse, but they all contain common elements. They all address what the person's goals are, what the person's style is like, and what the person's relationships are like. There are innumerable ways to work out these elements, but they all need to work in order for the overall picture to be complete. In this next section, you should try to create a role sketch for yourself.

There are two ways to go about this task. One is to reject your current personality and "start from scratch" by describing the person you really want to be. We do not feel this way of proceeding is a very good idea. Instead we recommend a second way of approaching the role sketch, which is to accept much of your current personality *but to improve it* by suggesting modifications. In this recommended approach, a role sketch should sound a lot like the person you are right now. If you are quiet and gentle like Sharon, don't write an "extrovert" profile like Joe's for yourself (unless you're willing to go through a long and very difficult process of change). Use the good qualities you already have as the core of a successful role sketch. Whichever approach you take, the role sketch should contain all the elements mentioned above: life goals, personal style, nature of relationships. These should be well worked out in a way that can succeed for you (not for your neighbor, or the person you were 10 years ago, or your "dream self"—they have to work for *you*).

Finally, the role sketch should describe the changes you will need to make to get from where you are now to where you want to be. How different from you is the successful, happy person you describe? If you've done the job as we recommend, the role sketch should be a lot like you, but it should have important, clearly definable differences from your current self-description. Those clearly defined differences will become the basis of your plans for change.

Here's a guide to help you put this all together. If you get confused, look back at the role sketches on the previous pages, and use them to give you ideas about how to get started. In addition, here is one more role sketch (Figure 14–1) about "Harry," who was formerly depressed but has become much happier as a result of working on his problems. In particular, he has increased his pleasant activities, learned to relax in social situations, and has changed some nonfunctional beliefs— for example, the belief that everyone must love him.

"Harry's" role sketch is systematically structured to give you a guide in putting together your own sketch. Use the form in Figure 14–2 to write your own role sketch.

Figure 14-1
Role Sketch of "Harry"

1. My highest priorities (life goals, major commitments, etc.)
   My greatest commitment is to my marriage and my family. I also
   hope to use my professional training well but would not sacrifice
   my family for it. I want to be cared for by those who mean the
   most to me, not necessarily by everyone.

2. Personal style
   I am soft-spoken, gentle, and generous. I enjoy having fun with a
   small group; I don't like big parties. I like doing active things—
   playing games, sports, hikes—more than sitting around talking. I
   work hard, because I enjoy accomplishment and coming through
   for people.

3. Relationships
   People don't get to know me easily, but once they do know
   me they like and trust me. I avoid relationships with people who
   "live for the moment." I like more intimate, long-lasting relationships.

4. Summary: I can be happy and successful because
   I fit my goals and social activities to my quiet style, instead of
   trying to force myself to be more outgoing. I am likeable for my
   warm, hard-working, reliable style, and I can really accomplish
   my goals with those qualities.

5. How is this person I hope to be different in clearly specified ways
   from my self description right now?
   1. I need to develop more of the giving warmth I describe here.
   2. I need to relax more at work and remember that I work to
      accomplish things, not to become famous and beloved.
   3. I've improved a lot in enjoying the company of others in
      small groups, but I could still work on this a little.

Figure 14–2
Role Sketch of _____

1. My highest priorities (life goals, major commitments, etc.)

2. Personal style

3. Relationships

4. Summary: I can be happy and successful because

5. How is this person I hope to be different in clearly specified ways from my self description right now?

TRYING OUT THE ROLE

Now you are ready to try out some life changes. There are several things to keep in mind as you do. First, this is just an experiment! You don't know for sure how these changes will work until you try, so don't worry about failure. If this role doesn't work out, you can try out another one. You will gradually find one that's right for you if you keep trying and keep modifying and adapting. It may help to tell yourself over and over that it is "only practice." You aren't in a tournament—you're just warming up and practicing a skill. If you don't do well, it just means you need a little more practice.

Second, remember to set realistic goals for yourself. You can't change your facial features by trying out a role sketch, nor can you become super self-confident overnight. You are not trying to become a new person; you are just trying to be a happier, more adaptive, more flexible one than you were before.

Third, use and reuse this book to help you reach your goals. Remember what you have learned about using social learning principles to guide change. Try out chapters that didn't seem crucial before if your role sketch suggests that they would be helpful now. Keep doing the things that have helped you thus far while you make your new changes.

LOOKING AT THE FUTURE

Throughout this chapter, we have suggested that life is a constant process of change and we have tried to show you how to change without fear in directions you choose for yourself. It might be a good idea to plan to make this a lifelong process. At regular intervals, for instance every year on your birthday, you might write out a role sketch for yourself using the format in this chapter.[1] Don't look at your previous role sketches until you have written your current one. Then go back and compare who you are now with earlier role sketches. This will show vividly both how you have changed and how you have built on what came before. Change and continuity should both emerge, forming a pattern.

SUMMARY

This chapter has discussed the need for continual change in your life. Even if you have successfully overcome your depression, you will still need to change as you grow older and your life circumstances change. We have discussed some fears that people report when they look ahead and consider the changes to come. We have tried to show that these fears are groundless and that you should embrace change, seeing it as an opportunity to experience new facets of life.

This chapter has also presented a brief method for thinking about what changes you need in order to become more like the person you really want to be. This role sketch method can be used throughout your life to help you follow the patterns of change and continuity that you experience.

REVIEW

_____ I have written a role sketch for myself.

_____ I have figured out how to work on the changes I still have ahead in order to be more like my role sketch. I will

[1] Another copy of the Role Sketch Form is included in Appendix B.

———— Use additional chapters in the book: Chapters ————————————————

———— Keep working on some things I have started, using Chapters ————————————

———— Use another self-help book: ————————

———— See a counselor.

———— Not be working systematically on anything for a while.

———— Other: ————————————————

———— I will rewrite my role sketch at the following regular interval: ————————————————

chapter 15

Planning
Your Future

As we come near the end of our book, we'd like to talk with you about what comes next. We have tried to share what we think are helpful ideas with you, and we hope these ideas will continue to have some influence in your life as the years go by. People often react to crises by putting new ideas into practice, but when the crises pass, they return to their old patterns. So we'd like to share these ideas with you:

1. Think preventively and in terms of positive mental health.

2. Planning is related to mental well-being.

3. Consider the high moments in your life, the "peak-experiences." Learn to recognize them and make room for them.

PREVENTIVE THINKING AND BEYOND

Many people only pay attention to their well-being when it shows clear signs of deteriorating. They have a picture of "average" or "normal" health in their minds, and when they fall below this norm they run hard to catch up with it. Once they feel they have reached an "average" state of well-being, they again neglect the factors that can give them even greater strength. By continuing to plan one's daily life from a "positive health" perspective, one can nourish one's physical and psychological potential, thus increasing one's enjoyment of life and forestalling serious consequences should a serious energy-draining crisis occur.

Psychological prevention is a much neglected area. There is so much need for giving services to people who are hurting that we do not take the time to prepare those who are not hurting to live life in effective ways. If we did, we might be able to prevent many from becoming casualties. The savings in therapy time and money—not to mention human suffering —could be enormous. Perhaps some day "psychological impact statements" will be as familiar to our ears as "environmental impact statements."

Much of the material in Chapter 13, *Maintaining Your Gains,* can serve a preventive function in your life. Note, in particular, the section *Major Life Events and Life Changes That Often Cause Depression.* But remember that the stress produced by change need *not* be destructive. If used well, these events can be beneficial to one's growth and fulfillment. By anticipating and preparing for them, we can increase the chances that we will be able to use them well.

Instead of waiting until we are being left behind and then running hard to catch up, we can keep up a steady pace that conserves energy for the really hard places. This involves looking ahead, of course, and it turns out that doing so is in itself healthy. But that is the second idea we wanted to mention.

PLANNING AND MENTAL HEALTH

Recent research attempting to discover factors related to psychological adjustment has determined that those people rated as well-adjusted are good at (1) knowing the consequences of their acts, and (2) planning ahead to obtain their goals.

This is not surprising, of course. After all, it makes intuitive sense that aimlessness is likely to be accompanied by boredom and feelings of worthlessness. Having a goal, a direction, seems to get one's body and mind in tune and one's energy directed harmoniously toward its destination.

As you consider the years ahead, it would be worth your while to think about how your plans are going to harmonize your values with your goals. Let's start by defining the last two terms.

Values are general principles or guidelines you consider desirable and worthwhile. *Goals* are specific ends toward which you direct your efforts. Hopefully, your goals will be compatible with your values, that is, your specific ends will follow from your general principles.

For example, if you have the protection of the environment as a value and the ownership of a large, high-powered automobile as a goal, you will have to do some thinking about how the two fit (or don't fit) together. You may decide that, to stay within your value system, you will have to buy one of the most gas-efficient cars available, and certainly not a big 8-cylinder gas-guzzler. Or, you may conclude that buying *any* kind of a car would go against your values, and instead decide to ride a bike to work.

If your value system includes enjoying the fruits of your labor as you see fit (and does not include environmental concerns), then you will not have to limit your search for a car in any way. If you have both sets of values, you probably will have to do some compromising or decide that one value has precedence over the other.

Note that your goal gets meaning and worth from your values. Even if you decide not to get a car, that decision has positive emotional tone when it stems from a clearly defined value. Compare it, for example, to not getting a car because you don't have the money. In both cases, you wind up with no car, but in the former case, you are likely to have a greater feeling of satisfaction than in the latter. Values (general guidelines) give meaning to goals (specific plans).

Sometimes values contradict each other. If you value a close-knit family and also value staying free of responsibility for others, one or the other value must change. In such cases, the most adaptive outcome will be to acknowledge both sets of values and choose between them or blend them into a realistic new value. In this case, for example, the new value might be an equalitarian family system in which everyone shares responsibility according to their age and capabilities. The goal for an individual with this value would probably be to find and attempt to become close to like-minded members of the opposite sex. Later, it would be to raise children who would be self-sufficient. Note that you would have to take on some responsibilities, but perhaps not as much as you originally feared. If you have to choose between the two values, at least you'll have the knowledge that you are giving up something for something even more desirable.

Another alternative, of course, would be to decide to abide by one value for a period of time and then focus on the other value. This is probably the most common choice in relation to raising a family: being single, then married with no children, then having children. The length of each of these periods probably varies with the importance of independence or family ties for the individual.

The important point is that awareness of conscious choice between such values makes it less likely that one would destructively berate oneself for not having heeded whichever value necessarily gets lower priority. Values that we have found to cause considerable conflict among depressed persons include:

- Wanting to be a good mother and wife *and* wanting to have a career.

- Wanting to keep the family together *and* wanting a divorce.

- Wanting to have money in the bank *and* wanting to help one's child through college.

- Wanting to be very successful in one's line of work *and* wanting to spend more time with one's family.

These are not easy choices to make, but we do make them, even by default. If a choice is proving very hard for you and if the indecision is becoming a source of serious stress, we recommend visiting a counselor or other mental health professional. They cannot make the decision *for* you, but they can help you see things more clearly and give some support as you make a clear choice.

Another source of difficulty can spring up when we fail to achieve a certain goal and, as a result of frustration, we give up both the goal and the value behind it.

> Phil valued family life and hoped to marry someone who would share that dream with him. However, after he fell in love with a girl named Jean, she decided that she did not want to marry him. Phil proceeded to get involved in a number of brief relationships and claimed he was sure he would never get married.

The unsatisfying, cynical flavor of these relationships finally convinced Phil that he was throwing out a *value* he still held when he gave up the *goal* of marrying Jean.

Only then was he able to enter into relationships with an open mind and allow himself to entertain seriously the possibility of a permanent relationship.

If a value change occurs in a deliberate manner, then the person has made a conscious choice for which he or she is responsible. If, however, the value change occurs as an automatic reaction to frustration (as when it occurs "out of spite") or in a "sour grapes" manner, then the person is losing a certain amount of freedom. Our values *are* subject to some degree of choice, and in making this choice we determine, in large part, whether or not we will obtain self-fulfillment.

Values are influenced by our upbringing, our education, our readings, the mass media, and our social group. Values can be reinforced symbolically, through encouragement for their verbal or behavioral expression. We have a hand in determining which values will be most important in our lives by placing ourselves in situations in which certain values are reinforced. For example, by attending lectures, reading books, or associating with people who believe in specific values, we can strengthen those values.

Since this is the case, we can maintain our freedom of choice in regard to values and associated goals by *deliberately arranging social support systems* that will motivate us to continue on a road we have chosen and by avoiding energy-draining individuals or groups that punish our pursuit of cherished goals.

We have talked about values in an abstract way thus far. To help clarify our discussion, we will now list some of the many goals human beings have at their disposal. These goals can be individual or interpersonal, short-term or long-term, or superordinate goals.

Individual Goals

These goals include:

1. Life-style (which involves choosing the kind of image one would like to fashion oneself into).

2. Spiritual, religious, or philosophical activities.

3. Economic pursuits.

4. Educational plans.

5. Vocational choices.

6. Physical activity level.

7. Recreational and creativity-oriented activities.

Note that in all of these areas there is no way to avoid making choices. For example, if you choose not to concern yourself with physical activity, you are probably choosing a low level of physical activity. The more aware you are of the many choices to be made, the less likely you are to merely drift into one of them.

Interpersonal Goals

These goals, by their very nature, involve interaction with others:

1. *Family life-style*: degree of closeness with parents, spouse, children, and other family members.

2. *Friends*: number of friends, degree of intimacy, source (work, hobbies, geographic closeness, political similarities, etc.).

3. *Romantic relationships*: seriousness, sexual involvement, financial understandings, exclusiveness vs. multiple relationships, equalitarian vs. "traditional" styles, expectations regarding the future, and so on.

4. *Group commitments*: degree of involvement with social and community groups, time priorities for group activities vs. personal or family activities, level of emotional dependence on groups.

5. *Leadership roles*: how much influence one wants to exercise on groups, how much responsibility one wants to undertake, how much recognition one wants to receive.

Take the time now to note briefly your present goals in each of these areas.

Individual Goals

1. Life-style _____

_____

2. Spiritual, religious, or philosophical activities _____

_____

3. Economic pursuits _____

_____

4. Educational plans _____

_____

5. Vocational choices _____

_____

6. Physical activity level _____

_____

7. Recreational and creativity-oriented activities _____

_____

Interpersonal Goals

1. Family life-style _____

_____

2. Friends _____

3. Romantic relationships _____

_____

4. Group commitments _____

_____

5. Leadership roles _____

_____

Short-Term Goals

These goals are the kind that can be placed on a "to do" list, such as meeting new people, completing a project, making an appointment, writing a letter, calling a friend, reading a book, and so on. These day-to-day goals are important because they have a great influence on one's daily mood shifts (see Chapter 7).

Long-Term Goals

These goals help to place the short-term goals in perspective. They also help you come up with short-term goals that will increase your chances of reaching your long-term goals.

You may come up with your own long-term goals by looking at the "individual" and "interpersonal" goal lists and answering these two questions regarding each of the items:

1. Where would you like to be in regard to each of the items 10 years from now? 20 years from now? 30 years from now?

2. In looking back 10, 20, 30 years from now, what kind of memories would you like to have about the present?

The first question should help you make plans for the future. The second question should help you make plans for now. Though you may not have thought about it before, you can arrange to have pleasant memories in the future by engaging in satisfying activities now.

Superordinate Goals

These are all-encompassing life goals. Some people find them very useful to give perspective to their present situations and to give direction to their lives.

These goals include "philosophies of life" or "reasons for living" such as religious commitments; political causes; humanitarian projects; struggles for economic security for one self and one's heirs; aesthetic pursuits; thirst for knowledge, pleasure, fame, power, justice, or enlightenment; the desire to love and be loved; and the decision to be open to existence.

Being aware of these goals helps many people to avoid aimless drifting. Superordinate goals help to provide order for the less inclusive goals mentioned earlier. They can be effective in getting people out of destructive ruts by organizing their energy and directing it toward a destination that they consider worthwhile.

Take a few moments now to jot down your "philosophy of life":

If I had to tell someone what life is all about for me, I would say:

_____

_____

_____

_____

_____

_____

_____

_____

_____

Do not read ahead until you take the time to fill out your philosophy of life. The following examples may bias your own ideas if you read them first. Put the book down now. Take some time to think about your life and then come back and jot it down.

My Philosophy of Life by Ana, a 46-year-old housewife.

The most important things in my life are to be good to my family and faithful to my God. I believe that raising my children to respect other people as well as themselves and to learn to take good care of themselves in this world are some of the best things a mother can do. I also believe that means setting a good example by taking care of myself and my needs. That's why I always set aside time for me and my husband to enjoy times together by ourselves. I'd like to be known as an interesting, likable woman who is a good mother and a good wife.

My Philosophy of Life by Gina, a 30-year-old lawyer.

I believe strongly in reaching the highest goals one can. My profession is my most important goal right now, and I'd like to dedicate myself to becoming well known and respected in my field. I also believe that I should use my knowledge and energy to help bring about societal change by working within the system. Having good companionship is something that I guess I consider important, but I have not spent much energy on it for a while, and I don't really feel a need to do so at present.

My Philosophy of Life by Mark, a 36-year-old waiter.

I guess I see my life as a time for learning and experiencing many things. I really don't know if there is life after death, and I don't spend time thinking about it much. I like to have time to travel, to eat good food, to meet and get close to many different women, to read, listen to music, etc. I like having money in my pocket and spending it any way I want to. I like feeling healthy, so I take good care of my body. If I ever have kids, I'd like to teach them to enjoy life the way I have.

My Philosophy of Life by Phil, a 26-year-old teacher

My basic philosophy of life is to be responsible but not per-

fectionistic. The most important people in my life are my
parents, my wife, and my kids. Next in line are my students.
I believe that the most worthwhile thing a human being can
do is learn about the world. To learn the most, one needs to
learn to read and to think; that's what I try to teach my kids
and my pupils. In order to have the luxury to learn, you have
to be secure, so having enough money is really important to
me. But, in a way, learning is still the most important because
having enough money is really the result of having learned to
earn it.

An essential element in planning involves learning to put
your goals in priority order. This involves the ability to dis-
criminate between more and less important goals as well as the
ability to winnow out destructive ones. To help you get a start,
we'll mention a few examples.

First, we consciously leave out destructive goals such as
perfectionism, (which is unattainable) and the goal of considering oneself either "the best" or "a failure" (which is a common destroyer of many fine human beings). Note that we do
not mean to condemn the goal of striving for excellence. We *do*
condemn the practice of equating failure to be "perfect" or "the
best" with "total failure" as a person.

Another common destructive goal is setting goals for others
and making *our* happiness dependent on *their* reaching them.
This is most often seen in parents who place all their expectations of fulfillment on their children or in teachers who feel
that they have failed if their students do not "make good" later
in life.

Having screened out goals that we consider destructive, we
can begin to consider constructive goals. As an example, let's
look at Abraham Maslow's hierarchy of motivators.[1] Maslow, a
famous humanistic psychologist, spoke of *physiological needs*,
such as for food and water; *safety needs*, such as for predictabil-

[1] Maslow, A. M., *Toward a Psychology of Being* (2nd ed.). New York: Von
Nostrand/Reinhold, 1968.

ity and ways to cope with danger; *belongingness and love needs,* such as being part of a community and being emotionally important to others; *self-esteem needs,* such as feeling pride in one's characteristics and one's accomplishments; and the *need for self-actualization,* which involves going beyond survival needs and reaching the highest level of human functioning.

Whether or not you agree with this list of human priorities, it can serve as a model in putting together your own. In particular, note that the list includes some goals we generally take for granted, such as enough to eat. Even if these goals are already being met, it may be worth your while to include them to increase your awareness of how much you are already accomplishing.

RECOGNIZING AND APPRECIATING "PEAK-EXPERIENCES"

This book deals with depression, a psychological state characterized by dysphoria. Thus far, we have tried to show you ways to bring this experience under control, returning your mood to normal levels. In this chapter, we have spoken about planning and prevention as ways to avoid deep depression in the future. But we have not addressed the other end of the mood spectrum, that is, the feeling of *euphoria.*

Webster's dictionary defines euphoria as "an often unaccountable feeling of well-being or elation." We think that by becoming aware of this experience when it occurs, you may learn to recognize the circumstances in which it is likely to come about. You may then learn to "set the stage" or facilitate its emergence.

To help you recognize this psychological state, we would like to use the descriptions Abraham Maslow collected from people talking about their happiest moments, ecstatic moments, the most wonderful experiences of their lives. These are the moments Maslow calls "peak-experiences."

Persons in the peak-experience feel more integrated, more unified, and yet more able to fuse with the world. They feel at the peak of their powers and have a sense of effortlessness and ease. They feel more self-determined, more responsible, and at the same time most free of inhibitions and fears. They are therefore more spontaneous and relaxed, and also more creative, novel, and fresh.

During the peak-experience, people feel unique, more purely different. They are "all there," more in the here-and-now than at other times. They feel less restricted by physical limitations, as though they were "pure psyche." They have a sense of non-striving, non-needing, and yet deeply appreciate their situation, wanting to express their reactions to it in a poetic manner that blends easily with a feeling of playfulness, delight, and happy, childlike joy. This is accompanied by a sense of gratitude, of being lucky, fortunate, of not having earned one's joy. And the experience seems complete in itself, without needing to look to the past or the future to give it importance.

"Peak-experiences" are an example of the opposite of depressive experiences. Individuals who have learned to focus on depressive feelings often do not recognize feelings of happiness or satisfaction. By describing them, we hope to help you recognize them and appreciate their value.

HAPPINESS AND SATISFACTION

Survey studies of subjective well-being have come up with an interesting finding. People seem to differentiate between "happiness" and "satisfaction." It seems that ratings of happiness are greatest during young adulthood and decrease (on the average) with age. Ratings of satisfaction are lowest during young adulthood and increase (on the average) with age. It may be that happiness is equated with emotionally charged enjoyment and satisfaction with more tranquil, peaceful (but probably equally deep) feelings of contentment.

Since this is the case, you may consider how this may affect "peak-experiences." During youth, they may be much more easily recognizable because the emotional arousal may be more intense. As you grow older, your peak-experiences may be more mellow, and thus easier to overlook. It may be important, therefore, to learn to recognize and appreciate both types.

One thing should be clarified: The survey findings do *not* mean that highly charged feelings of happiness disappear as people grow older, nor that young people never feel satisfied. What they do indicate is that "happiness" is more frequent in younger people and "satisfaction" is more frequent in older people.

A FINAL NOTE

As you consider putting into practice some of our suggestions we would strongly advise you to consider the importance of *deciding*. Deciding on a course of action helps you feel more in control of your life. It is also a way to bear hard times when they come, because a decision made consciously has meaning behind it. Then, even if the decision doesn't lead to the best possible outcome the meaning behind the decision gives it more intrinsic worth than a haphazard event. In addition, making a decision about your personal values and goals is a way to reduce the tendency to compare yourself to everyone else. No one else has exactly the same values and goals that you have. Thus, your efforts cannot be strictly compared to others' efforts.

Decide to follow or to put aside our suggestions and make

this decision consciously. Decide even *not* to decide. We wish you success in your efforts and satisfaction with your continual progress.

REVIEW

———— I have read about prevention and know what it is.

———— I understand that planning is related to mental health.

———— I have thought about my values and my goals, and I understand how they differ from one another.

———— I realize how we strengthen or weaken our values by what we choose to come in contact with.

———— I have written out

    ———— My individual goals.

    ———— My interpersonal goals.

    ———— My philosophy of life.

———— I have read about "peak-experiences," and I think I could recognize a "peak-experience" if I had one.

———— I understand the difference between happiness and satisfaction.

———— I have *decided*

    ———— To try the suggestions in this book.

    ———— Not to follow the suggestions in this book.

    ———— Not to decide.

appendix A

Suggestions for Further Reading

DEPRESSION

AKISKAL, H. S., AND McKINNEY, W. T. "Depressive Disorders: Toward a Unified Hypothesis," *Science*, 182 (1973), 20–29.

ANNELL, A. L. *Depressive States in Childhood and Adolescence.* Stockholm: Almquist & Wiksell, 1972.

ANTHONY, J. E., AND BENEDEK, T. *Depression and Human Existence.* Boston: Little, Brown, 1975.

BECK, A. T. *Depression.* New York: Harper & Row (Hoeber Medical Division), 1967.

BECKER, J. *Depression: Theory and Research.* Washington, D.C.: V. H. Winston & Sons, 1974.

BECKER, J. *Affective Disorders.* Morristown, N.J.: General Learning Press, 1977.

DAVIDSON, P. O. (Ed.). *The Behavioral Management of Anxiety, Depression, and Pain.* New York: Brunner/Mazel, 1976.

FANN, W. E., KARACAN, I., POKERNY, A. D., AND WILLIAMS, R. L. *Phenomenology and Treatment of Depression.* New York: Spectrum Publications, 1977.

FIEVE, R. (Ed.). *Depression in the 70's.* Amsterdam: Elsevier-Excerpta Medica, 1971.

FRIEDMAN, R. J., AND KATZ, M. M. *The Psychology of Depression: Contemporary Theory and Research.* Washington, D.C.: V. H. Winston & Sons, 1974.

GAYLIN, W. *The Meaning of Despair.* New York: Science House, 1968.

GREENACRE, P. (Ed.). *Affective Disorders—Psychoanalytic Contributions to Their Study.* New York: International Universities Press, 1953.

GRINKER, R. R., MILLER, J. SABSHIN, M., NUNN, R., AND NUNALLY, J. C. *The Phenomena of Depressions.* New York: Paul B. Hoeber, Inc., 1961.

JACOBSEN, E. *Depression—Comparative Studies of Normal, Neurotic, and Psychotic Conditions.* New York: International Universities Press, 1971.

*KLINE, N. S. *From Sad to Glad.* New York: Ballantine Books, 1975.

LEVITT, E. E. AND LUBIN, B. *Depression.* New York: Spricyes Publishing Co., 1975.

LEWINSOHN, P. M. "Clinical and Theoretical Aspects of Depression," in *Innovative Methods in Psychopathology*, Calhoon, K. S., Adams, H. E., and Mitchell, K. M. (Eds.). New York: John Wiley & Sons, 1974, pp. 63–120.

---

* References of special interest to the nonprofessional reader.

LEWINSOHN, P. M. "The Behavioral Study and Treatment of Depression," in *Progress in Behavior Modifications,* Hersen, M., Eisler, R. M., and Miller, P. M. (Eds.). New York: Academic Press, 1975, pp. 19–64.

LEWINSOHN, P. M., AND YOUNGREN, M. A. "The Symptoms of Depression," *Comprehensive Therapy,* 2 (1976), 62–69.

MENDELS, J. *Concepts of Depression.* New York: John Wiley & Sons, 1970.

NEVRINGER, C. (Ed.). *Psychological Assessment of Suicidal Risk.* Springfield, Ill.: Charles C Thomas, 1974.

OSTOW, M. *The Psychology of Melancholy.* New York: Harper & Row, 1970.

SECUNDA, S. K., KATZ, M. M., FRIEDMAN, R. J., AND SCHNYLER, D. *Special Reports, 1973: The Depressive Disorders.* Washington, D.C.: Department of Health, Education and Welfare, Publication No. (HSM) 73–9157.

SELIGMAN, M. E. P. *Helplessness.* San Francisco: W. H. Freeman, 1975.

SCHNEIDMAN, E., AND ORTEGA, M. (Eds.). *Aspects of Depression.* Boston: Little, Brown, 1969.

SILVERMAN, C. *The Epidemiology of Depression.* Baltimore: Johns Hopkins Press, 1968.

"Symposium on Age Differentiation in Depressive Illness," *Journal of Gerontology,* 31 (1976), 278–326.

WEISSMAN, M. M., AND PAYKEL, E. P. *The Depressed Woman: A Study of Social Relationships.* Chicago: University of Chicago Press, 1974.

WILLIAMS, T., KATZ, M., AND SHIELDS, J. (Eds.). *Recent Advances in the Psychobiology of Depressive Illness.* Washington, D.C.: Government Printing Office, 1972.

WINOKUV, G., CLAYTON, P., AND REICH, T. *Manic-Depressive Illness.* St. Louis: Mosby, 1969.

ZUBIN, J., AND FREYHAN, F. A. (Eds.). *Disorders of Mood.* Baltimore: Johns Hopkins Press, 1972.

SOCIAL LEARNING THEORY

BANDURA, A. *Principles of Behavior Modification.* New York: Holt, Rinehart, & Winston, 1969.

*BANDURA, A. "A Social Learning Interpretation of Psychological Dysfunctions," in *Foundations of Abnormal Psychology,* London, P., and Rosenhan, D. (Eds.). New York: Holt, Rinehart, & Winston, 1968, pp. 293–344.

*BANDURA, A. *Social Learning Theory.* Morristown, N.J.: General Learning Press, 1971.

BANDURA, A. *Social Learning Theory.* Englewood Cliffs, N.J.: Prentice-Hall, 1977.

KANFER, F. H., AND GOLDSTEIN, A. P. (Eds.). *Helping People Change.* New York: Pergamon Press, 1975.

*KRUMBOLTZ, J., AND THORESEN, C. *Counseling Methods.* New York: Holt, Rinehart, & Winston, 1976.

BEHAVIORAL SELF-MANAGEMENT

GOLDFRIED, M. R., AND MERBAUM, M. (Eds.). *Behavior Change through Self-Control.* New York: Holt, Rinehart & Winston, 1973.

KANFER, F. H., AND GOLDSTEIN, A. P. (Eds.). *Helping People Change.* New York: Pergamon Press, 1975.

*MAHONEY, M. J., AND THORESEN, C. E. *Self-Control: Power to the Person.* Monterey, Calif.: Brooks/Cole, 1974.

THORESEN, C. E., AND MAHONEY, M. J. *Behavioral Self Control.* New York: Holt, Rinehart & Winston, 1974.

* References of special interest to the nonprofessional reader.

*Watson, D. L., and Tharp, R. G. *Self-Directed Behavior: Self-Modification for Personal Adjustment*. Belmont, Calif.: Wadsworth, 1972.

RELAXATION

*Rosen, G. M. *The Relaxation Book*. Englewood Cliffs, N.J.: Prentice-Hall, 1977.

*Benson, H. *The Relaxation Response*. New York: Avon Books, 1975.

SOCIAL INTERACTION

General References

*Gambrill, E., and Richey, C. A. *It's Up to You. The Development of Assertive Social Skills*. Millbrae, Calif:. Les Femmes, 1976.

*Johnson, S. M. *First Person Singular: Living the Good Life Alone*. Philadelphia: Lippincott, 1977.

Weissman, M. M., and Paykel, E. S. *The Depressed Woman: A Study of Social Relationships*. Chicago: University of Chicago Press, 1974.

Youngren, M. A., and Lewinsohn, P. M. "The Functional Relationship between Depression and Problematic Interpersonal Behavior," in press.

*Zimbardo, P. G. *Shyness: What It Is, What to Do About It*. Reading, Mass.: Addison-Wesley, 1977.

*Zunin, L., and Zunin, N. *Contact: The First Four Minutes*. New York: Ballantine Books, 1972.

* References of special interest to the nonprofessional reader.

Assertion

*Alberti, R. E., and Emmons, M. *Your Perfect Right* (2nd edit.). San Luis Obispo, Calif.: Impact, 1974.

*Bower, S. A., and Bower, G. H. *Asserting Your Self: A Practical Guide for Positive Change.* Reading, Mass.: Addison-Wesley, 1976.

Cotter, S. B., and Gruerra, J. J. *Assertion Training.* Champaign, Ill.: Research Press, 1976.

*Fensterheim, H., and Baer, J. *Don't Say Yes When You Want to Say No.* New York: Dell, 1975.

Kazdin, A. E. "Effects of Covert Modeling and Model Reinforcement on Assertive Behavior," *Journal of Abnormal Psychology,* 83 (1974), 240–252.

Kazdin, A. E. "Covert Modeling, Imagery Assessment, and Assertive Behavior," *Journal of Consulting and Clinical Psychology,* 43 (1975), 716–724.

*Phelps, S., and Austin, A. *The Assertive Woman.* San Luis Obispo, Calif.: Impact, 1975.

Rich, A. R., and Schroeder, H. E. "Research Issues in Assertiveness Training," *Psychological Bulletin,* 83 (1976), 1081–1096.

*Smith, M. J. *When I Say No, I Feel Guilty.* New York: Bantam Books, 1975.

Nonverbal Behavior

Ekman, P., and Friesen, W. V. "Nonverbal Behavior and Psychopathology," in *The Psychology of Depression: Contemporary Theory and Research,* Friedman, R. J. and Katz, M. M. (Eds.). New York: John Wiley & Sons, 1974.

* References of special interest to the nonprofessional reader.

PLEASANT EVENTS

MacPhillamy, D. J., and Lewinsohn, P. M. *Manual for the Pleasant Events Schedule.* (Mimeographed) Eugene, Ore.: University of Oregon, 1975.

MacPhillamy, D. J., and Lewinsohn, P. M. "Depression as a Function of Levels of Desired and Obtained Pleasure," *Journal of Abnormal Psychology,* 83 (1974), 651–657.

Lewinsohn, P. M., and MacPhillamy, D. J. "The Relationship between Age and Engagement in Pleasant Activities," *Journal of Gerontology,* 29 (1974), 290–294.

Lewinsohn, P. M., and Libet, J. "Pleasant Events, Activity Schedules and Depression," *Journal of Abnormal Psychology,* 79 (1972), 291–295.

Lewinsohn, P. M., and Graf, M. "Pleasant Activities and Depression," *Journal of Consulting and Clinical Psychology,* 41 (1973), 261–268.

Lewinsohn, P. M. "Activity Schedules in the Treatment of Depression," in *Counseling Methods,* Thoresen, C. E., and Krumboltz, J. (Eds.). New York: Holt, Rinehart & Winston, 1976, pp. 74–83.

Lewinsohn, P. M., Youngren, M. A., and Grosscup, S. C. "Reinforcement and Depression," in *The Psychobiology of the Depressive Disorders: Implications for the Effects of Stress,* Depue, R. A. (Ed.). New York: Academic Press, in press.

COGNITIVE APPROACHES

Anton, J. L., Dunbar, J., and Friedman, L. "Anticipation Training in the Treatment of Depression," in *Counseling Methods,* Thoresen, C. E., and Krumboltz, J. (Eds.). New York: Holt, Rinehart & Winston, 1976, pp. 67–73.

*ELLIS, A., AND HARPER, R. A. *A Guide to Rational Living.* No. Hollywood, Calif.: Wilshire Book Co., 1973.

JACKSON, B. "Treatment of Depression by Self-Reinforcement," *Behavior Therapy,* 3 (1972), 298–307.

*KRANZLER, G. *You Can Change How You Feel.* Eugene, Ore.: University of Oregon Press, 1974.

LAZARUS, A. A. "Learning Theory and Treatment of Depression," *Behaviour Research and Therapy,* 6 (1968), 83–89.

MAHONEY, M. J. "The Self-Management of Covert Behavior: A Case Study," *Behavior Therapy,* 2 (1971), 575–578.

MAHONEY, M. J. *Cognition and Behavior Modification.* Cambridge, Mass.: Ballinger, 1974.

MEICHENBAUM, D. "Self-Instructional Methods," in *Helping People Change,* Kanfer, F. H. and Goldstein, A. P. (Eds.). New York: Pergamon, 1975.

MEICHENBAUM, D. *Cognitive Behavior Modification: An Integrative Approach.* New York: Plenum Press, 1977.

MEICHENBAUM, D., AND CAMERON, R. "The Clinical Potential of Modifying What Clients Say to Themselves," in *Self-Control: Power to the Person,* Mahoney, M. J., and Thoreson, C. E. (Eds.). Monterey, Calif.: Brooks/Cole, 1974.

STAMPFL, T. G., AND LEVIS, D. J. "Essentials of Implosive Therapy: A Learning-Theory-Based Psychodynamic Behavioral Therapy," *Journal of Abnormal Psychology,* 72 (1967), 469–503.

CHANGING YOUR PERSONALITY

KELLY, G. A. *The Psychology of Personal Constructs,* Vols. 1 & 2. New York: Norton, 1955.

* References of special interest to the nonprofessional reader.

BEISER, M. "A Study of Personality Assets in a Rural Community," *Archives of General Psychiatry,* 24 (1971), 244–254.

CAMPBELL, A. "Subjective Measures of Well-being," in *Primary Prevention of Psychopathology. Vol. I: The Issues,* Albee, G. W., and Joffee, J. M. (Eds.). Hanover, N.H.: University Press of New England, 1977.

CAPLAN, G., AND GRUNEBAUM, H. "Perspectives on Primary Prevention: A Review," in *The Critical Issues of Community Mental Health,* Gottesfeld, H. (Ed.). New York: Behavioral Publications, 1972.

KESSLER, J., AND ALBEE, G. W. "Primary Prevention," *Annual Review of Psychology,* 26 (1975), 557–591.

MASLOW, A. H. "Peak Experiences as Acute Identity-Experiences," *American Journal of Psychoanalysis,* 21 (1961), 254–260.

MASLOW, A. H. *Toward a Psychology of Being* (2nd edit.). New York: Van Nostrand Reinhold, 1968.

MASLOW, A. H. *Motivation and Personality* (2nd edit.). New York: Harper & Row, 1970.

MUÑOZ, R. F. "The Primary Prevention of Psychological Problems," *Community Mental Health Review,* 1 (6) (1976), 1–15.

MUÑOZ, R. F., AND KELLY, J. G. *The Prevention of Mental Disorders.* Homewood, Ill.: Richard D. Irwin, 1975.

SHURE, M. B., AND SPIVACK, G. "Means-Ends Thinking, Adjustment, and Social Class among Elementary-School-Aged Children," *Journal of Consulting and Clinical Psychology,* 38 (1972), 348–353.

MISCELLANEOUS

Alcohol Problems

*MILLER, W. R., AND MUÑOZ, R. F. *How to Control Your Drinking.* Englewood Cliffs, N.J.: Prentice-Hall, 1976.

Memory Problems

*HISBEE, K. L. *Your Memory: How It Works and How to Improve It.* Englewood Cliffs, N.J.: Prentice-Hall, 1977.

*LORRAYNE, H., AND LUCAS, J. *The Memory Book.* Briarcliff Manor, N.Y.: Stein & Day, 1974.

*YOUNG, M. N. AND GIBON, W. B. *How to Develop an Exceptional Memory.* Hollywood, Calif.: Wilshire Books, 1973.

Phobias

*ROSEN, G. *Don't Be Afraid: A Program for Overcoming Fears and Phobias.* Englewood Cliffs, N.J.: Prentice-Hall, 1976.

Sex and Marital Problems

*BARBACH, L. G. *For Yourself: The Fulfillment of Female Sexuality.* New York: Doubleday, 1975.

*GOTTMAN, J., NOTARIUS, C., GONSO, J., AND MARKMAN, H. *A Couple's Guide to Communication.* Champaign, Ill.: Research Press, 1976.

*HEIMAN, J., LoPICCOLO, L., AND LoPICCOLO, J. *Becoming Orgasmic: A Sexual Growth Program.* Englewood Cliffs, N.J.: Prentice-Hall, 1976.

---

* References of special interest to the nonprofessional reader.

Zeiss, R., and Zeiss, A. Prolong Your Pleasure: A Couple's Treatment Guide for Premature Ejaculation. New York: Pocket Books, in press.

Sleeping Problems

Coates, T. J., and Thoresen, C. E. How to Sleep Better. Englewood Cliffs, N.J.: Prentice-Hall, 1977.

---

* References of special interest to the nonprofessional reader.

appendix B

Extra Forms

Cut along the dashed lines and have additional copies of all of these forms made for your future use.

Beck Depression Inventory [a]

Instructions: This is a questionnaire. On the questionnaire are groups of statements. Please read the entire groups of statements in each category. Then pick out the one statement in the group which best describes the way you feel *today,* that is *right now.* Circle the number beside the statement you have chosen. If several statements in the group seem to apply equally well, circle each one.

Be sure to read all the statements in the group before making your choice.

[a] The authors wish to thank Aaron T. Beck, M.D., for granting permission to reprint the Beck Depression Inventory.

Beck Depression Inventory

A. (SADNESS)

0   I do not feel sad

1   I feel blue or sad

2a   I am blue or sad all the time and I can't snap out of it

2b   I am so sad or unhappy that it is quite painful

3   I am so sad or unhappy that I can't stand it

B. (PESSIMISM)

0   I am not particularly pessimistic or discouraged about the future

1   I feel discouraged about the future

2a   I feel I have nothing to look forward to

2b   I feel that I won't ever get over my troubles

3   I feel that the future is hopeless and that things cannot improve

C. (SENSE OF FAILURE)

0   I do not feel like a failure

1   I feel I have failed more than the average person

2a   I feel I have accomplished very little that is worthwhile or that means anything

2b   As I look back on my life all I can see is a lot of failure

3   I feel I am a complete failure as a person (parent, spouse)

D. (DISSATISFACTION)

0   I am not particularly dissatisfied

1a   I feel bored most of the time

2a   I don't enjoy things the way I used to

2b   I don't get satisfaction out of anything any more

3   I am dissatisfied with everything

Beck Depression Inventory *(cont.)*

E. (GUILT)

0 I don't feel particularly guilty

1 I feel bad or unworthy a good part of the time

2a I feel quite guilty

2b I feel bad or unworthy practically all the time now

3 I feel as though I am very bad or worthless

F. (EXPECTATION OF PUNISHMENT)

0 I don't feel I am being punished

1 I have a feeling that something bad may happen to me

2 I feel I am being punished or will be punished

3a I feel I deserve to be punished

3b I want to be punished

G. (SELF- DISLIKE)

0 I don't feel disappointed in myself

1a I am disappointed in myself

1b I don't like myself

2 I am disgusted with myself

3 I hate myself

H. (SELF-ACCUSATIONS)

0 I don't feel I am worse than anybody else

1 I am critical of myself for my weaknesses or mistakes

2 I blame myself for my faults

3 I blame myself for everything that happens

Beck Depression Inventory (*cont.*)

I. (SUICIDAL IDEAS)

0   I don't have any thoughts of harming myself

1   I have thoughts of harming myself but I would not carry them out

2a   I feel I would be better off dead

2b   I feel my family would be better off if I were dead

3a   I have definite plans about committing suicide

3b   I would kill myself if I could

J. (CRYING)

0   I don't cry any more than usual

1   I cry more than I used to

2   I cry all the time now. I can't stop it

3   I used to be able to cry but now I can't cry at all even though I want to

K. (IRRITABILITY)

0   I am no more irritated now than I ever am

1   I get annoyed or irritated more easily than I used to

2   I feel irritated all the time

3   I don't get irritated at all at things that used to irritate me

L. (SOCIAL WITHDRAWAL)

0   I have not lost interest in other people

1   I am less interested in other people now than I used to be

2   I have lost most of my interest in other people and have little feeling for them

3   I have lost all my interest in other people and don't care about them at all

Beck Depression Inventory (*cont.*)

M. (INDECISIVENESS)

0   I make decisions about as well as ever
1   I try to put off making decisions
2   I have great difficulty in making decisions
3   I can't make any decisions at all anymore

N. (BODY IMAGE CHANGE)

0   I don't feel I look any worse than I used to
1   I am worried that I am looking old or unattractive
2   I feel that there are permanent changes in my appearance and they make me look unattractive
3   I feel that I am ugly or repulsive looking

O. (WORK RETARDATION)

0   I can work as well as before
1a   It takes extra effort to get started doing something
1b   I don't work as well as I used to
2   I have to push myself very hard to do anything
3   I can't do any work at all

P. (INSOMNIA)

0   I can sleep as well as usual
1   I wake up more tired in the morning than I used to
2   I wake up 2–3 hours earlier than usual and find it hard to get back to sleep
3   I wake up early every day and can't get more than 5 hours sleep

Q. (FATIGABILITY)

0   I don't get any more tired than usual
1   I get tired more easily than I used to
2   I get tired from doing anything
3   I get too tired to do anything

R. (ANOREXIA)

0   My appetite is not worse than usual
1   My appetite is not as good as it used to be
2   My appetite is much worse now
3   I have no appetite at all

Beck Depression Inventory (*cont.*)

S. (WEIGHT LOSS)

0 I haven't lost much weight, if any, lately
1 I have lost more than 5 pounds
2 I have lost more than 10 pounds
3 I have lost more than 15 pounds

T. (SOMATIC PREOCCUPATION)

0 I am no more concerned about my health than usual
1 I am concerned about aches and pains or upset stomach or constipation
2 I am so concerned with how I feel or what I feel that it's hard to think of much else
3 I am completely absorbed in what I feel

U. (LOSS OF LIBIDO)

0 I have not noticed any recent change in my interest in sex
1 I am less interested in sex than I used to be
2 I am much less interested in sex now
3 I have lost interest in sex completely

Figure B–1
Daily Mood Rating Form

Please rate your mood for this day (how good or bad you felt) using the 9-point scale shown. If you felt really great (the best you have ever felt or can imagine yourself feeling), mark 9. If you felt really bad (the worst you have ever felt or can imagine yourself feeling), mark 1. If it was a "so-so" (or mixed) day, mark 5.

If you felt worse than "so-so," mark a number between 2 and 4. If you felt better than "so-so," mark a number between 6 and 9. Remember, a low number signifies that you felt bad and a high number means that you felt good.

very   very
depressed   1   2   3   4   5   6   7   8   9   happy

Enter the date on which you begin your mood ratings in Column 2 and your mood score in Column 3.

Monitoring Day	Date	Mood Score	Monitoring Day	Date	Mood Score
1			16		
2			17		
3			18		
4			19		
5			20		
6			21		
7			22		
8			23		
9			24		
10			25		
11			26		
12			27		
13			28		
14			29		
15			30		

Figure B-2 Daily Monitoring–Relaxation

Relaxation Rating: 0 = Most relaxed you have ever been
10 = Most tense you have ever been

Date: _____ to _____

	Monday	Tuesday	Wednesday	Thursday	Friday	Saturday	Sunday	Average Score (add your scores and divide by 7)
Average Score for the Day								
Least Relaxed Time								
Score								
When								
Where								
Situation								
Most Relaxed Time								
Score								
When								
Where								
Situation								
Occurrence of Tension Symptoms								
H = Headache SA = Stomachache SP = Sleep problem								
Relaxation Practice								
When								
For how long								
Score before								
Score after								

331

Figure B-3 Daily Monitoring–Relaxation in Problem Situations

Relaxation Rating: 0 = Most relaxed you have ever been
                    10 = Most tense you have ever been

Dates: _____ to _____

Problem Situations	Monday	Tuesday	Wednesday	Thursday	Friday	Saturday	Sunday
1.							
2.							
3.							
4.							
5.							
6.							
7.							
8.							
9.							
10.							

Figure B-4 Activity Schedule

Activity

	Day																													
	1	2	3	4	5	6	7	8	9	10	11	12	13	14	15	16	17	18	19	20	21	22	23	24	25	26	27	28	29	30
1																														
2																														
3																														
4																														
5																														
6																														
7																														
8																														
9																														
10																														
11																														
12																														
13																														
14																														
15																														
16																														
17																														
18																														

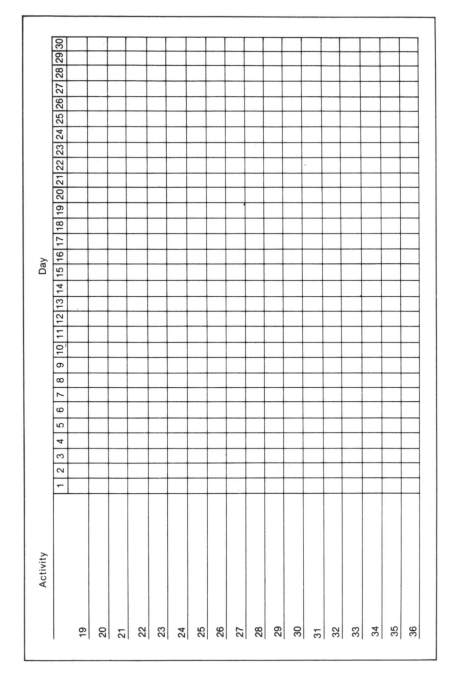

334

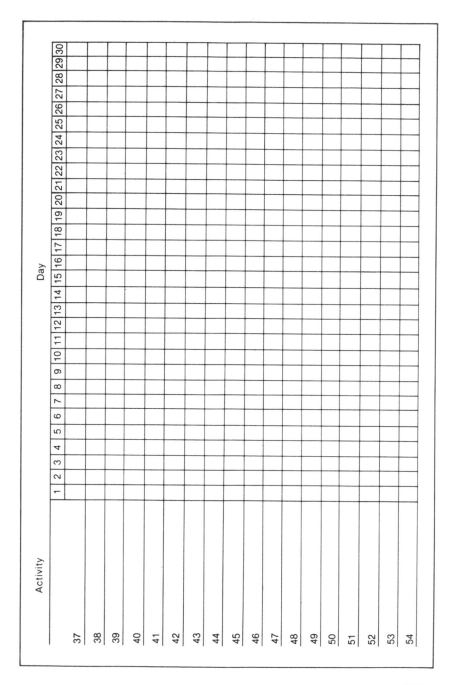

335

Day

Activity	1	2	3	4	5	6	7	8	9	10	11	12	13	14	15	16	17	18	19	20	21	22	23	24	25	26	27	28	29	30
55																														
56																														
57																														
58																														
59																														
60																														
61																														
62																														
63																														
64																														
65																														
66																														
67																														
68																														
69																														
70																														
71																														
72																														

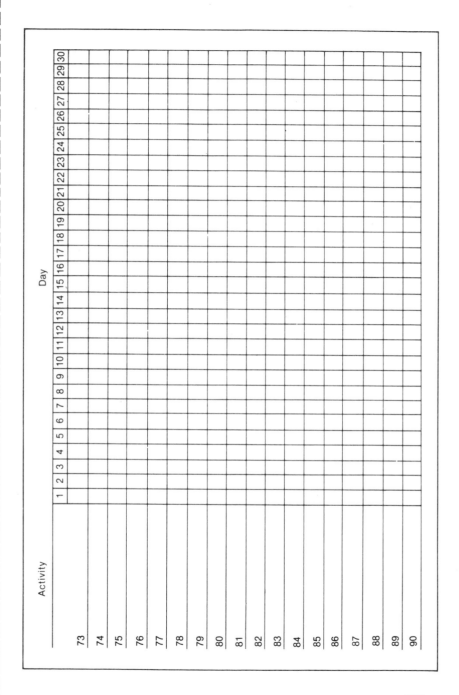

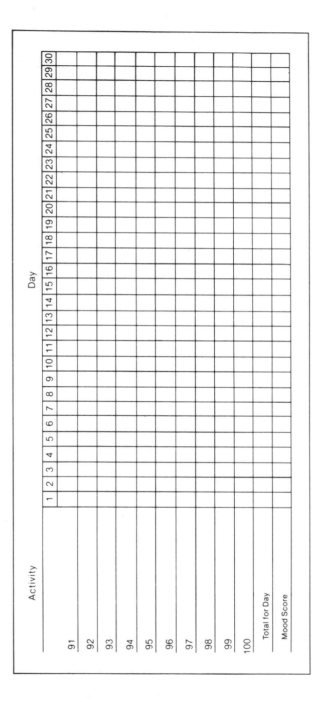

338

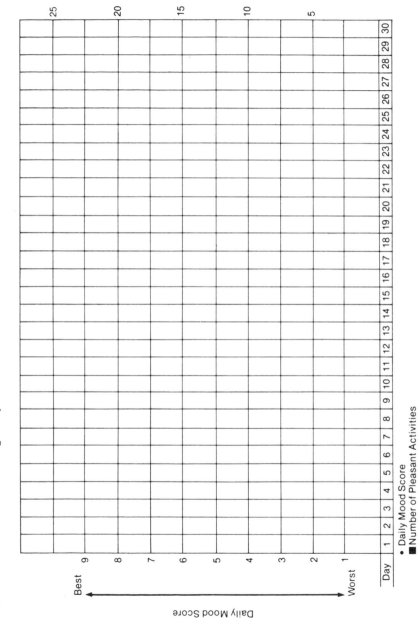

Figure B-5 Chart for Recording Daily Pleasant Activities and Mood Scores

Number of Pleasant Activities

- Daily Mood Score
- ■ Number of Pleasant Activities

339

340

Figure B-6 Weekly Plan

Date:							
Time	Monday	Tuesday	Wednesday	Thursday	Friday	Saturday	Sunday
8:00							
9:00							
10:00							
11:00							
12:00							
1:00							
2:00							
3:00							
4:00							
5:00							
6:00							
7:00							
8:00							
9:00							
10:00							

Figure B–7
Self-Monitoring of Assertion Form

Situation	Comfort	Skill in Asserting Myself
1.		
2.		
3.		
4.		
5.		
6.		
7.		
8.		
9.		
10.		

Figure B–8
Social Activities to Increase

Month: _____

Item Date:								
1.								
2.								
3.								
4.								
5.								
6.								
7.								
8.								
9.								
10.								
11.								
12.								
13.								
14.								
15.								
16.								
17.								
18.								
19.								
20.								
Daily Totals:								

Goal for Increasing: _____ per _____ .

Average Increase Achieved: _____ per _____ .

Figure B–9
Interferences: Activities to Decrease

Month: _____

Item Date:								
1.								
2.								
3.								
4.								
5.								
6.								
7.								
8.								
9.								
10.								
11.								
12.								
13.								
14.								
15.								
16.								
17.								
18.								
19.								
20.								
Daily Totals:								

Goal for Decreasing: _____ per _____ .

Average Decrease Achieved: _____ per _____ .

Figure B–10
Daily Monitoring Form [a]

Daily Monitoring Form[a]

Date _____

A. Activating Event

(Briefly describe the situation or event that seemed to lead to your emotional upset at C.)

B. Beliefs or Self-Talk

(List each of the things that you said to yourself about A.)

1.

2.

3.

4.

5.

(Now go back and place a checkmark beside each statement that is non-constructive or "irrational.")

C. Emotional Consequences

(Describe and rate how you felt when A happened.)

I felt: _____

_____

Rating (0 = mildly upset; 5 = extremely upset): _____

D. Dispute of Self-Talk

(For each checked statement in Section B describe what you would ask or say to dispute your non-constructive self-talk.)

[a]*Note:* You should first complete Section C. Then go back and complete Section A and Section B. After the first week of self-monitoring, also complete Section D.

Figure B–11

Role Sketch of _____

1. My highest priorities (life goals, major commitments, etc.)

2. Personal style

3. Relationships

4. Summary: I can be happy and successful because

5. How is this person I hope to be different in clearly specified ways from my self description right now?

Index

A

A–B–C method, 245–48
  activating event, 245
  belief about activating event, 246
  consequences, 246
  self-talk, nonconstructive, 248
  steps in, 247
Activity, pleasant, 122–70
  and depression, 123
  likelihood of being seen as such, 124–25
  mood-related, 125
  and self-change plan, 126
Alberti, R. E., 188
Alcohol and drug problems, 94–95
  and depression, 95

Antecedents, 153–58
  and anxiety and discomfort, 156
  examples, 155
  and lack of care in activity choice, 154–55
  and life changes, 155
  and pressure from unpleasant needs, 154
  and tension, 156–57
Antecedents, discovering, 60–62
  avoiding of, 61
  Eileen, example of, 62
  examples, 60–61
Assertion, 173–88
  Jack, example of, 173
  nature of, 173–74
  questionnaire, 175–77

Self-talk, disrupting of (*cont.*)
  overgeneralizations, 252
  "shoulds" and "oughts," 251
  "terribles" and "awfuls," 251
Sleep problems, 96
Social learning, 23–32
  and curiosity about behavior, 23
  and depression as learned be-
    havior, 25
Social Learning Theory:
  and control of self, 29–30
  implications of, 30–31
Social skills, use of, 197–216
  bad habits list as tool, 204
  inadequate rewards, 210–11
  inadequate stimulation, 202–3
  information gathering, 209–10
  Janet, example of, 197–98
  pleasant activities, increasing,
    209
  progress monitoring, 212
  ruts, 198
  scoring of, 202
  self-evaluation, 198–99
  social attitudes questionnaire,
    200–202
  social participation problems,
    199, 202–4, 209–12
  success story, sample, 213–14
Starting, where to, 96–99
  importance vs. change difficulty,
    97
  pleasant activities, 97–98

T

Thoresen, C. E., 96
Thoughts, control of by self, 217–39
  accomplishments, noticing of,
    233–34
  blow-up technique (ridiculous
    exaggeration), 231

Thoughts, control of by self (*cont.*)
  characteristics of, 218–19
  counting of, by type, 227
  identifying, 224–26
  Marsha, example of, 230–31
  priming of self, 232
  self-assessment, of patterns of
    thought, 219–23
  self-rewarding thoughts, 234–35
  silent "Stop!" yell, 229
  Theresa, example of, 217–18
  thought interruption, 228–29
  time projection (mental time
    travel), 235–36
  using cues to self, 233
  worrying time, 229–30
Toward a Psychology of Being
  (Maslow), 308

V

Values and goals, conflicts between,
  298–301
  blending of, 299
  conflicts in depressed people,
    300
  contradictions between values,
    299
  deliberate change of values, 301
  and emotional tones, 299
  Phil, example of, 300–301
  successive values, 299–300
Vocational problems, 93–94
  loss of job satisfaction, 94

Y

You Can Change How You Feel
  (Kranzler), 247
Your Perfect Right (Alberti and
  Emmons), 188